Further Praise for *Go Back to Where You Came From*

"Wajahat Ali writes with effervescent verve, an easy wit, and a bracing moral clarity. This book made me laugh out loud, tear up, giggle, google recipes for Pakistani food, and think long and hard about what it means to be an American and whom we include in that category. Easily the most enjoyable book I've read in years. Now if only it had recipes."

       —Julia Ioffe, journalist and author of *Motherland* (forthcoming)

"Raw, funny, honest, and, most important, all-American"

         —Kim Ghattas, author of *Black Wave*

"A tender, knife-sharp analysis of racism, America, and the wick of power, language, and culture—personal, painful, familial, and global. Read this text. Feel its rebel blades. A hard-won offering to all. . . . Wajahat Ali leaves no assault, lie, or fakism unturned."   **—Juan Felipe Herrera**, United States Poet Laureate Emeritus

"A lovely book full of wisdom and compassion, not to mention Ali's signature humor. As educational as it is entertaining. I wish my nine-year-old immigrant self had had this book when the playground kids were telling me to go back to where I came from."

       —Gary Shteyngart, author of *Our Country Friends*

"A gifted playwright and media star, Wajahat Ali mines the sheer comedic potential of being brown and Muslim in America and dissects the dynamics of bigotry in all its aspects, including Islamophobia and white nationalism. He captures the tragic realities of life in America and lauds its potential wonders, which help him still believe the journey is worthwhile."

    —Carla Blank, author and editor (with the Before Columbus Foundation)
    of *Rediscovering America: The Making of Multicultural America, 1900–2000*

"In prose at times hilarious and at other times deeply moving, Wajahat Ali chronicles a uniquely American experience. All will benefit from reading his story."

         —Representative Ilhan Omar

"With characteristic wit and humanity, Ali captures something essential—even universal—in this hilarious, sweet, sad, unexpectedly hopeful, and timely memoir. There was something that resonated with me on every page—and not just as a fellow South Asian. Everybody should read this book."

    —Meena Harris, best-selling author and founder and CEO of Phenomenal

"Timely and engrossing, *Go Back to Where You Came From* balances Wajahat Ali's sharp satire and deep empathy by chronicling his personal story of growing up as a first-generation Muslim-American. His brilliant, hilarious, and eye-opening book will make any reader want to come to his block party."

—**Sunny Hostin**, *New York Times* best-selling author of *I Am These Truths*

"A candid story of growing up Muslim in America, *Go Back to Where You Came From* reveals the pain of loving a nation that doesn't always love you back."

—**Laila Lalami**, author of *Conditional Citizens*

"With wit and charm, Ali has delivered a masterful meditation on growing up brown in America. Like the superheroes he dreamed of in his youth, Ali has a keen moral compass. His love for his large Pakistani-American family helps him press ever forward as he overcomes great personal challenges, and ultimately claims his place in a country that both embraces and reviles him. An intoxicating rejection of cynicism in the face of existential threats to multiracial democracy. An American memoir, and a clear-eyed call to arms against the forces seeking to stop the expansion of American democracy. An affirmation of the country America could be."

—**Mara Gay**, *New York Times* editorial board member and MSNBC political analyst

"With humor, empathy, and insight, Wajahat Ali unwinds what it means to be 'Amreekan' at a time when the future of the nation feels urgently up for grabs. Ali is, above all, a master storyteller who leads readers through some of the most pressing questions facing the United States—What is the power of plurality? Why do we get derailed by racism? Who gets to write our story?—in engaging, thought-provoking ways. *Go Back to Where You Came From* is a tour de force coming-of-age tale of homeland and belonging, one that shows us who we can vibrantly be if we harness the power of our collective energies, and what we lose when we fail to live up to our collective ideals. This book is required reading for anyone concerned with how America came to this moment of promise and of impasse, and about where on earth we go from here."

—**Jonathan Metzl**, author of *Dying of Whiteness*

"I love a good Trojan horse and this book offers all the satire and political commentary one hopes for, but not without delivering a tremendously earnest gut punch to the soul."

—**Thi Bui**, author of *The Best We Could Do*

"*Go Back to Where You Came From* is an American story shorn of its legends. Powerful. Funny. Biting in its honest criticism and hopeful in the end. In telling his story, Wajahat Ali helps us imagine this country anew—this book is an amazing gift in these troubling times."

—**Eddie S. Glaude Jr.**, author of *Begin Again*

"A compelling, harrowing account of growing up brown in America. Also, a love letter to that same America. I couldn't put it down."

—**Gene Luen Yang**, author of *American Born Chinese*

"Funny is what gets into the heart, and Wajahat Ali has written an unflinchingly honest and hilarious book. This is a book of our times and for our times, and I'm grateful to have read it." —**Jose Antonio Vargas**, author of *Dear America*

"The world needs more truth-tellers like Wajahat Ali who can educate us all with love and humor. As you laugh throughout this book, you will also learn that this most imperfect nation has yet to fully accept its own truths. Waj delivers like a Steph Curry three." —**Julio Ricardo Varela**, founder of Latino Rebels

"I didn't expect to be laughing out loud as I read *Go Back to Where You Came From*, but I should have. Wajahat Ali's foremost talent is delivering lessons on racism, civil rights, history, politics, and policy with unmatched wit, wisdom, and, somehow, comedy. Ali has written a brilliant, poignant, and urgent memoir of the immigrant American experience in his authorial debut, interweaving his personal history with the history of how America has treated its Muslim citizens. I immediately recognized my own story in the contours of Ali's story, and I found hope for the future of our children here, in America, which is where they come from."

—**Rabia Chaudry**, author of *Adnan's Story*

"This book is—appropriately enough—Wajahat Ali in book form: smart, hilarious, very into food, and deeply empathetic. He's the very best of America, and this book can help you be, too."

—**Franklin Leonard**, founder of The Blacklist

"Lots of people can write solemn, heavily-footnoted books on immigration, Islamophobia, the American Dream and the threats that could take it down, and the Pakistani-American experience. It takes a singular talent to tackle such issues deftly and disarmingly, but Ali has the stats, courage, and comedic gifts to deliver. Nuanced yet hilarious, brave, and bracingly revealing, *Go Back to Where You Came From* is so entertaining that one forgets how much one learns as one races through its pages."

—**Carla Power**, author of *Home, Land, Security*

Go Back to Where You Came From

Go Back to Where You Came From

★ *And Other Helpful Recommendations on How to Become American*

Wajahat Ali

W. W. NORTON & COMPANY
Independent Publishers Since 1923

Copyright © 2022 by Wajahat Ali

For information about permission to reproduce selections from this book,
write to Permissions, W. W. Norton & Company, Inc.
500 Fifth Avenue, New York, NY 10110

For information about special discounts for bulk purchases, please contact
W. W. Norton Special Sales at specialsales@wwnorton.com or 800-233-4830

Manufacturing by Lakeside Book Company
Book design by Lovedog Studio
Production manager: Lauren Abbate

Library of Congress Cataloging-in-Publication Data

Names: Ali, Wajahat, author.
Title: Go back to where you came from : and other helpful recommendations
    on how to become American / Wajahat Ali.
Description: First edition. | New York, NY : W. W. Norton & Company, [2022] |
    Includes bibliographical references.
Identifiers: LCCN 2021037426 | ISBN 9780393867978 (hardcover) |
    ISBN 9780393867985 (epub)
Subjects: LCSH: Ali, Wajahat. | Children of immigrants—United States—
    Biography. | Pakistani Americans—Biography. | Political activists—
    United States—Biography. | Journalists—United States—Biography. |
    United States—Ethnic relations. | United States—Social conditions—1980–
Classification: LCC E184.P28 A45 2022 | DDC 305.8914/122073092 [B]—dc23
LC record available at https://lccn.loc.gov/2021037426

W. W. Norton & Company, Inc., 500 Fifth Avenue, New York, N.Y. 10110
www.wwnorton.com

W. W. Norton & Company Ltd., 15 Carlisle Street, London W1D 3BS

1 2 3 4 5 6 7 8 9 0

For Ibrahim, Nusayba, Khadija, and the next generation of Amreekans.

Contents

Go Back to Where You Came From

Introduction

Assalamu Alaikum. Peace be upon you.

Fan Mail #1: *Go back to where you came from!*

Fremont, California? I'd love to, but I can't afford the rent. I'm priced out. (Damn you, tech overlords!) Cursed be my fate. Oh, if only I had listened to Mother and become a doctor instead. (Silent weeping.) Thank you, though, I appreciate the helpful recommendation!

Fan Mail #2: *Why don't you shut up and go fuck a goat, you Moslem terrorist!*

Always with the goats and camels. Why limit my options? Two legs good, four legs good. But, no thank you, I'm happily married to a woman. Also, it's *Muslim* terrorist. Unless you're referring to muslin, which is a versatile cotton fabric originally hailing from Mosul, Iraq, and typically has not been associated with overt acts of violent extremism. Nonetheless, I appreciate the helpful recommendation.

Fan Mail #3: *Your a real smart-ass, Gandhi.*

My parents are from Pakistan, not India, but it was all one country pre-Partition, so I'll allow it. Also, thank you for comparing me to a beloved icon of nonviolent resistance who helped overthrow British imperialism. But Gandhi was also racist and a proponent of the oppressive caste system, so even Gandhi had much self-work to do on his path toward progress. Still, I appreciate the helpful compliment. *You're welcome.

Fan Mail #4: You . . . are literally the biggest fucking race baiting, scumbag, loser moron on the face of the planet. Thanks for guaranteeing Trump's reelection though. Go fuck yourself clown.

Trust me, if I could, I would. As a teenager, I tried, but I eventually gave up. I appreciate you referring to me as the "biggest fucking race baiting . . . moron." For so long, I was runner-up. A Salieri to all the Mozarts of the race-hustling game. But now the student has become the master. Thank you for noticing. I appreciate you using the word "literally" the way it was, literally, meant to be used. Also, Trump lost.

Fan Mail #5: You speak so well and you are actually a moderate and not a radical!

Thank you! I also actually read well, am lactose intolerant, and am only wanted in three states. We moderates are an endangered species, but we few who remain try to be civil.

The Best Fan Mail: I saw you agitating for a race war against White people (European-descended people). What are you waiting for, little man? Your people have accomplished nothing. Backwards goat fuckers. It's telling that you would rather invade White spaces and live off White cultural capital than return to your own ancestral lands and try to make a difference there. No, you are just a parasite. . . . We are onto you, you degenerate mud. We know your game.

You have a good day.

Cordially,
Brock Strongballs
College Conservatives

Dear Mr. Strongballs,

I am in awe.

After reading, and rereading, this inspired masterpiece, I had to pause and collect myself. I felt like a lady from the Antebellum South, flushed and out of breath, muttering "Oh, my" and fanning herself upon receiving a most generous compliment from a slaveholding gentleman with amorous intentions. One of your heroes, or ancestors, I imagine.

I remain floored by the profundity and depth of this epic missive that has serendipitously graced my in-box. It is indeed *The Odyssey* of fan mails, Mr. Strongballs, and I assure you I am no man of hyperbole or flattery! Your prose sings like the Sirens and drives me mad with desire.

In honor of your elegant, incisive thoughts, allow me, with the limited capacity afforded to me and my fellow "mud" people, to retort to your poetry:

Mr. Strongballs, you begin with an assumption, a compliment, and a question:

I saw you agitating for a race war against White people (European-descended people). What are you waiting for, little man?

Thank you. I have indeed lost a lot of weight since childhood and no longer wear Husky pants. However, you are far too kind. I am by no means "little" and can afford to lose the dad bod.

I am neither agitating for nor plotting a race war against the "White people," whom you have helpfully defined as the "European-descended people." In fact, some of my favorite people are white people, especially the European-descended kind. My preferred white people are the Moderate Whites of European descent.

I assume you had a small typo and meant "rice war," correct? Indeed, in the spirit of camaraderie, I will wager my basmati against your gruel.

Your people have accomplished nothing.

Contrary to popular belief, we left-handed people are a highly productive and successful minority who have left a mark on history with our south-paw. My people include US presidents, such as my Muslim brother, President Barack Hussein Obama, and legendary thespian, President Ronald Reagan. Supreme Court Justice Ruth Bader Ginsburg (RIP RBG) banged her gavel with the left hand, author and America's lasting conscience James Baldwin wrote with his left as well, and Jimi Hendrix shredded "The Star Spangled Banner" at Woodstock. We helped influence Western and "European" civilization with the likes of Alexander the Great, Charlemagne (the emperor, not tha God), Julius Caesar, and Napoleon Bonaparte, whose humiliating loss nonetheless inspired a catchy ABBA classic. With the left hand, my people even painted God as a naked white man on the Sistine Chapel, something I know you'd appreciate.

Backwards goat fuckers.

I had never imagined "backwards" goat sex. Is it similar to reverse cow-girl? You seem like an expert, so I hope you don't mind me asking.

It's telling that you would rather invade White spaces and live off White cultural capital than return to your own ancestral lands and try to make a difference there.

It is true. I have spent some time at Whole Foods, admiring the endless selection of artisanal cheeses and overpriced, organic fruit spreads. I once entered an Abercrombie & Fitch at the Valley Fair Mall, but I assure you I only window-shopped. I purchased nothing! I do not put raisins in my potato salad and have yet to own a single pair of cargo shorts. However, I do confess to enjoying the first two seasons of *Girls* and owning (and loving) a Sarah McLachlan CD. So, you got me there. As I told an earlier fan, I would love to move back to my ancestral land of the Bay Area, California, but only if you can help subsidize my rent.

No, you are just a parasite . . .

Thank you! Parasites get a bad rap, but did you know some of us actually help protect the host from infections, diseases, and ailments? In the case of America, we protect this country from eating bland food, doing manual labor, competing in spelling competitions, driving around NYC, engineering, performing their own surgeries, economic collapse, and making fools out of themselves when they attempt to wear a sari without guidance.

We are onto you, you degenerate mud.

Are two people writing this email now? Or are you using the imperial "we"? If so, "we" is the color of mud, so "we" appreciate you noticing. "Degenerate"? Please. "We" is married. Don't talk dirty to us. (You saucy minx!)

We know your game.

Word? You're into Carrom also? I'll bring the board, you bring the pieces, and I'll take home the queen.

You have a good day.

> **Cordially,**
> **Brock Strongballs**
> **College Conservatives**

And a good day to you, sir.
> Gracefully,
> Wajahat Ali
> Mud Degenerates

✳ ✳ ✳ ✳

Assalamu Alaikum. Aloha. Salaams. Shalom. Marhaban. Chào bạn. Namaste. Kamusta. Nǐ hǎo. Hujambo. Ola. Oi. 'Sup. Ciao. Howdy. Hallo. Hi. Hei. Hej.

These are numerous ways human beings greet and welcome each other around the world. You don't even need words. You can just make eye contact and tilt your head briefly to acknowledge an individual's presence. However, if you're special like me, you'll often get hit with an endearing "Go back to where you came from!"

Some people cry, some rage, and some laugh when they are always asked to be welcoming but are still never welcomed to the American BBQ. Each emotional response is valid in processing and dealing with the daily pain of knowing your own country doesn't want you.

I try to find some dark humor embedded with the perpetual discomfort and absurdity. Humor, both sublime and silly, sophomoric and sophisticated, unleashed with purpose, can often help communicate very real, hard truths about American society.

Humor helps me process and find moments of much-needed catharsis, a release. Aristotle believed catharsis was an integral part of tragedy, allowing the audience to purge themselves after experiencing fear and pain. The character's fatal flaw, or hamartia, inevitably dooms the hero to their tragic fate, but at the very least the hero, along with the audience, experiences an epiphany toward the end.

In 2016, 63 million Americans voted for Donald J. Trump, a racist vulgarian, a failed businessman, and a gaudy reality-TV show host with zero political experience who appealed to racial anxieties and white resentment. He promised to "Make America Great Again" by building a wall and enacting a Muslim Ban. His presidency was a historic failure that resulted in two impeachments, multiple scandals, job losses, a rise in the debt and deficit, a misguided trade war, over 600,000 Americans dead from COVID-19, and international humiliation. This only meant that 11 million more Americans voted for him in 2020 than in 2016. White supremacy remains stubborn, persistent, and self-destructive until the end.

In 2022, we are still reeling from the horrors of this mistake, recovering from a debilitating recession and a deadly pandemic, and rebuilding our frayed institutions.

A record number of Americans came out during a pandemic to elect Joe Biden and Kamala Harris in 2020. That was our short-term cleanse.

Like many great works of theater, I believe America is simultaneously a riotous comedy and a heartbreaking tragedy. Our hamartia, our fatal flaw, is racism. It haunts us every day.

Thankfully, our last Act is unwritten.

The question remains: Who will be allowed to hold the pen and write the rest of the American story?

What I do know is that many communities in America are still waiting for their catharsis, their release.

Some are just hoping to breathe.

My name is Wajahat Ali.

I am what Diversity and Outreach coordinators refer to as a "Muslim man of color." I am neither white nor Black. Instead, I belong to a growing, miscellaneous tribe known as "people of color." Recently, I've been informed that I've been inducted into something called BIPOC. It's an acronym for Black, Indigenous, and People of Color. It also sounds like a malevolent cybernetic entity from a dystopian science fiction novel or an advanced breathing apparatus for people suffering from sleep apnea.

I apparently belong to the POC part of BIPOC.

I have also been affiliated with "Other" and "Asian" during high school. I briefly flirted with "Pacific Islander" in college, but who doesn't experiment in their youth?

I was born and raised in the Bay Area, California, in the year of *The Empire Strikes Back*, or 1980. I was also blessed with a trisyllabic name. Today, people at least tell me my name is unique and memorable, even as they insist on pronouncing it incorrectly.

The story goes that my Dada (paternal grandfather), Mirza Mustafa Ali, decided on the name Wajahat after he opened the Quran, closed his eyes, and randomly put his finger down on a page. His index finger serendipitously landed on the Arabic vowel و (pronounced "wow"). So, he chose a name starting with و, Wajahat, which means "esteemed" and "one of good face."

Yes, over the years, I shamelessly used the line "I'm Wajahat with a wow. It means one of good face." The ladies rarely agreed, but at least I tried.

However, nobody who knows me calls me Wajahat.

I am Wajoo to my family. Waji to elementary school friends. Waj to my college and law school buddies. Sir Waj-a-lot, Whatcha Want? and, my personal favorite, Waja-the-Hut to my childhood bullies. Online, I'm Wajass, Asshat, or Goat Fucker to my many admiring fans.

Growing up, I wondered why Dada's finger couldn't have landed on م (pronounced "meem") and turned me into a Muhammad instead? America eventually loved Muhammad Ali, even though it initially hated him for converting to Islam, embracing black nationalism, and protesting the criminal Vietnam War.

Or even Mufasa? America loves *The Lion King* so much they just digitally repainted the animated movie, added Beyoncé, and released it again to a gross of over one billion dollars.

Or how about Mike? It's strong and sturdy, the oak tree of American names. For every Pence and Huckabee, there's a Jordan and The Mechanic.

For a few weeks in first grade, I desperately wanted an "American" name and begged my mom to consider changing Wajahat to Wally or Wilbur. (I checked and those were definitely not Pakistani names.) She entertained my plea for the amount of time it took her to curtly say, "No." Desi mothers and fathers operate only in two modes: blunt and very blunt.

By the way, Desi refers to people who hail from the Indian subcontinent. I'll be using it frequently in this book.

I am the son of two Pakistani immigrants who came here from Karachi thanks to the 1965 Immigration and Nationality Act (INA). This federal law eliminated restrictive quotas based on national origin implemented in 1924. Back then, America wanted to keep out the "invaders," that is Asians, Italians, Eastern European Jews, and other undesirables who at the time were not accepted as "white" even though many of them are now considered to be Brock Strongballs's "European-descended people"—you know, the real Americans.

The act also allowed for family reunification, now branded as "chain migration," and sought skilled and educated labor from abroad. My father, a young graduate student who arrived in 1966, eventually brought along most of his family, just as Melania Trump brought her parents.

Some immigrants "burned the boat" when they arrived and decided to assimilate into "mainstream" (white) culture as quickly as possible. Instead, my family decided to bring the boat inside the suburban home. I grew up in a traditional setup. My grandparents lived with us until they passed away. I ate fresh Pakistani food every night because my family refused to order "nonsense" like McDonalds and Pizza Hut. I prayed the five daily prayers (I missed the early morning one because I was lazy and it was hella early), and all the while nobody thought it was important to teach me English.

Until the age of five, I spoke only Urdu peppered with three words and phrases of English:

1. Shut Up! (Because my mother used to say, "Shut Up!")
2. Idiot! (Because my mother usually used to follow "Shut Up!" with "Idiot!")
3. Uh Oh, Pasghettio! (This was the best I could do to repeat the classic commercial line "Uh Oh, SpaghettiOs!")

I was also shy, sickly, overweight, and prone to life-threatening accidents. Unlike some of my peers, I could never blend and melt into this magical American pot. I was always too Desi, too Muslim-y, too Husky. I avoided root beer until the age of nine, because I thought it was an alcoholic beverage. My carpoolers Ankur and Amit laughed at me while drinking a delicious can of root beer. Amit's mom found out and then she laughed. They offered me a sip and I hesitantly tasted the sugary goodness.

I learned early on that I always had to explain, educate, and at times defend my very being. I often became the token Pakistani and Muslim friend for many of my peers who had never met someone who fasted during Ramadan and didn't eat pork. Once, I ordered a slice of pepperoni pizza and took off all the pepperoni except a small piece embedded in the side of the cheese. It was delicious, but for the rest of the week I felt like a cursed character in a Poe short story, wracked by guilt, convinced Allah would punish me. My friends were curious as to whether I'd go to hell if I ever ate pork. I assured my friends that the earth would not swallow me up whole if they poured bacon bits on my salad during lunch. (They did it anyway. I did not go to hell. Well, I haven't . . . yet.)

I was always the odd duck. I went to an all-boys Jesuit Catholic high school in the Bay Area, where I dominated the yearly religious studies classes to the point that Father Allender almost wept when reading out the highest grades in the class: Wajahat Ali, the Muslim, followed by Kalyan, the Hindu. I carpooled with Brian, a Jew, Gaurav, a Hindu, and Allen, a Christian son of Nigerian immigrants. My America was a United Colors of Benetton ad.

In the '80s and '90s, my parents used "Amreekans" synonymously with white people. It's almost as if they knew, without consciously realizing, they still weren't part of the tribe.

"Amreekans say, 'I love you' all the time. After waking up, going to the bathroom, going to school, on the phone. What is this nonsense?" my mother asked. My parents are not "I love you" people. To this day, I've never said it to them or heard them say it to me. My parents weren't Spartan or miserly with their love; I always felt it, but they just have their own way of showing it. My father still slobbers me with big wet kisses on the cheek and my mother smothers me with hugs. They do this in public, alongside giving me unsolicited, critical comments about my wardrobe, fluctuating weight, and thinning hair.

They always thought "I love you" was superfluous nonsense goras did that cheapened the sentiment. Gora is what we use for white people. (Ghora is the word for horse, so be careful.)

Goras also celebrated Thanksgiving and Christmas. We didn't. Christmas was easy because it was a Christian holiday and my mother told me point blank at the age of four that Santa Claus was not going to give me presents because he didn't exist and was simply created by goras to sell toys. She then told me I should be grateful for all the toys I already had. That same year, she decided to become the serial killer of all imaginary creatures. I was informed the tooth fairy and the Easter bunny also weren't real, and they would not be bringing me quarters or chocolate.

My parents appreciated Thanksgiving and the entire tradition and concept of showing gratitude. However, they did not indulge in the customary dinner because they refused to cook this "strange," "tasteless," "dry bird" that goras inexplicably loved. By the early twenty-first century, however, they were hosting their own Thanksgiving parties, deep-frying the dry bird, respecting it with a proper masala base, and also adding achaar and chicken korma on the side.

Eventually, they too became Amreekan.

I always knew I was Amreekan, and also a brown-skinned kid with a strange name. I was awkward and creative.

But that same dorky, shy kid who couldn't speak English ended up graduating with an English degree from UC Berkeley, practicing law, and eventually grew up to write "so well" for the *New York Times* and speak "so well" on CNN. I also married way up.

My wife, Sarah, is smarter, kinder, and better-looking than me. I know this because my parents remind me. "Beta, you know she's better than you, right? Don't mess this up," my father warns me once a week. Remember, I am an only child, so this makes the advice that much more cold-blooded. She's also a doctor, a former athlete, and a former cheerleader, and somehow she has still retained her abs despite birthing three children. If you are the person who gains weight simply by looking at food, then you are my brother and sister in this cruel journey called

"Life Without Metabolism" and share my frustration at the unfairness of it all.

I still fast during Ramadan, try to watch every Warriors game, and do an awesome Yoda impression for my kids. I have learned how to make my mom's excellent Pakistani and Hyderabadi dishes during quarantine.

I'm about as American as chicken korma, apple pie, and chai, but even after forty years I'm *still* told to "go back."

Where, exactly?

In America, who (and what) are you when you're both "us" and "them"? When I'm a native but seen as a foreigner? When I'm a citizen but also seen as a perpetual suspect? When I'm your neighbor but also seen as an invader? When I'm a cultural creator but also seen as an eraser of white identity and European civilization?

According to mainstream code, I will never be "ordinary" or "a real American" from the "Rust Belt" (unless you consider California the heartland, which, let's face it, no one does). My parents are seen by some as potential terrorists because they're from Pakistan, even though they've lived in this country for over forty years.

Can I be a "real" American when I'm not white no matter how much Fair & Lovely cream I slather on my skin? The answer in 2022 is "Yes, but with conditions."

But I don't want conditional love. I want more from America and my fellow Americans. I am not content being the token, the diversity hire, the moderate Muslim, the magical minority, or "that one brown guy" who gets the invite to the prestigious festival or space on the cover of the brochure so the company and university can show the world they are open-minded and tolerant.

With the resurgence of radicalized white power movements, many are now forced to confront the reality called white supremacy that the rest of us have had to deal with our entire lives.

For many, resisting meant protesting. For the rest of us, our resistance is simply walking out of our house and breathing, just holding our head up, smiling, having hope, and telling our children that America belongs to them.

For us, surviving is an act of resistance.

There are forces that have always attempted, and ultimately failed, to make America static and rigid. But America has proven to be elastic. Our ancestors have always had to push and stretch America to accommodate its many residents and communities. We now have to do our part.

If any of you have been active students of US history, you know that with every two steps we march forward toward progress, we always get pushed one step back. The racially anxious men and women with hoods, tiki torches, and business suits will do everything in their power to violently chokehold and drag America back to 1953. This is the year before the Supreme Court in *Brown v. Board of Education of Topeka* ruled that segregation in public schools was unconstitutional. I'm convinced that 1953 is also the year that many enemies of diversity and progress believe America was allegedly "great."

You might disagree with me, sometimes passionately, about my opinions, choices, and what the appropriate path is for America to move forward toward becoming "great again." But boring an audience is a grave sin. I believe God said in one of the Holy Books, "Verily, thou shan't boreth an audience or thy Lord shall smite thee and make ye eat stale naan."

Bismillah.*

---

* In Arabic, "Bismillah" means "In the name of God." People generally use it to invoke a beginning. If you've already said it, you've become a Muslim. Gotcha.

Chapter 1

Create Your Own Superhero Origin Story

I always felt like I was slightly undercooked.

It's like God sneezed and took his eye off the ball during a crucial molding process, and instead of going back to correct the flaws, he thought it would be hilarious to see what would happen if he shipped me out of the kitchen with all defects intact.

First, I'm an only child, which makes me a brown unicorn. We South Asians are a breeding people. If you don't believe me, check out the world population statistics. Out of the top ten most populous countries, India ranks second with 1.3 billion, Pakistan comes in fifth with 238 million, and Bangladesh lands in eighth with 164 million. Like I said, we handle business.

Growing up, it was rare to find a fellow Pakistani only child. It was like discovering that one white friend who also took off shoes in their home—they belonged in a museum, protected and preserved for the world to witness.

Most people assumed my parents were either so disappointed with the initial result that they decided just to retire and make peace with the L, or they were cheap and didn't want to afford another kid, or there was nazr or jadu that prevented my mother from having more kids. Nazr is the evil eye, usually when someone sends bad vibes in your direction inspired by jealousy. Jadu refers to magic, usually when someone hires individuals to put a specific hex on you.

My mom actually had two miscarriages after me and could never become pregnant again. Whether it was nazr, jadu, nature, or disappointment remains an Unsolved Mystery.

Second, I am the only left-handed person in my entire family, and this was not seen as a praiseworthy characteristic. I was also known as "very healthy" and "mashallah." "Healthy" is a nice way of saying "fat." Mashallah is an Arabic word that means "Allah has willed it." You can say it after giving a sincere compliment. You also say it when you are incapable of giving a compliment. "Yes, your baked chicken without spices was . . . mashallah." I inherited my father's unique back-hair patterns, which my college friends to this day refer to as "the Batman symbol." I also have a giant dent in the middle of my forehead as a result of a hit-and-run accident when I was a kid.

The interior matches the busted exterior.

I inherited a heart condition from my paternal side known as supraventricular tachycardia, which almost killed me as an adult. I also inherited OCD, an anxiety disorder, from my father. I had terrible allergies as a child that required weekly shots and a hardcore dosage of antibiotics to control. I sweat profusely. I have constant stomach pain. I was shy and initially unable to raise my hand and talk in the classroom (cue the sweating). Recently, a podiatrist told me that I am flat-flooted and don't have a normal arch, which explains why I wobble slightly when I walk.

Clearly, I was born a winner.

When screenwriters sit down and imagine the protagonist of the movie, I am obviously their archetype, the Pakistani Adonis. I am Captain Islam. I am the Muslim superhero who saves the day, but only after sunset prayer and not during the thirty days of Ramadan. Just give me a cape, a leotard, prayer beads, and a magic janamaz (a prayer rug) and point me in the direction of a pork factory.

At a young age, I looked around and realized America's master narrative does not include a kid like me as one of its superheroes. At best, I could only hope to be a sidekick, a Hadji Singh to help Jonny Quest. We never saved the day or kissed the hot girl. Hardworking, awkward, endearing Desi kids who ate with their hands were never bitten by a radioactive spider or tussled with a pharaoh or threatened a criminal while holding a .44 magnum. Thankfully, Charlton Heston was there to play Moses in *The Ten Commandments* and a Mexican in the great Orson Welles movie *Touch of Evil.*

We Muslims and South Asians were at best neutered, goofy sidekicks or ethnic wallpaper, peppering the background. During the '90s, we were given complexity in the form of Apu, a 2D cartoon from *The Simpsons* voiced by Hank Azaria, a white actor. Often, we were the cardboard villain, a lazy composite of every Orientalist fantasy assembled into a convenient brown, bearded bogeyman whose emotional range existed somewhere between belligerent and irritable.

Or worse: we were completely excised from the story.

Call me skeptical, but I just don't trust others to truly understand the challenges of having turmeric-stained fingernails as a five-year-old in preschool or explaining to high school friends why your mom's hamburgers had "green stuff" inside them. So, the first recommendation on your hero's quest to become American is to create and share your own superhero origin story.

The Amreekan Dream

Once upon a time, a young student, with a full head of hair, decided to leave his family behind in Karachi, Pakistan, and travel to Amreeka with his older brother on a student visa to attend college. Both were excellent academic students and envisioned being the first in their family to "make it" in Amreeka, enjoying a slice of this deliciousness called the Amreekan dream.

My dad, Zulfiqar Ali, and his older brother, Sultan, arrived in San Francisco, California, as teenagers in 1966, in the midst of the civil rights movement. Protests and riots were erupting across America. MLK was still alive and the Beatles had just declared themselves more popular than Jesus. President Lyndon B. Johnson was sending more soldiers to the escalating Vietnam War. The first ATM was introduced. *The*

Sound of Music won Best Picture, as Julie Andrews and the von Trapp family sang memorable songs while escaping Nazis in Europe. Meanwhile, in Dallas, Texas, George Lincoln Rockwell of the American Nazi Party carried placards in the street that read: "Race Mixing is Financed and Led by Jews!" Alas, some leopard spots never change.

The Ali brothers immediately ditched their kurtas and crew cuts for bell-bottoms and shoulder-length hair. Growing up, I assumed my father was born bald, in khaki Dockers, and with glasses that accentuated his large eyes. I refused to believe he had hair, let alone "hippie hair." However, I have seen the photos, they are not doctored, and I remain traumatized.

Both brothers enrolled in Hartnell, a two-year college, and then Abu, which is what I call my father, transferred to Cal State University in Los Angeles to obtain his bachelor of science degree in finance. In 1971, he received a scholarship to attend Northern Illinois University as a graduate student in econometrics, with an emphasis in data analytics. He also obtained a job at the university as a graduate student instructor.

The nerd game was strong in him.

Contrary to popular myths, South Asian immigrants aren't genetically predisposed to academic excellence. Our mother's breast milk isn't laced with an extra supply of organic DHA-Omega 3 for brain health that grants us superior advantages in spelling. Also, you should take comfort in knowing there are many South Asians, such as yours truly, who are terrible spellers. (I am a shanda to my people.) The reality is that most people of color learn early in America that we will have to work twice as hard to get half as far, and when we fail, no one will help us fall up.

Immigrants, people of color, and women learn early that in order to make it in Amreeka you have to daft punk it through life. You have to do everything harder, better, faster, stronger, and smarter. Those are just the rules. The streets of Amreeka aren't paved with gold; they're paved with blood. As an immigrant, you'll take a beating but you'll be like Rick Ross and keep hustling. If Bob works eight hours a day, you work ten. If Samantha works late on Friday, then you work on Saturday. You go twenty feet just to get to ten feet.

My father learned this while applying for his visa extension to attend Northern Illinois University. Abu's academic excellence couldn't erase his brown skin or protect him against America's original sin: racism. According to him, he walked into the U.S. Citizenship and Immigration Services office in Chicago for what he assumed would be a routine procedure to extend his F-1 student visa.

There his achievements meant nothing. He was just another young brown man without citizenship, without whiteness. As soon as he saw the white officer's contemptuous glare, he knew there would be trouble. The man briefly reviewed Abu's application, muttered under his breath, and then, looking my father in the eye, said he didn't think Abu was a serious student or had any real intention of pursuing graduate studies. My father was stunned. Still trying to process the situation, my father asked the officer why he believed he had no intention to pursue graduate studies. Upon hearing this, the officer snapped, "You Arabs come here only to fuck our American girls."

Bigots aren't really nuanced when it comes to their racial anxiety. An Arab might as well be a Pakistani who looks like a damn Indian who comes roughly from the same place as a goddamn Chinaman, who, like all Black people, originally come from shithole countries and invade America to just take, take, take this country's resources, especially its most prized possession: "American girls," which refers only to white women.

Now, if you've been paying attention, you know that we are Pakistani and not Arab. Pakistan is a country in the Indian subcontinent, and the major languages spoken include Punjabi, Urdu, Saraiki, Balochi, Pashto, Sindhi, and English. Abu is not nor has he ever been Arab. Second, my father was admitted, with a scholarship, to a graduate school and brought along all the necessary evidence.

Abu was indeed very handsome in his youth, but he wasn't really messing around with girls due to his sober, studious, nerdy disposition.

His sister once told me her brother Sultan and his friends finally pressured him into having one gori girlfriend named Cassandra who was very sweet. My father insists she was "just a friend," there was no romantic relationship, and she simply "volunteered" to buy clothing and household items for his mother and sister, who were visiting from Karachi.

Most kids of Desi immigrants just assume all our elders were sexless robots who rejected foreplay and flirting for good credit and stable degrees. Only years later do we realize that some of our most pious and stern elders actually had gori girlfriends before marriage. Some also used to drink, party, and wear bell-bottoms to the disco. Again, this is still never acknowledged; however, one thing that has been confirmed is that no Jews were involved in the financing of this alleged race mixing.

So, maybe, he was with a gori—according to my aunt at least—but it was a harmless, sweet friendship that was not illegal, no concern of the immigration officer, and not justifiable ground for deportation. Also, unlike with the British colonizers of South Asia, there was no exploitation, pillaging, raping, or looting of this country's women or wealth. If anything, my parents' generation has only helped America with its labor, academic brilliance, and contributions to finance, science, health, and engineering. Abu also probably taught his alleged gori girlfriend Pakistani recipes, and her children and grandchildren should thank us forever. We helped feed future generations khatti daal and keema.

STAMP!

Visa extension DENIED. Deportation ORDERED.

The immigration officer told Abu he had to leave within a week. He went to every lawyer he could in Chicago, all of whom, according to him, basically said, "Sir, you're fucked."

My father packed his bags and bought his one-way ticket back to Karachi, Pakistan. His flight left on a Saturday night. The day before, he decided to try one more lawyer whom he recalls was located in Hoffman Estates, a suburb of Chicago. He told his story to the seasoned attorney, who echoed the hopelessness, and my father left his office resigned to his fate.

On the way out of the building, a young lawyer, a white man by the name of John, ran and caught up to him. He was working at the law office and awaiting his bar results. He had overheard the story, felt bad for my father, and thought of a solution: the "Einstein visa."

This special visa grants employment-based permanent residency in the United States for foreign nationals who have "extraordinary abilities," or to "outstanding professors or researchers." The Einstein visa allowed Melania Trump to remain in the US, where she eventually obtained her citizenship. My father was a brilliant researcher who received a scholarship, a grant, and a teaching position at a graduate university. Melania Trump was a Slovenian model who at the time, in 2000, was dating Donald Trump and appeared naked on a fur rug on the cover of *British GQ*. Both Abu and Melania obviously had "extraordinary abilities" valued by the United States of America.

The young attorney told my father to ditch the flight to Karachi and that he'd accompany him, for free, in front of the immigration judge with a petition for a permanent resident visa for academic achievement. Abu recalls that the elderly judge, a Jewish man presumably due to his last name, shook his head with disgust at the nonsensical deportation order, canceled it, then looked up and said, "I will approve this application. Kindly get it submitted within ten days."

Less than three months later, Abu received a call from the dean's office telling him his visa application had been approved on an expedited basis. Five years later, he became a citizen.

"Our entire family's trajectory would have changed if I'd been deported," my father tells me. He said one American's racism and another American's kindness helped chart our future in this country. That push and pull, the perpetual tug of war between xenophobia and acceptance, is a perfect microcosm of the lived experiences of so many Americans who are still told to "go back."

You're "us" until you're suddenly "them."

Indeed, if it wasn't for a serendipitous act of kindness from a stranger balancing out a callous act of racist cruelty, I'd be watching Hollywood movies on my smartphone in Karachi, wondering how such a mighty country, which had more than 600,000 COVID-19 deaths, succumbed during a pandemic. Or, I'd still be spermatid waiting for my chance to swim. Either way, I wouldn't be here writing this story, or probably any story, because I'm a terrible swimmer.

The Interesting Girl from Karachi: A Marriage Story

After obtaining his graduate degree, Abu sponsored my Dadi, or grandmother, who arrived with Dada, my grandfather, and my father's youngest sibling, his sister Yasmeen, whom I call Phuppo. They all started wearing bell-bottoms. Dadi loved listening to the Doobie Brothers while cooking nihari and reciting her devotional hymns. She was also very open about her crush on Tom Jones. She put her sewing material and jewelry in Royal Dansk cookie tins, which immigrants of every ethnicity universally agree is the true calling and purpose of the round blue receptacles. Yasmeen Phuppo, a brunette, dreamed of having Farrah Fawcett's hair from *Charlie's Angels* and becoming a singer of Urdu and Hindi songs. She was known for her beautiful voice.

My grandfather was basically retired but helped my father out in his business activities. He was a punctual and jovial man with a set routine. He'd wake up in the morning, have chapati for breakfast, and go for his daily power walk in his Kangol and gray sweats, with his thumbs up, his arms swaying up and down with each stride as if he were skiing. Let it be known, he never skied. There's not much snow in Karachi. My family is not a skiing, camping, or hiking family. These were considered exotic "gora people activities" when I was growing up. My parents believed they worked too hard in this country to go out and sleep and shit in the woods voluntarily, for fun.

At night, Dada relaxed on his La-Z-Boy and watched Clint Eastwood Westerns. He was also incapable of subtlety, like everyone else in the Ali family. He used to warn my aunt to watch her weight during her first marriage because her doctor husband was surrounded by beautiful, flirtatious nurses. "Beti, the young generation isn't like us old-timers. Your mother, whom I love, let herself go and gained weight. She knows I'll never leave her. But this generation? No man wants to come home and see a buffalo moaning on the bed."

Obviously, this did not go over well with the women of the house. Something about being compared to large mammals generally has that negative, polarizing effect. According to my mom, who was horrified but also thought it was hilarious, Dada refused to apologize and instead expressed shock as to why anyone would be upset at him for simply stating the truth.

Both of my grandparents were social butterflies with numerous acquaintances and the gift of the gab at parties. Abu, unfortunately, is physically incapable of making small talk and would rather self-immolate if given the option. In fact, he has actively self-expelled himself from social parties throughout his life.

Abu's idea of heaven would probably be staying at home, researching, doing chores in his boxers and chappals while listening to Nusrat Fateh Ali Khan, watching TV for about thirty minutes, reading his wazifas, a litany of Quranic verses, and going to Costco every two weeks to buy enough toilet paper in bulk to last us until Yawm al-Qiyamah, the Day of Judgment. He was the exact opposite of his elder brother Sultan, a ladies' man, who teased my father relentlessly. Their mutual friends referred to Abu only as "Brother" because of his serious disposition and the fact that he rarely joined them in their bachelor revelry. By 1977, the clan had moved from Chicago to Dayton, Ohio, where my father went to work at Wright Patterson Air Force Base. He was recruited by the Fairchild Aircraft Company as a program manager to assist the head of the United States Air Force System Program Office (SPO) that was responsible for A-10 Attack Aircraft acquisitions. (Note: a Pakistani Muslim American helping the country's national security and defense program would, forty years later, be seen as a member of a religion that is a unique threat in need of a ban.)

My father was nearing the *Dead Zone* age of eligibility for South Asians: thirty. My grandparents were giving him subtle hints to find a wife and settle down—that is: "Get married, now." Dada used to read the *Jang* newspaper, shipped to him from Pakistan. One day, Abu picked it up and noticed a black-and-white photo of an "interesting girl" who finished first in her master's test results in the field of nutrition. Her name was Sameena Roohi Hashmi, daughter of Commander Iqbal Ahmed Hashmi, retired from the Pakistani navy. My father casually asked my grandfather about this "interesting girl." Dada instantly recognized Commander Hashmi as one of his old college friends from Osmania University in Hyderabad, India. Yasmeen Phuppo remembered the "interesting girl" as one of her elder classmates during their time in the College of Home Economics in Karachi. To this day, my father never says, "As soon as I saw her, I knew she was the one," or the usual stockpile of worn clichés. Instead, he just says, "She was interesting."

In fact, I've only heard him comment on women's beauty twice: The first time, commenting on Sophia Loren, who was the universal gold standard for most boys born between 1945 and 1950. The second time was after an interview with actress Teri Hatcher during the height of her *Lois and Clark: The New Adventures of Superman* fame, when he said to no one in particular, "She has a very . . . symmetrical face."

Dada thought my mom was both "symmetrical" and smart, and he did some old-school sleuthing and discovered that her professor was married to his longtime friend Himayat Ali Khan. He decided to use him as an intermediary to do initial reconnaissance because Himayat uncle was closer to Nana, my mom's father. He mailed him my father's "biodata" as a potential rishta, a marriage prospect, with a personal letter to be delivered to the commander.

"What's a 'biodata'? Does it include blood samples and a urine test?" you ask. South Asian arranged marriages are now basically accelerated dates between individuals, and their extended families, with the intention of deducing compatibility for marriage. "Biodata" is like your résumé, Tinder profile, LinkedIn, or Topps Baseball Card with all your best stats that you unleash on the first date. The prized categories in the South Asian biodata are as follows:

~ "Good job." Translation: Doctor, engineer, businessman, or inherited wealth.

~ "Good family." Translation: Everyone is married, civil, and able to smile and behave properly at social events, and you are able to hide or lie about all your family's dysfunction, divorces, mental health issues, arrests, temper tantrums, and otherwise normal family chaos.

~ "Fair skin." Translation: Your skin color is white but not white. You are light, which means you are right. You can never be Black, and you must try very hard to never be dark.

To this day, South Asian elders in America and abroad casually say the following: "Oh, she's so pretty, but, bichari [poor girl], she is dark," or "Oh, she's lovely, laikin [but] she is kum rang [dark]." Kum rang literally translates to "less color," which makes it even more absurd when it's used to describe dark skin. The phrase for light skin? Saaf rang, which literally translates to clean skin color.

My mother did not have saaf rang. In fact, she barely resembled her newspaper photo and she complained it was false advertising. She was an athlete who used to play tennis on the varsity team and spent most of her hours in the Karachi sun, which darkened her skin and gave her mother, my Nani, panic attacks. "No one will marry you! Look how dark you've become! Stay inside!" she begged my mother, who used to ignore her and continue playing.

Himayat uncle did his job and passed on my father's biodata to Nana, who remembered Dada from their college days and was intrigued by Abu's potential. He unleashed his own counterintelligence operation and asked his eldest son, Masood Mamoo, who was finishing his chemical engineering master's degree at MIT, to go check out the Alis.

Mamoo is a genial, mild-mannered dude with a wry sense of humor that masks his otherwise sharp, cutting intellect. The Alis are all hot-tempered, passionate, garrulous eccentrics who lack filters. Mamoo visited all of them in Dayton, Ohio, and stayed for three days.

Abu spent that long weekend "eating my brother's brain," according to my mom. He grilled him with every hypothetical scenario imaginable and asked Mamoo to deduce how Ami would react in each situation. Dada was so embarrassed and exhausted by the interrogation that he told Mamoo, "Listen, I'm sorry, I don't know how you can stand this. If my son did this to me, I'd kick his ass out of the house."

Mamoo took it in stride, collected all of his thoughts and observations in a detailed ten-page analysis, and mailed it back to Ami. In hindsight, Ami said he perfectly described and predicted the personality and characteristics of every single family member. She vividly remembers his description of Dadi: "She always has her tasbih [prayer beads]. She has her own rocker. She listens to naats [devotional hymns], and she loves Tom Jones."

A few months later, in March 1978, Abu had a business trip to Abu Dhabi. Dada encouraged him to stop over in Karachi and at least meet this "interesting girl." Abu brought along the entire Karachi clan to my Nana's home. They all made the usual, awkward, formal chitchat. Chai and sweets were served. My mother and father of course did not talk to each other, and then everyone left.

This was considered a success.

My father then asked Nana if he could have his permission to talk to my mother. This was agreed. He returned to the house. My mom came out to meet him.

Silence.

More silence.

"Well, you've asked to talk, so talk. Why aren't you talking?" my mom asked.

Nani attempted to murder her with a glare. Ami deflected it and continued looking straight at Abu.

He cracked a faint smile.

Five minutes later, he got up and left.

Less than a week later, they were married.

A week after that, Sameena, who would become my Ami, landed in America for the first time, arriving in NYC for her green card, then finally stopping in glorious Dayton, Ohio. She was twenty-three years old and part of the Alis.

The Arrival, Or the Golden Child Who Wasted His Face

My mother had a difficult pregnancy and labor. Before I was born, she had a dream she was praying at the Prophet's mosque in Medina, Saudi Arabia. Masjid Al Nabawi is the second-holiest mosque for Muslims after Masjid al Haram, which houses the Kaaba, the black cube you see Muslims circle around during Hajj. She was accompanied by Patata Dadi, who was my grandmother's sister-in-law. I called her Patata Dadi because I pronounced "paratha" as "patata," and when as a child I visited her in Pakistan, she used to make amazing animal-shaped parathas, which are a glorious, layered flatbread that will put you in the best food coma. The name stuck forever.

Ami always found it strange that in this dream she wasn't accompanied by her mother, or her three sisters, or her mother-in-law, but instead by a woman she had just met and befriended after marriage. They were seated in the prayer row and a stranger came up to her and placed a big bouquet of white flowers in her lap on top of her crossed legs.

And then she woke up.

The tafseer (interpretation) of this dream according to the elders was that her child would be a blessing for the family. It could also have meant that Ami really wanted Abu to get her some flowers, but let's stick with the story that makes me sound like the Chosen One.

I was born in November 1980 in El Camino Hospital. A brilliant flash of light did not illuminate the hospital hallways. No choir of angels could be heard singing high-pitched opera. The birth was notable only for being a painful, intense delivery that required a C-section. I had to come out the unorthodox way even during my arrival.

Dada was given the honor to name me, and he did the Eeny-Meeny-

Miny-Moe with the Quran and settled on Wajahat, which means esteemed and handsome. Unfortunately, I was neither. My mother said I was a pretty ugly baby. She loved me, but it wasn't because I was cute. Currently, my mother laments that I have not taken advantage of my alleged good looks by working out, building muscles, dressing appropriately, and using my jawline to act in Hollywood: "Allah gave you such a nice face, and you wasted it." My mother also believes she is the most subtle and diplomatic member of our family.

I was the first Scorpio in the family as well. Both my maternal and paternal side to this day say, "Oh, watch out, he's a Scorpio," which is strange because they aren't into astrology and I have yet to unleash the Scorpio sign's patented jealousy or anger. I am, however, intense, passionate, loyal, secretive (but I'm writing a memoir, so I guess I'm changing), and a stubborn bakra (goat) according to Mom, and if you betray my trust, you are dead to me for life.

The first Wajahat of the family arrived home, which at the time was a house in Milpitas, California, shared by my parents, my grandparents, my aunt and my father's brother, his wife and their two kids. We were the Desi Bunch and our squad had a deeper bench than the Bradys.

The Left Hand Is Only Used for One Thing

My left hand led me astray. For the first few years the only thing setting me apart from my cousins was the fact that I was an only child and a "bit healthy" and "big boned." Then I started catching and throwing with my left. I drew stick figures and my Baby Picassos with my left. At first, there was no cause for premature alarm. Not until I started eating with my left. That was Defcon 5.

It's already difficult being a left-handed minority in a right-dominated world. Our entire lives we've been systematically oppressed by right supremacy. We have to write from left to right and endure smudge marks on our left palms and mockery from the right-handed elite. We have to tuck in our elbows and contort our bodies to sit in desks at school to accommodate the right majority and not trigger right anxiety. We stare in confusion as the right-handed scissors don't work in our left hand. We learn to throw and catch with our right hand, because schools rarely have extra left-handed baseball mitts for after-school activities. Right privilege doesn't see right-hand bias. Rightness thinks all handedness matters.

It's especially shameful to be left-handed in many Muslim and Asian communities, because we are told from childhood that "the left hand is only used for *one thing*." How can one hand that is used to clean one end be used to feed the other? It's unimaginable.

There is no verse in the Quran that knocks left-handedness. Trust me, I've checked multiple times.

In Islam, Muslims follow the Quran, our Holy Book we believe was revealed to the Prophet Muhammad, and the Sunnah, the traditions and actions of the Prophet during his lifetime. Hadith are a collection of sayings, actions, and traditions attributed to the Prophet Muhammad. Hadith have a chain of narration and system of ranking that classifies them based on their reliability. The top-shelf hadith is known as sahih, which establishes an unbroken narrative chain that identifies all the narrators as being of sound mind and good character, and it can be connected all the way back to the Prophet. A da'if hadith is seen as "weak" because there's a gap in the narrative chain and one of the narrators is not seen as reliable.

As you can tell, this vast body of literature can lead to multiple, sometimes conflicting, interpretations.

Several hadiths, however, do reveal that the Prophet encouraged his companions to eat with the right hand, because the left was exclusively for the toilet. According to one sahih hadith, the Prophet allegedly said, "No one among you should eat with his left hand or drink with it, for the shaytaan eats with his left hand and drinks with it." Shaytaan is also known by his stage name, Satan. The Prophet also allegedly said, "One ought not to eat with one's left hand or drink with one's left hand unless there is good cause." Another sahih hadith. One would assume being born left-handed is pretty damn "good cause" and that settles the conversation.

Of course not.

If the world starts heading toward a global religious war, it seems the world's major monotheistic religions can make peace over their shared history of fearing the left hand, dominant in nearly eleven percent of people worldwide.

The word "sinister," an apt description for the Devil and his malevolent intentions, is derived from a Latin word that means "on the left side." In the Old Testament, it is written that humans have two impulses: the one inspiring righteousness is on the right, and the one inclining you toward wickedness is on the left. During the Spanish Inquisition, the Catholic Church at times condemned and executed my left-handed tribe. During the Salem Witch Trials, left-handedness was one of the signs of witchcraft.

I had no idea my desire to eat Fruity Pebbles with my left hand was the demon's mark revealing my inherent disposition toward villainy. I just wanted sugar posing as cereal in my He-Man bowl.

Ami and Dadi, my mother and grandmother, hatched an ingenious conversion plan to save my damned soul, and one that thankfully didn't involve electroshock therapy or bloodletting. Ami would hold my left hand behind my back as Dadi would throw tennis balls directly at my body. The idea was that, eventually, I would begin catching the balls with my right hand and thus avoid being assaulted and battered.

That was the plan.

Unfortunately, I'm a stubborn Scorpio, and humans plan but God laughs. One day, my father's youngest brother, Wasif Chacha, who at the time was studying to become a doctor, walked in and saw tennis balls bouncing off my shapely stomach as his mother kept throwing them at my body and my mother forcefully held my arm back.

Disturbed and slightly amused, he dashed their strategy. "Let it go. Let it go. It's over. He's left-handed," he told them.

My mother and grandmother resigned themselves to my cursed fate.

To this day, when I'm at a large Muslim social event and take food from the buffet table with my left hand, or God forbid eat with my left hand, I get reprimanded. My aunt, Yasmeen Phuppo, on numerous occasions has decided to inform me, loudly, in front of the entire party, "Wajahat. The left hand is only used for *one thing!*"

Freakmont and the Suburban Utopia

In kindergarten, I started attending James Leitch Elementary School, situated on the mean, suburban streets of Fremont, California. I take immense pride in my Fremont roots—for no other reason than I basically spent my entire life, except for four years at UC Berkeley and three years at UC Davis, living there until I left to be with my wife in Virginia.

The Bay remains my first home, and I must rep and defend it until the end even though it broke my heart.

The city is also a reminder of the original sins of white nationalism and American imperialism in all its hubris, violence, and absurd contradictions. In 1846, John Frémont was sent by the U.S. War Department on an ambitious expedition to survey California. Like most colonizers before and after him, he took credit for discovering something that already existed. Isn't that wild? I just admire the chutzpah and confidence of walking into somebody's house and saying, "Yeah, that belongs to me. God willed it. Oh, by the way, since this is the first time I'm seeing it, that means I discovered it. Your presence and history are not valid and no longer needed. However, thanks for cultivating the land. Now, you can either stay as my slave or I'll kill you. God bless."

The inhabitants of the land, Native Americans, were apparently not part of God's plan. In order to ensure they'd be erased from the story, Frémont and his men presided over not one but several massacres of Indigenous people along the way to their destiny. None of his men were charged or punished for their crimes.

Instead, for his role in massacring Native Americans, John Frémont was later rewarded with being elected as one of the new state of California's first senators. He also ran for president of the United States in

1856 under the newly created Republican Party, but he lost to James Buchanan. If he were a Confederate general and traitor, he would have been celebrated with many more statues and schools named after him, but alas, he was just a Union general during the Civil War.

I wonder how Frémont and his merry band of murderers would react knowing that in the twenty-first century, the town named after him is one of the most ethnically diverse cities in the Bay Area and populated by brown and Asian immigrants who came from shithole countries? (It's the little things that give me joy.) It is home to a ridiculous number of Desis and also Afghans, many of whom settled in the city as refugees escaping the brutal Russian invasion of Afghanistan.

"Freakmont," as it is affectionately known by some, still doesn't get love or respect. We're seen as the drive-by city between San Jose and Oakland. A quiet, boring, suburban town where middle-class and upper-class immigrants and Silicon Valley workers reside for the expensive houses, great weather, excellent public schools, and delicious "ethnic" food. We also take pride in being the hometown of Olympic gold–winning figure skater Kristi Yamaguchi.

We don't have the Golden Gate Bridge, but we have Pakwan, Shalimar, and De Afghanan Kabob. (If you're ever in Fremont, tell them I sent you. The workers knew me as "Ali bhai" and recognized my voice on the phone.)

During my youth, in the '80s, Fremont had yet to experience the Silicon Valley tech boom and population growth. There was still plenty of affordable land and even many white people. My father had achieved the coveted "upwardly mobile" middle-class status a few years before most of his Pakistani peers and was able to invest early. We moved from Milpitas to my childhood home on Curtner Road, which at the time fellow Desis in my community looked upon with awe as "the big triangle house."

My grandparents and my mother in particular were quite social, and our old home is still fondly remembered for these festive Quran khatams and old-school music parties where community members and my aunt sang ghazals and Bollywood classics. My mother and aunts were trained by my Dadi to cook up a feast on the drop of a dime. They worked like an efficient army unit and were able to make a delicious spread for a hundred people in a day. People were always staying with us, some of them family and others just random folks who stayed six months or a year or two because they were related to my parents' friends and needed a place to stay when first arriving in Amreeka.

To most this would seem like a chaotic halfway house for itinerant Pakistanis, but to me it was perfectly normal. I thought all homes were like this, filled with several generations of eccentric family members, religious functions mixed with social gatherings, giant pots of food, Urdu and Saturday morning cartoons, He-Man action figures and Sunday school where the religious teacher would come to our home and teach the neighborhood kids how to read the Quran.

We even had a huge wraparound yard, a separate garage in the back, and a giant eucalyptus tree in front of the sidewalk. It was Xanadu for us first-generation kids.

Dada decided to gift the family a Mercedes Benz, and we even bought a big-screen TV, which back in the day was the size of a tank, took up the entire corner of our family room, and weighed five hundred pounds. We kept our Honda, and my father felt more comfortable driving that because immigrants are all about efficiency and getting the most mileage for the buck. We baptized our new TV system with *Top Gun*, which had just been released on VHS.

By 1987, my parents had achieved the Amreekan dream. They had checked off all the boxes for the barometer of Pakistani immigrant success:

~ A marriage. ✔
~ A child. ✔
~ A nice suburban home. ✔
~ A Honda, Mercedes, BMW, and/or Toyota. ✔ ✔ (Double check!)
~ A big-screen TV. ✔
~ A job that somehow affords all this. ✔

All that was left for them to do was go to Hajj and become more religious to prepare for retiring from Earth, having fulfilled life's purpose. They literally could have died in 1987 and community members would have said, "Those Alis. They had a big-screen TV *and* a Mercedes. Mashallah. They made it. Those bastards."

In many South Asian communities, personal fulfillment and desires take a back seat to "log kya bolingay," the sole question that never receives an answer but nonetheless drives immigrants to participate in a relentless, panicked race that eventually leads them to their graves.

"What will people say?"

My friend Hasan Minhaj had a similar experience and mentioned this in his Netflix special *Homecoming King*. (Yes, all South Asians in the media know each other and are related and have the same story and look exactly the same. In fact, my real name is Fareed Zakaria.)

We spend our entire lives hijacked by "what will people say?" We are obsessed with it. We do everything we can to show our good "face," even sabotaging our own happiness in the process. We give up so much for people who really don't know us or care about us and who won't even come to our funeral, because they're too consumed and self-absorbed, running the same race, asking themselves, "What will people say?"

If you live in an apartment when all your peers live in a house, what will people say? If your kid was born in this country and went to school and was unable to get a "good job," what will people say? If you're above the age of thirty and you're unmarried, what will people say? If you get divorced, what will people say? If you eat with your left hand at parties, what will people say?

My parents never drilled the checklist into my head. In fact, I never heard them obsess over the size of our house or compare our cars with our friends. This conversation never came up in my house, but it smothered my generation nonetheless. It covered us like a thick blanket of smog. It was inescapable. We breathed it in, observing what our community elders valued, how they valued us, how they were judged, how they judged others, how people were ranked. All that was left was for me to go to a "good college," get a "good degree," get a "good job" with a "good salary," marry a "good girl," produce "good children," and then pass on this recipe of success to my "good children" so the goodness could be replicated until the end of times. Happiness is optional.

But happiness defined my childhood. Our old triangle house was my personal playground, my fortress of solitude, my Wayne Manor, where I had my toys, my backyard, and my secret hiding spots. It was a sanctuary from all the horrors and problems of the world, a warm, safe bubble that kept me well-fed and was populated by grandparents, parents, family members, and random people who stayed in the guest bedroom and showered me with attention and love.

I thought this was the norm, not the suburban exception. Ignorance, no matter how well intentioned, is one of the unfortunate handicaps and setbacks of privilege.

Success, or the appearance of it, has its own toxic baggage. All eyes are on you. Especially when you have the biggest house in the community, your Dada is driving a Benz, and your parents have allegedly "made it" before everyone else. Compliments are now laced with poison. Guests enjoy the haleem and the kheer after the music party, but a few ask, "Why them? Why not me?" Passive-aggressive cuts are delivered with wide smiles in between pleasantries.

During junior high, a friend from school moved into one of the beautiful, multi-million-dollar mansions that started to quickly replace the vineyards on nearby Mission Hills. Many of my parents' contemporaries had literally moved on up. Our house was now quaint compared to their spacious palaces. We were still content with our triangle house with the big-ass eucalyptus tree in front. No complaints. I congratulated my friend on the move.

"Now *we* have the biggest house," he responded. His demeanor and voice were tinged with anger and pride, a cocktail mixed with vengeance and triumph, as if some cosmic wrong was righted. It shook me. I had no idea there was a competition. I wished someone had informed me while I was playing my Sega Genesis.

For those who nurtured similar resentment for years, their patient commitment would one day be rewarded.

We'd eventually lose the house, the Benz, and "the checklist."
We'd lose everything.
"Log kya bolingay?"
A lot apparently.

ESL Boys and Elementary School Girls

As our entire class walked from the playground back to homeroom, they would take me and three other children out from the single-file line to a small room for our unofficial English as a Second Language class, effectively marking us for social death.

In first grade, I was still the token Muslim, and although there was a smattering of brown kids, I was holding down representation for the entire subcontinent in my homeroom. The teachers were lovely, not an evil jinn among them, but I was reminded daily how I was "unique" for my ethnic eccentricities. I also sported a bowl haircut, always trying to cover my forehead.

I had a giant scar as a result of a hit-and-run confrontation with a motorcycle in Karachi, Pakistan, that left my forehead looking like a wrinkled map of Pangea. In college, I used to call it my Klingon scar. In my twenties, I called it my Harry Potter scar, and it eventually became a great ice breaker with women. But for six-year-old Wajahat, this was just another damning mark of my otherness, a literal sign on my forehead that yelled, "FREAK." I was so self-conscious about it that I frequently patted down my hair over my forehead, which ended up inviting people to ask, "Hey what's that thing on your head?"

But at least I could hide it—sometimes. What I couldn't hide was my slight accent. It was crippling my ascension on the social ladder, and it prevented me from talking to Jennifer, my first crush. She was the Helen of First Grade, a blonde, blue-eyed, white American princess with golden locks that were kept in perfect condition and held up by the angels. She gave my stomach the "googly tinglies." That's how I described the butterflies that flew in my gut each time I'd catch a glimpse of her in homeroom or during recess while sitting on the dome climber with my two friends, Chris and Greg, who also pined for her.

None of us were cool, outspoken, charming, or had any other friends. It's like when you befriend or marry someone by default. We found each other by virtue of our dorkiness, and the fact that no one else would hang out with us.

The only girl who talked to me was Mercedes, who was Mexican-American. She was the first girl I ever made laugh. We all were the last in line during lunch, waiting to get our food from the cafeteria. We started talking about our favorite beverages. Naturally, I chose Coke, the correct choice. Mercedes went for Fanta, and Chris came in with the curveball, Dr. Pepper. Like an amateur Seinfeld, I just started riffing on the word. "What's Dr. Pepper? Is it a Doctor or a Pepper? How can it be a drink?" (Thank you, thank you. I'll be here all week. Tip the staff, please.)

Mercedes laughed out loud, eyes focused on me, and I kept going. "I mean, where's Doctor Salt? Is that a drink?" She snorted and even Chris had to admit it was funny. A real girl was voluntarily hanging out with me, enjoying my corny jokes, not mocking me for my accent and brownness and "big bones," and inspiring me with her infectious laughter. She even came up and talked to me after school as we waited for our parents during pick-up. As she walked away with her mom, she turned around and waved.

Still, she wasn't Jennifer. I only had the attention span for one crush. I had to choose between them, so I went with the popular girl, the one who looked like the women on TV and in cartoons. I was convinced I would somehow make her like me. She would accept me. She would be mine.

My first crush also inspired my first nemesis. Let's just call him Chad, a tall, skinny, white kid with blonde hair who looked like the promethean Aryan child, molded from the aspirational dreams of white nationalists everywhere. Despite accomplishing nothing of significance in his six years of life, Chad was a cocky bastard who walked like a mediocre white man who woke up every day thinking he pissed excellence.

There was an unspoken acknowledgment in the homeroom that Jen-

nifer and Chad were destined to be together. They fit the quintessen-
tial mold of the Hollywood couple, the prom king and queen from '80s
movies, or Samantha and Jake, the leads from the 1984 classic *Sixteen
Candles*. We were Ted, the über-geek, Anthony Michael Hall's character who kept hitting on Samantha only to be rejected, or worse, Long
Duk Dong, the foreign exchange student, a walking caricature of every
ridiculous and humiliating Asian stereotype. Either way, I knew I wasn't
getting Jennifer with my poor, accented English.

In ESL, around a small desk, was me, the Pakistani Muslim kid who
was still learning English, two Asian-American girls who had recently
arrived in America and didn't know English, and a Black kid who
seemed to be there for no discernible reason other than he was the
token Black kid.

"Wajahat, just like yesterday. We are going to work on your 'W's and
'V's, OK?" the teacher informed me. "Now, repeat after me: Whatever."

"Whatewer," I responded, trying my best to copy her.

In the Urdu language, which uses the Perso-Arabic script, there is
no letter for "V." We at least have a letter for "P" so we can say "Pepsi,"
which is known as "Bebsi" in Arab-majority countries.

"No, it's Whatever."

"Whatewer."

"Listen. It's What—Ever," she repeated, frustrated, accentuating the
word.

"Vat-Ewer."

"WHAT. WHAT, OK?" she stressed. "WHAT—EVVVER."

"WHAT—EWWWER."

This went on for days.

Words with both "V" and "W" are Desi kryptonite. They have humbled giants among us, regardless of their education and literacy. Some
Pakistanis will fearlessly take on a lion with their bare hands (and sub-
sequently be eaten in the process), but if you tell them to get in front of
an audience and say "Volkswagen," they'll bring out a white flag. To this
day, I've stumbled with my "V" and "W" words, even on television and
during speeches.

Here are ten "V" and "W" words that can be used to dismantle your Desi nemesis:

1. Well-versed
2. Whatever
3. Volkswagen
4. Westworld
5. Vagina
6. Veggie
7. Vivacious
8. Inventive
9. Harvard
10. Wow or Vow

I will still laugh when I hear or say, "Wagina." Why? Because it's hilarious. My mother to this day says, "Har-ward," and we laugh; she could care less and shoots back, "Yeah, yeah, laugh. Come to Pakistan and speak Urdu, saala."

During childhood, my wife Sarah and her siblings used to make my mother-in-law say "Wow" so they could laugh at her pronunciation. She lovingly indulged her kids' immaturity. During our first year of marriage, I told a story using a Desi accent. We all chuckled. My mother-in-law went quiet behind her smile. Later, Sarah told me her mother has always been self-conscious about her accent. No matter how hard she tried to nail the "V" and "W," they still got the better of her after forty years. I was mortified and offered to apologize, but Sarah said acknowledging it would just make it worse.

Growing up, we had both teased our parents for their accents and loved doing it, for our amusement but also as an ownership of our roots. I was never embarrassed by it. However, my generation had the benefit of code switching. I can inflect my accent and engage in Urd-ish, Urdu and English, while talking to South Asian elders, then I can unconsciously flip a switch and sound like an American kid born in the suburbs. I could pass as white by sounding white—that is, mainstream, "real" American. If you only heard me speak but didn't see me, you'd never be able to tell I'm the son of Pakistani immigrants who took ESL as a kid.

I eventually discarded the accent as I grew up. My parents' generation never could. Their "whatewer," like my forehead scar, marked them for life. A telltale sign that, despite all their successes, their investment and time spent in this country, they were still foreigners and immigrants, a punching bag and a punchline.

My mother-in-law eventually got her revenge against Sarah, who went to Egypt after college to learn Arabic with her brother, Faraz, who now speaks it fluently. My wife's Arabic is notorious for being atrocious. It makes wild animals howl at night. It is so painful that she's banned from speaking it out loud in the house. Once, while my mother-in-law was in the next room praying, Sarah started reciting something in Arabic. My mother-in-law burst out laughing, which ruined her prayer. She got up, ran into the room, and playfully admonished Sarah, "I told you! Don't speak Arabic! At least not while I'm praying! I can't concentrate."

Whenever most Pakistanis recite the Quran during prayer, Arabs grit their teeth and recoil. No matter how hard we try, we just can't pronounce the "ع" ("ain"), which I'm convinced exists within some special portal hidden deep within the roof of the mouth, beyond the reach of us mere mortals unable to access the root of Arabic power.

We all have accents.

If you go to Boston, you'd think the locals don't know that the English alphabet contains the letter "R." Go down South to some parts of Virginia and ask for directions and you'd swear Foghorn Leghorn stepped out of a Looney Tunes cartoon to tell you to get on Interstate 64. Head over to New Orleans and you'll hear vowels being violently flattened. Move on to the Midwest and laugh as a grown man refers to a Coke bottle as "soda pap." Hug Highway 1 and drive to LA overlooking the Pacific Ocean and visit Arnold Schwarzenegger's house, push the intercom button, and just try to understand what he's saying with his thick Austrian accent. That didn't stop the former bodybuilder from becoming the governor of the state of California.

Like I said, we all have accents, but only some of us are deemed foreigners.

I never mustered the courage to talk to Jennifer. Each time I made the intention, sweat poured and my throat went dry. As predicted, Chad and Jennifer started "going out." This meant they giggled with each other for a few minutes during school and after school. During lunch one day Chad told me to come with their squad to the field. I was shocked. The cool kids wanted to hang out *with me?* My Ramadan prayers came true. Allah forgave me for being left-handed. The social ladders descended from heaven. This was all that I ever wanted. To be accepted by cool kids. To be invited to a gora friend's house and run around without taking off my shoes. To eat this mysterious dish called meatloaf and see how they talked back to their mothers.

Instead, two of Chad's friends held me and then Chad asked the only person of color in his crew, a Mexican kid, to punch me in the stomach. He hesitated. He met my eyes for a brief moment as if to say, "Hey, sorry, man, but I gotta do this. You know how it is. I'm getting my stripes today."

BOOM.

Right in the fleshy gut. I think he pulled his punch, but I felt it. Everyone else laughed as I caught my breath, trying to figure out what I did to deserve this punishment. Chad never knew of my harmless infatuation with Jennifer, and I never wronged him or any of his friends. They just decided to pick on me that day because they could, because it gave them a laugh.

This entire experience, although seemingly harmless in the grand cosmic scheme of life, was a perfect microcosm of the American dream. The good minority earned his rank by beating up the bad minority—a tale as old as the founding of this country. You try to gain as much proximity to whiteness and as much distance as you can from Blackness or the villain of the day, in order to become accepted by the mainstream. Benjamin Franklin loathed the Germans in the eighteenth century. Fifty years later, those same Germans, now natives, bullied the Irish. Fast forward to the twentieth century, and the Italian kids and Eastern

European Jews were the ones taking the beatings. Later, as those communities moved toward whiteness, Latino kids took over their spot. Historically, Black kids always occupy the lowest rung. The playground is where you first learn your rank in the American hierarchy.

Years later, I recognized my mistakes. I had the lessons in front of me the entire time thanks to *Teen Wolf*, the 1985 movie starring Michael J. Fox. He played a good-hearted, shy teenager who ignored the advances of his neighborhood friend, the girl who loved him, and instead desperately pined for the vain, blonde cheerleader. Puberty kicks in and overnight he transforms into a wolf. Instead of a bloodthirsty creature of the night, he becomes a hairy, charismatic jock, beloved by the school, and ends up dating the cheerleader. Meanwhile, he loses his humility, abandons his real friends, and ignores his true love. Only when he relinquishes the wolf persona and decides to be himself again does he make the game-winning shot and get the girl who believed in him from the start.

Why didn't I appreciate and value Mercedes, the girl who laughed at my Dr. Pepper joke and waved at me?

Choose Your Pants Wisely

I needed new pants.

If I only changed my pants, then I'd become popular overnight, and the cool boys would invite me to their homes to eat meatloaf and the pretty girls would smile at me.

Costumes are critical for superheroes. They serve multiple functions, namely aesthetics, protection, and a cover for a secret identity. They allow Superman and Batman to disguise their alter egos and fight villains in spandex, while always looking *fabulous*. Capes, once considered a necessary sartorial touch in the crime-fighting vocation, have since been deemed optional. Edna from *The Incredibles* declared, "No capes!" after recounting the tragic mishaps that befell caped superheroes: capes caught in missiles, capes stuck in airplane engines, accidental choking to death due to a cape, and so forth.

However, pants are never optional. For "healthy kids" like me, wearing pants was a daily jihad and a humiliating reminder of our "big bones."

South Asian cultures often operate like Jane Austen novels but with frequent episodes of outward bluntness justified as "keeping it real." Elders, the aunties in particular, are skilled serial killers who murder their enemies through a lifetime of passive-aggressive cuts. Some rudely tell you exactly what's on their mind and often share their unsolicited opinions on your weight, while others apply a more subtle, surgical touch.

To some elders, I was "mota," which means "fat." To others, I was "bohot mota," which means "very fat." To those who were civil, however, I was "healthy" and "big boned." They used to look at me and say, "Oh, he is very healthy. Mashallah." I was so "healthy" and "big boned" that I was forced to wear Husky pants, which any overweight child in America immediately recognizes as a source of enduring trauma.

The product namers probably consulted a South Asian aunty.

My mother and grandmother used to buy me the OshKosh B'gosh stretchy pants for kids my age. That worked until I wore my red pants to kindergarten one day. The teacher told all of us to sit down "Indian" style.

I obliged.

Rip! Now everyone could see my colorful superhero underwear. I had leaned in and suffered for it.

My mom then bought pants from the older kids section. Although they fit on my "healthy" waist, I still had short, five-year-old legs. My mom tried rolling the overlong pants into multiple folds around my ankles. This technically solved the problem but created another one: I looked like a child clown who had escaped the circus with the weight dragging me down.

Finally, we went to the dreaded "Husky" section of the clothing store. These roomy pants stretched out, a match made in heaven for my brown shanks. I could finally exhale, run, and play without fear of Hulking out again. However, the gods must be cruel. Every fortune has its price. On the backside of these pants, smack dab on the butt, there was a giant tag that read: "HUSKY." It was like in 96 Times New Roman font, made to be seen from space, the Great Wall for Big and Tall clothing. I felt like a branded cow.

This was the 1980s. Unlike today, 40 percent of American adults weren't obese back then. Us fat kids didn't have the Dove Soap Real Beauty campaign, which promoted body positivity. We didn't have conversations in school about fat shaming and the data that shows shaming only leads to harmful consequences, making overweight people feel worse about themselves, causing low self-esteem, binge eating, and more guilt. There were two size categories: normal and fat. One was accepted and the other was ridiculed. America kept rooting for Oprah to keep her weight down, mocking her when she gained it back, and then applauding her when she lost it again.

For fat kids, every day in school was like World War III. You had to survive knowing you could get pulverized at any moment. A small jab from your local bully comparing you to a whale, the locker room snickering as you quickly changed your clothes to hide your "healthy" stomach, the easy joke during lunch when someone would wave food at you or invite you to eat their leftovers. We were the human piñata for all the freaks, geeks, and nerds.

To this day, when I see myself in my head, it's often the shy, overweight kid wearing Husky pants, even though my wife assures me I'm a pretty handsome, middle-aged dude with a dad bod. I joke about it during speeches, but the trauma runs deep for many. After every event where I mention my experiences with Husky pants, someone comes up to me, glancing over their shoulders, and in a hushed voice, like a criminal confessing a crime, they say, "Hey . . . I also wore Husky pants."

During a brief fat reprieve, between first grade and fourth grade, I had a shot to leave behind my lowly social caste.

Every two weeks, my grandfather and I ventured out in our reliable Honda Accord, the preferred vehicle of South Asian immigrants, where he would haggle with the sellers at the local flea market and buy me a small toy. (I was his favorite.)

One fateful day, five-year-old Wajahat spied shiny, black, leather pants hanging from the stalls. These would be my magical armor, a costume that would instantly change me from a shy, ignored wallflower into the dashing hero, a mini Michael Jackson at the height of his post-*Thriller* fame. I would finally be noticed by my new unrequited love, Samantha. I begged my grandfather to buy them, and he obliged. The pants were about three sizes too large. No problem! My mother rolled up my pant legs and cinched the pants, which had no belt openings, with . . . pins. (It seemed like a brilliant, creative solution at the time.)

I wore my Michael Jackson leather pants with confidence and swagger. Recess arrived. I stood in the middle of the playground, right at the time Samantha would roll through during her daily Radio Flyer trip. She would see my Michael Jackson leather pants. She would be entranced. She would be mine.

Everything was going according to plan. I stood, gallantly, beaming, in my tight Michael Jackson leather pants. Samantha, right on cue, whizzed by on her red wagon.

A gust of wind.

Laughter.

I looked down.

My pants were on the ground.

In second grade, I transferred to Harker, an elite private school in Saratoga where we all wore uniforms. Someone made the genius decision to have us wear green sweaters, green pants, and white-collared shirts. I looked like a brown hobbit, but the uniform saved me from potential humiliation because we all looked ridiculous. In third grade, we would change into gym shorts for our PE class and then sit on our assigned numbers waiting for roll call. I changed my clothes and went and sat on my spot next to Timothy, a student from England with a British accent. I enjoyed the quiet and was surprised by the soft cool breeze that swept over my legs.

"Look!! He's got no pants! He forgot his pants!" I heard Timothy yell in between laughs.

"Who?" I wondered. Then I saw him pointing at me. I had forgotten my shorts.

The entire class laughed.

My gym teacher, who looked like Coach Buzzcut, couldn't help but chuckle. He quickly stifled his laugh and motioned me to stand up and come over to him. He gave me the locker room keys and said, with pity, "Jesus, Waji, just go put on your shorts. Come on, man."

The sixty-second walk of shame felt like an eternity.

Outside school, I tried to flex a new look with my local Muslim and South Asian community. In 1990, Z Cavaricci pants were all the rage— a staple of the cocaine-fueled '80s along with mullets, leg warmers, Mr. T, and *Pee-wee's Playhouse*. They were high-waisted, pleated pants with unnecessary buttons and loops and "Z Cavaricci" written on a small white label. It took me months of begging my parents for this high-priced monstrosity, but they finally caved and bought me a pair. I wore them with a silk shirt to a community wedding. The cool kids, my older cousin's friends, would surely notice and invite me to join their circle. They did—only to laugh at me for looking ridiculous. Z Cavaricci pants were already out of style.

From high school to law school, I stopped trying to impress anyone and fit into any social circles. I more or less gave up on fashion altogether and evolved into a "Karachi uncle" aesthetic, which was basically a T-shirt or collared shirt from Mervyn's, Dockers khakis, and sneakers. I was only twenty-three, but people assumed I was a thirty-five-year-old married man with kids and asked me advice about how to achieve good credit. I made peace with all my awkwardness and eccentricities. I owned them fully, and that brought about a quiet confidence that attracted both women and friends.

But that could happen only after I discovered and honed my superhero power.

How I Discovered My Superpower

In order to be a hero, you usually need a superhero power.

Superman's near-invulnerability is because his alien DNA is powered by the Sun. Spider-Man's powers of climbing walls and spidey sense resulted after a bite from a radioactive spider. Hulk's superhuman strength came from a gamma ray accident. Mutants, like Wolverine and Jean Grey, were born with special powers that manifested at puberty.

My powers were unlocked when I was in the fifth grade and was asked to write an original story.

As a person of color in America, you need to fly to reach the hallowed gates of wealth and mainstream success while others can just walk. "Good" is not good enough. You have to be exceptional, especially when you don't have the legacy admissions, the generational wealth, the mentors who look like you and come from your communities, and an entire system that benefits one skin color and gender at the detriment of others. Again, you have to daft punk it through life. It reminds me of that classic Chris Rock bit where he's talking about his neighbors, all of them who are the crème da la crème of Black talent. There's him, Eddie Murphy, Mary J. Blige, and a white dentist. Just an old, regular, "yank yo tooth out" dentist. Rock says that in order for a Black dentist to live there, "he'd have to invent teeth."

Human beings remain the only storytelling animals in existence. It's how we make sense of the chaos of this intricate, mad puzzle called life. It's how we understand ourselves and share our values, our histories, even our religions. Everything, from science to politics to love, becomes a story shared by humans. It's how we choose to introduce, name, describe, and place ourselves in this universe.

Around the world, people often ask someone they've just met, "Hey, what's your story?"

At the time, my only superhero power was the impressive ability to eat more than most adults and sweat profusely when talking to girls. But I already knew that, in America, if you aren't writing your story, your story will always be written for you. If you aren't telling your story, your story will always be told to you.

Until the age of ten, my story would have been a silent movie or a blank page. I was still paralyzed by shyness in front of large crowds, strangers, or new settings. But Mrs. Peterson, my Kentucky-born fifth grade teacher, had an unorthodox approach. On the first day of class, she gave each of us a paper with an intricate maze. She instructed us to pick up the pencil and draw a line from the center of the maze all the way to the top. I kept looking at the maze. There was no way to draw a line from the center to the top without violating the lines. We were all confused. She repeated, "Pick up the pencil and draw a line from the center of the maze to the top."

I was terrified of disturbing the sanctity and order of this beautiful, pristine maze. Apparently, I wasn't alone. Most of us students just kept staring at the page.

She took the paper and in front of us drew a line from the center, straight up to the top, going right through the walls, lines, and borders of the maze without any hesitation or fear. "See? That was easy," she said.

I was shocked. It was a brave new world. It's like she saw the world with the mysterious third eye, giving her a sight beyond mortal gaze. She was granted basirah, what the Sufis refer to as spiritual foresight. I felt like Neo from *The Matrix* when he realized that "there is no spoon." I couldn't bend reality, but I could change myself and my perceptions.

"There is no maze."

Mrs. Peterson invested most of our class time working on nearly two dozen ambitious, creative projects. This included dressing up as a historical figure and memorizing and delivering a speech in character. (I was Thomas Edison.) She also asked us to make puppets and put on a show. (I made sure to make some puppets of color.) She grouped us into teams and we even had to create a diorama of the wagon trail. (Our diorama was kick-ass and won first prize.)

At the time, I had missed more than thirty days of school. I had horrendous allergies, and the school was about to kick me out and make me do the year over again. My father intervened using old-school negotiation skills, and we finally found a competent allergist who put me on a heavy dose of medications and weekly shots. Eventually, I was able to rejoin the class after spending the afternoons catching up with a tutor. Mrs. Peterson was not impressed with my absence or my lackluster participation.

My first assignment upon returning was to write an original one-page short story. I ended up writing a ten-page epic inspired by Robin Hood—the version starring Kevin Costner in the title role as the English outlaw with an American accent.

Still, the movie introduced us to Azeem, a badass Muslim played by Morgan Freeman. He prayed in a way no Muslim had ever prayed before, but it didn't matter to us because he was such as a badass, who had a badass sword, and helped save the day.

My own rendition of *Robin Hood* was a wild, scatalogical romp blending fantasy and action, borrowing from classic tales. In my version, Maid Marian was trapped in the tower like Rapunzel, and her tears caused a flood of biblical proportions. Robin Hood was like the Sub-Mariner and had to swing through snot and mucus while razing Sheriff Nottingham's aquatic goons with a volley of arrows and underwater swashbuckling.

I hesitantly brought it to school and submitted the epic. I assumed Mrs. Peterson would admonish me. During a classroom activity, she quietly read all the stories as we worked through another creative project. "Wajahat, come here please," she told me in a serious tone.

"Crap, she's going to yell at me," I thought to myself.

"This . . . is brilliant. Fantastic stuff," she said with a huge smile on her face. "I'm giving you an A+!"

"What? An A+?" I asked, incredulous.

"OK, fine. An A++++," she said, writing the extra "+" marks at the top in her red pen.

Validation. After nearly half a year of dismissing me, Mrs. Peterson not only complimented my story, but it earned the only "A++++" in the class.

"Wajahat, I'm going to make you recite the story in front of the homeroom," she added. Wait. What? This was not part of the deal. I was supposed to receive my A++++, feel amazing for the day, go show off to my parents, and then eat food.

"Mrs. Peterson, that's OK. I'd rather not. Thank you," I replied sheepishly.

"Oh, nonsense. They'll love it. Everybody, Wajahat got an A++++ on his story. He's going to read it for all of you. Pay attention," she announced to the class.

All eyes on me. Time froze. My heart stopped. I forgot how to swallow. Had Mrs. Peterson asked me to punch myself in the stomach and inject bleach into my veins instead, I would have said yes without hesitation. I felt like the character who is surrounded by bad guys and is forced to come out and face them with his hands up and all the laser sights pointed at his chest. Unlike in the movies, I wouldn't escape but instead would end up shredded by the firing squad.

I said "Bismillah" under my breath and began reading. About thirty seconds in, I paused and looked up. No one had snickered or mocked me. I was waiting, expecting my bullies to hit me. Nothing. Silence. I kept reading. About two minutes in, I paused and checked again. "Yo, you can hit me now. Anyone? Anyone? Bueller?" Nope. All eyes still on me. Most faces had smiles. Eyes were widened. A few girls were leaning forward. They laughed at all the right places. They caught (most of) the jokes. They dug the action scene, and by the time I finished, Mrs. Peterson didn't even have to tell them to give me a pity clap because they were all applauding. My sweat came from adrenaline and joy. I sat down amid nods of respect from some of my usual bullies, whose daily part-time job was to make a cheap, easy jab about my weight.

"You're gonna have to do this for the upcoming talent show," Mrs. Peterson said, assuming her role as my Colonel Tom Parker. That was the one with the fifth, sixth, and seventh graders. All of the older kids. I said, "No, thank you," but she told me I had to do it.

Next thing you know, a few weeks later I'm on stage in front of hundreds of students, including the elders. My Eminem 8 *Mile* moment had arrived. With the same enthusiastic response. I had discovered my superhero skill. I had found a voice.

I went home and gave my parents the short story. My father read it while drinking chai at the table. After finishing, he said it was very good and told me I should consider becoming a writer. My mom, over-hearing the conversation, rushed from the kitchen and said, "Yes, but first become a doctor!"

Chapter 2

Say Hello to America's Oldest Friend

My job here is to help you become American, and as such I want to make the journey as easy, accessible, and entertaining as possible.

Unfortunately, your enemies are legion.

They range from the comical microaggressions—for example, when people think SPEAKING ENGLISH AT A HIGHER VOLUME AND A SLOWER PACE will somehow make a person of color magically understand the language—to the frustrating ones, for example, when people assume you don't speak or understand English just because of your name or ethnicity.

Your enemies include, but are not limited to, the following: online trolls who tell you to "go back to where you came from" and mock your "ethnic" last name; lazy stereotypes and conspiracy theories weaponized by politicians to scapegoat entire communities of people; managers who refuse to hire you or pay you less because of your skin color; shopkeepers who stick to you like sweat, eyeballing your every move, assuming the worst of your intentions; and friendly, educated, suburban neighbors who call the cops to investigate Black and brown people doing normal activities like selling lemonade, enjoying a barbeque, bird watching, or jogging in broad daylight.

If we analyze white supremacy from the philosophical lens of *Star Wars*, then it is all the Sith Lords, the Empire, and the First Order commanded by the Dark Side of the Force. It wants to dominate and impose its will on all galaxies, even those far, far away. Let's just call this insidious force THE WHITENESS.

The Whiteness's ability to inspire fear and anger is so strong that it corrupted many well-intentioned people, including people of color, to vote for an incompetent vulgarian in 2016 and 2020. It deludes many liberal and "moderate" whites into believing that they are the "good" ones who are committed to social justice as they talk about white privilege but never actually give up any of it. Still, they'll have these discussions about racial equality with their white friends in establishments with white patrons from white neighborhoods—without including the rest of us.

The Whiteness has always played for all the marbles. It's not interested in diplomacy, a representative government, free and fair elections, equitable pay, and a delicious buffet of meals from a multitude of countries. It needs a border wall, a Muslim Ban, and affirmative action for wealthy white students at Yale University. It's a system, a structure, a paradigm, an ideology whose ultimate goal is domination and submission by any means necessary. The Whiteness also discovers foods that have always existed, such as hummus, and gives them a new twist and sells them overpriced at restaurants and gentrified neighborhoods. Hello, artisanal chocolate hummus!

Yet white people are human beings, who like me belong to the genus species Homo sapiens. They simply have different levels of melanin than people of color. From my lifetime of observing them, with enough field research to earn me an honorary doctorate, I have deduced that many of them seem to like juicing, turtlenecks, Peloton bikes, excessive stickers on their bumpers, and donating to NPR. Verily, none of these are criminal acts. Every tribe has their own fascinating rituals and customs. For example, Pakistanis are genetically predisposed to transforming into wild, ravenous beasts at the sight of ripe, sweet mangoes, willing to sacrifice their young for a chance to enjoy the gooey nectar of the gods.

Who am I to judge?

White people are not the Borg, an alien, cybernetic species that share a hive-like consciousness. There is no one white world, white community, white narrative, or other convenient catchall that absorbs all the whites of the world into one bland, nondescript monolith. (White supremacists would beg to differ on that. Its core adherents believe that "white people" are descended from Norse gods, etched from their Viking ancestors who all happen to resemble Thor and Scandinavian models.) White people come in different shapes, genders, nationalities, political persuasions, and personalities.

In fact, many who are now part of the Whites in America weren't even considered white back in the day. They were excluded from the club. Just talk to Irish Catholics and Italian Americans who know their history.

Skin color itself is a product and spectrum of natural selection, evolution, and human migration in relation to our interaction and duration with sunlight. As you've heard by now in countless school lectures and public service announcements, the whole concept of race is just a social construct. The colonial records reveal there were no "white" people in Virginia when African slaves arrived in 1619. They made their first appearance about sixty years later. In America, "white" as a racial category was invented by the ruling class to create a system of racial privileges, control, and power for themselves at the expense and exploitation of others, namely "Black" people.

In my experience, each time topics like white supremacy, the Whiteness, white privilege, the caucasity, goras, and wypipo are discussed, some whites take it as a personal assault and an insult. They feel I'm slapping them across their face with my chappal. They bite their lips, their faces tighten, their bodies become tense, they cross their arms and lean back, flustered and hot.

They shut down.

Or, they hit back, defensive, holding back tears, making an impassioned case for their wokeness—oftentimes literally saying, "I'm woke!"—and insisting through use of specific life examples how they are not in any way privileged or racist but instead have lived through hardship, succeeded despite setbacks, have always tried to be allies of people of color, and have just managed to succeed due to their own merit.

During these speeches, you can expect to hear some of the following citations:

~ I'd totally march with MLK if I were alive back then.

~ I went to the Beyoncé concert and loved it.

~ I once had an Asian boyfriend/girlfriend.

~ I love Indian food, even the spices!

~ I hated the white family in *Get Out* and clapped when they died!

~ I convinced my friends not to wear blackface/brownface/yellowface or a culturally appropriated costume for our neighborhood Halloween party.

~ I voted for Obama.

~ I read Michelle Obama's *Becoming*. I made my mom read it.

~ I read Ta-Nehisi Coates. I made my dad read *Between the World and Me*.

~ I love Rumi and Sufism.

~ White people suffer too; just read *Hillbilly Elegy*.

~ I don't see race.

And those are just examples of some of the pleasant encounters.

Others hit back harder. They suggest that I am in fact the *real* racist for talking about race in the first place. They accuse me of being an antiwhite racist who only sees race, who can't see past race, who is stuck, swimming, bathing in racism, because I'm a professional race baiter and race hustler whose vocations and extracurricular activities involve peddling my brown skin to make a quick buck by sucking the ever-flowing teat of white, liberal guilt.

(It's delicious by the way. Salty, but delicious.)

As you can tell, this isn't my first rodeo. So, I assure you, the enemy is not white people.

But if we don't acknowledge and name the real enemy, how can we confront and fight it, oh fellow traveler who so desperately yearns to taste the fried glory that is America?

Hiccups are to be expected; roadblocks and potholes are routine on this eventful journey to the American dream, with the occasional fatal police stop. My parents, who came as immigrants, said it was normal to encounter the casual racist joke, the mocking of accents, or "the great lumping." The great lumping sounds like a kinky and adventurous tantric sex act, but it's what happens when your unique ethnicity and story are flattened and lumped into the giant burlap sack of brownness. Every Pakistani and Bangladeshi now becomes an Indian, who might as well be an Arab, because, hey, close enough, and we all look the same and geography is not America's strong point, so let's just stop being so sensitive!

The Whiteness doesn't want us to be American. But since it can't remove all of us, it will always find ways to dominate the rest of us and make our lives uncomfortable. Sometimes it's easier not to resist and fight back, but just to give in.

If that's your chosen strategy, then allow me to share this helpful guide on how to give in to the Whiteness, assimilate, and become a model Amreekan.

How to Be a Model Amreekan

1. Censor your babies' "ethnic" names. Instead, ask yourself, "What American names will white people like?" Adam and Laila are safe bets.
2. Study the Rust Belt and endlessly interview white undecided voters in Midwestern coffee shops to understand white grievance.
3. Be an "essential" worker during a pandemic, but never demand or expect essential wages, benefits, or health care.
4. Assume that wealthy and white immigrants are "expats"

while poor brown and Black immigrants are "foreigners" and a "public charge" who should go back to their "shithole countries." Lust after white immigrants from Norway— preferably the ones who look like Vikings and Thor.

5. Say you're drinking chai tea and eating naan bread, otherwise known as tea tea and bread bread.

6. Whine about liberal college kids and being "canceled" by woke activists from the platforms of influential newspapers, magazines, podcasts, and talk shows.

7. Applaud the curiosity and bravery of your white colleagues for tackling subjects in which they have zero expertise while the person of color with the actual experience is relegated to work on "ethnic" stories and "diversity issues." Always assume your white colleague is neutral and professional, and your colleague of color is biased and emotional.

8. Support free speech by trying to ban critical race theory from being taught at schools. Protect your children from turning into godless Marxists who hate gender pronouns and white people.

9. Be the one token person of color at school or work who does all the work in educating everyone about history, culture, racism, and diversity without asking anyone to do any homework or heavy lifting on their own.

10. Refer to the children of Latino immigrants as "anchor babies" and the children of white immigrants as "babies."

11. Celebrate wealthy white men with silver spoons for "keeping it real" when they challenge you by being "politically incorrect," but when a person of color challenges you, call them uppity and angry.

12. See John McCain (born in Panama) and Ted Cruz (real name Rafael, born in Canada) as red-blooded Americans, while suspecting Black people like Barack Obama and Kamala Harris, both born in America, as being foreigners.

13. Rail against Mexican immigrants and "welfare queens" for

being lazy and taking handouts, but whine and complain when the government takes away the Medicare and Social Security of "real" hardworking Americans.

14. Refuse to accept Santa Claus, a fictional character, as anything other than an old, bearded, white man, become enraged over the fake War on Christmas, and ignore the real War on Terror that has killed and devastated tens of thousands of innocent lives.

15. Demand immediate racial reconciliation, but never the truth.

On our journey toward becoming American, we must always be vigilant. If you're a person of color, you can't ignore the Whiteness. You will be tempted by its power, coveting its warm, comforting embrace, even if it means renouncing your identity, cultural roots, and community. You might voluntarily allow yourself to melt into its giant, bland, tasteless pot, deluding yourself into believing the Whiteness actually likes your "ethnic" smell and "exotic" flavor.

You will wear blue contact lenses, shorten your name to "Mo," and tell people you're Mediterranean even though you are brown-eyed Muhammad from Lahore who couldn't find the Mediterranean Sea on a map if his life depended on it. You will complain about those "lazy blacks" and "goddamn Mexicans" who take welfare and don't work hard as you hire those very same people on minimum wage because their labor keeps your successful business afloat. You will complain about Islamophobia and demand that other groups help your community push back against hate as you continue supporting homophobic and racist politicians who pass laws that harm other marginalized communities.

You will spend four years whining about Trump and his hateful rhetoric but end up quietly voting for him because you love his tax cuts. You will complain that America is going to hell and that nobody teaches their kids morals or selflessness and then proceed to throw extravagant weddings and parties during a pandemic.

You will always complain about the goras behind their backs but never, ever criticize the Whiteness publicly, because you don't want to rock the boat, even after you have attained power and wealth and status and can actually help reform the system.

You will feel anxious when any other person of color succeeds in your workplace and threatens to take away your coveted token status. You will go full Highlander and insist that "there can be only one" from your community—you—who can succeed.

You would rather go into debt and suffer from crippling anxiety and stress than give up your successful lifestyle because you will be obsessed with "what will people say?"

As you desperately try to hide all your problems, frustrations, and dysfunctions, you will smile wide with your white teeth showing and make sure your partners and kids do the same at social events, so everyone can see and celebrate you as a perfect, Amreekan family.

Chapter 3

Do Something Useful

As far as I can remember, I always wanted to be a storyteller.

However, I was the only son of Pakistani immigrants, and in our community the occupations consisted of the Holy Trinity.

To refresh your memory, they are the following:

1. The doctor
2. The engineer
3. The businessman who somehow makes enough money to buy a two-story house, a nice car, marry a nice wife, produce 2.1 good children and send them to a good school.

The only other possible occupation was:

4. Failure.

This is the immigrant checklist of success. Successfully accomplish and check off the boxes and then smile and nod in front of community gatherings and you will have accomplished the Amreekan dream.

Early on in my writing career, several uncles and aunties in my community used to ask me to my face, "Beta, why don't you do something useful?"

I always wanted to reply by asking them how being a software engineer was "useful" in helping our people and saving the world, but I was unfortunately raised too well thanks to "chappal diplomacy."

Chappal is another word for chancla or slippers. They are the primary murder weapon of choice for immigrant mothers. Imagine a gunslinger able to make their revolver dance and twirl before and after executing the perfect bull's-eye shot and then sliding it back into the holster. It's like all that but with a chappal.

The looming, impending threat of the chappal that could and would strike at any infraction was psychological punishment in itself. The mandatory minimum for talking back to your elders, even if they weren't family members, was at least one chappal slap or at the very least a terrifying, menacing standoff between you and your mother holding the chappal. The threat alone was enough to make me back down.

To this day, grown-ass men will pause and wince on seeing a chappal, taken back to a childhood moment of disobedience.

Some families use the switch or the belt. Personally, I think using physical violence against children is detrimental and does nothing but cause trauma. The people who always brag about how they "turned out right" and lament about today's kids being too spoiled usually are deeply messed up and traumatized. They just never admit it. Still, all communities around the world can unite in the dysfunctional, and sometimes hysterical, ways our parents tried to literally and figuratively beat us down and strip away our hopes, dreams, and desires.

My parents were different from many immigrant parents when it came to nurturing my artistic side. They actively encouraged me but hoped I'd also get "insurance"—a degree that would provide a "stable" backup. We South Asians just didn't have that many examples of success in the dramatic arts and media.

There was Art Malik, the brother of a family friend. Art was born Athar ul-Haque Malik in Pakistan. You've seen Art Malik opposite Arnold Schwarzenegger, the former governor of California, in the movie *True Lies*. He was Salim Abu Aziz, the leader of the terrorist group Crimson Jihad. James Cameron's 1994 blockbuster is extremely

enjoyable, absurd, and also deeply problematic in its anti-Muslim cari-
catures. Malik is clearly Pakistani, playing what seems to be some composite of angry, brown Muslim extremists who shoot their bullets in
the air and yell. This is entirely unrealistic, because Art—playing a
foreign terrorist and being an immigrant himself—knows that no self-
respecting child of immigrants would be so wasteful. The movie is out-
dated, and his character is a one-dimensional Muslim bogeyman, but we
still thought it was great to see Art uncle on-screen.

A few years earlier, he played an Afghan mujahideen ally of James
Bond in the underrated *The Living Daylights*, starring a more serious
and edgy Bond played by Timothy Dalton, who was sadly twenty years
ahead of his time. Here was a fellow Pakistani with a positive role and a
rather large speaking part in a Bond movie! We thought it was incredibly cool, and we proudly claimed Art uncle through our friendship with
his brother. (To this day, I have never met Art uncle.)

Still, Art uncle alone wasn't enough to justify encouraging your child
to pursue a "useless" degree. After all, our parents didn't leave their
family, their country, their security, traveling thousands of miles, enduring hardship and humiliation, so their son could become a theater arts
major.

Years later, while I was in college, my Dadi asked my mom what
I was studying for hours at night, reading all those thick books. My
mom said I was most likely going to major in "the humanities." Dadi
froze. We feared she had had a ministroke. She slowly covered her
shocked mouth and said, "But in Pakistan only the duffers and idiots
do the humanities."

It's not like Pakistani uncles and aunties don't love and respect
poetry. The tradition and culture of Sher Shayari (Poets and Poetry)
in South Asia is deep, and many immigrant uncles in our community fancy themselves amateur poets, eager to hop on to any stage
to entertain us with their verses in Urdu and Punjabi. They have
memorized volumes of poetry by Rumi, Iqbal, Faiz, and Amir Khusro,
among others. The written and oral traditions are passed down and

venerated to this day, even in the mean suburban streets of Fremont and Saratoga.

Unfortunately, some Muslims forced our MVP to prematurely retire. I'm of course talking about Cat Stevens, who converted and renamed himself Yusuf Islam. Our white knight, our Daywalker, our hero with all of our strengths and none of our weaknesses, who gave the world *Peace Train*, decided to support Ayatollah Khomeini's ridiculous fatwa against writer Salman Rushdie and quickly fell out of favor with fans and the industry. He even gave up his greatest gift, his music, deciding it was non-Islamic. He finally picked up his guitar and returned twenty-eight years later, still a staunch Muslim but more humble, wiser in an open, healthy, and I would say traditional form of Islam that encouraged and celebrated such beauty.

I think of how many years Yusuf Islam lost, and I reflect on that scene from *The Bourne Identity* where a brainwashed assassin sent to kill Matt Damon's character mournfully says before dying, "Look at this. Look at what they make you give."

The first cut is indeed the deepest.

I always told myself I'd never go out like that.

I was suffocating in a community that loved art but said just don't pursue it as a career or try making a living off of it. Instead, we were commanded, "Beta, do something useful."

But as far as I can remember, I always wanted to be a storyteller.

Growing up, my daily sustenance consisted of inhaling Pakistani food and Hollywood pop culture. I spent years imagining directing movies on a studio lot with the respected actors of that era, walking the red carpet with my wife, Winona Ryder, to attend the premiere of my movie, and practicing my humble-shocked face when the camera zoomed in on me as Jim Carrey called my name from the dais to accept my Academy Award, as the first Pakistani and Muslim to win Best Director, Writer, and Editor.

That was going to be my summer job. During the fall and winter, I would of course be a starting member of the Golden State Warriors, the first Desi to dunk alongside Run TMC, and on Sundays I would throw game-winning touchdowns as the quarterback of the San Francisco 49ers, going down in history for "The Catch 2." Like Bo Jackson and Deion Sanders, I'd be able to play multiple sports simultaneously, also donating my nonexistent athletic talents to the San Francisco Giants *and* the Oakland A's, where I'd hit, pitch, and field with my colleagues Will Clark, Rickey Henderson, and the Bash Brothers. I would play on both sides during the 1989 Battle of the Bay World Series. They would make me invincible in the Tecmo Bowl and RBI Baseball video games on Nintendo.

As you can tell, I had a very fertile imagination that some psychiatrists would deem delusional. However, to an adolescent boy, these fantasies are perfectly reasonable. As a teenage boy, you are the star, the hero, and the protagonist of your dreams. Every beautiful woman you desire not only accepts your invitation for sex but often aggressively initiates the torrid encounter, coveting your unbridled potency and lusting for your Husky butt that the world has foolishly ignored and shunned.

In reality, I had terrible allergies, was overweight, had limited arm strength, and couldn't dribble, and all my school friends and family members knew it. As the fat kid, I was always picked last for teams. The greatest days were when I was picked second to last, barely edging out fellow awkward freaks and geeks who possessed zero skill in sports.

But I didn't need to be athletic to be a storyteller. I could flex my mind and imagination.

I created stories where I commanded the spotlight. I was no third-string terrorist or Salim Abu Aziz who died after shooting and wasting bullets in the air. I was not the goofy cabdriver with a fake Pakistani accent who exists only in movies. I was not erased, stereotyped, mocked, or villainized.

No.

I was Indiana Jones with a fedora and a whip battling Mola Ram, avoiding arrows, barely hanging on for life on the rickety bridge, telling him, "Thum Shiva Ke Vishwasth Karthe Ho!!!" I was Marty McFly riding my skateboard listening to Huey Lewis and the News and hitting 88 mph in my DeLorean to go back in time. I was the billionaire playboy by day and superhero at night, my nonexistent jawline underneath the cowl with Pakistani takeout in the back seat of my Batmobile.

But back in the day, there were very few close-ups of South Asians and Muslims in movies, TV, or video games, and when they did come into focus, the image was rarely positive or reflective of my family and friends. Forget the close-up, I would have been happy with a wide-angle shot that included someone like me in the margins. Just give me a blurry brown arm, a leg, and a partial neck, and I'd freeze the frame and point at it with pride. Then came Apu, a fictional, 2D, animated character on *The Simpsons*, who is from India and is a Hindu, but the pickings were slim, and we were desperate, so most fellow Desi Muslim kids accepted him. We applauded as a family when we saw the 1985 comedy *Spies Like Us* where Dan Aykroyd and Chevy Chase ended up in a totally unrealistic depiction of Pakistan. Even during college, I used to pause the screen whenever I saw a brown actor and then I furiously Googled to check if they were of South Asian descent. We didn't have Mindy Kaling or Hasan Minhaj or Riz Ahmed or Kumail Nanjiani back then.

Instead we had to settle for Peter Sellers in *The Party*, a silly '60s comedy directed by Blake Edwards featuring Sellers in brown makeup. This movie would *never* get made in the twenty-first century. Sellers plays Hrundi V. Bakshi, an affable idiot who is accidentally invited to a fancy Hollywood party where he causes havoc. Eventually, he becomes the toast of the party and walks away with the heroine.

Even though the movie is classic brownface and utterly inappropriate today, it is passed down from generation to generation in South Asian families. My parents and their friends love it, still giggling at the line "Birdie Num Num." We can quote entire sections by heart.

I once mused with a producer, a son of Iranian immigrants, about why our parents' generation loved this movie so much. "It's because even though he's an idiot, he's the hero," he told me. "Hrundi is the hero of the movie, and everyone loves him in the end. That's what's key." When you're starving for meaningful representation, you'll celebrate Peter Sellers in brown face.

Short Circuit, released in 1986, featured the positive character of Ben Jabituya, an immigrant with an accent who is a brilliant scientist and Steve Guttenberg's assistant. He even became the lead in the ill-fated sequel released a few years later. My cousins and I enjoyed the movie, but we were mostly amazed that a South Asian character had such a huge role: It wasn't until the early '90s that I realized the actor, Fisher Stevens, is a white dude. My jaw dropped. I think I even said, "Daaaaamn!" out loud. Aziz Ansari devoted an entire episode to this revelation in his Netflix show *Master of None*.

It was like when I found out root beer wasn't alcoholic or the time I found out braces were actually orthodontics. My mother used to point out a young teenage grocery clerk at our neighborhood store who had braces and say, "See his black teeth? See what he has in them? Go look. That's what happens to you when you lie to your parents. Go look." My cousins and I, curious and terrified, slowly approached him and kept waiting for him to say something while he bagged our groceries. He finally opened his mouth and that's when we saw the metallic punishment forged by Satan himself. We ran back to my mom and promised we would never lie. I was shocked when I discovered that the true purpose of braces was to straighten teeth. My mother would have been an excellent torturer or propagandist for an authoritarian government. She wouldn't use violence but instead the power of persuasion to fill your head with horrors.

We had seen Ben Kingsley as *Gandhi* in brownface, but we gave him a pass because we all knew he was born to a Desi father, a doctor no less, and that his name at birth was Krishna Pandit Bhanji. Plus, he kicked all sorts of ass as the Hindu ascetic who preached nonviolent resistance to the colonial rule of the haramzaday British.

Still, this Fisher Stevens reveal was less of a betrayal and more of a sense of confusion and wonderment: how could we have been so fooled? "What else were they hiding from us?" I asked.

In 2022, I know some Americans continue to delude themselves into thinking we live in a post-racial society because Barack Hussein Obama was elected twice and because Hollywood released *Black Panther* and *Crazy Rich Asians*. America has rushed to address its "diversity problem" following the mass Black Lives Matter demonstrations across the country in the summer of 2020, so I guess I shouldn't complain any further. Yes, we have improved but we still have a ways to go.

Historically, if you're a storyteller of color, you either work in the service of a white man or you don't work at all. According to the 2020 Hollywood Diversity Report, 91 percent of studio heads are white and 82 percent are male. Similarly, among all senior executive positions, 93 percent are held by white people and 80 percent by men. I once asked TV producer and showrunner David Guarascio, "How does a person of color make it in such a white industry?" He was promoting his show at the time, *Aliens in America*, about a Pakistani Muslim exchange student who is sent to live in a white Wisconsin town. "It starts more from [the writing room] and from behind the camera," he told me, acknowledging that the writing staff is overwhelmingly white—not due to intentional exclusion, but because friends usually worked with people they knew or who were already in the business.

Do white men and women in power ever look outside their own social bubble to search for talent of color? It's so much easier to say, "We looked everywhere and we just couldn't find anyone," or rationalize, "Well, it's just a meritocracy where anyone can make it if they work hard." We sent them names. We gave them résumés, and clips and reels, and nothing ever changed until the spotlight was put on all industries after 2020 to acknowledge the diversity gap and actively *do* something to address it.

"Minorities," the rest of us, buy the majority of tickets that keep Hollywood humming and churning out content that ignores us, stereotypes us, and silences us. In 2019, we bought the majority of tickets to eight of the top ten films.

I've been told by so many white creatives that casting should be race neutral and that the talent and bankability of the actor should determine if they get the role. In an ideal world, this sounds beautiful. So many Black actresses would love a chance to play Cleopatra or even Queen Elizabeth—why not? A Thai actor would love to show off his singing skills as King Mongkut in *The King and I* or even King George.

A Persian actor would love to be the *Prince of Persia* instead of Jake Gyllenhaal (not Persian) or a prince of Europe. Any actor of Middle Eastern descent would have loved those plum roles in *Lawrence of Arabia* played by Alec Guinness and Anthony Quinn or any role where they aren't trying to blow up infidels. Middle Eastern actors rarely get the chance to play Jesus or Moses in a big-budget movie or TV series.

One of the many advantages of being white in America is not only do they get to tell our stories, they get to play *our* protagonists as well.

A Brief Hall of Fame and Tour of Recent Whitewashing:

~ Scarlett Johansson in *Ghost in the Shell*, a Hollywood adaptation of a Japanese manga comic where the setting is Japan, most of the characters are Japanese, and her character's name is Motoko Kusanagi.

~ Emma Stone as Captain Allison Ng, the half-Asian love interest of Bradley Cooper's character in Cameron Crowe's *Aloha*.

~ The white kids in *The Last Airbender*. This one hit hard because they destroyed a fantastic cartoon series with Asian and Native American characters: *Avatar: The Last Airbender*. It was directed by M. Night Shyamalan, a Desi, who should've known better. (Come on, man! I even defended you after *The Happening*, and this is how you repay us?)

~ Joel Edgerton, an Australian white dude, as the Egyptian pharaoh, and Christian Bale, a Welsh white dude, as the Prophet Moses in *Exodus: Gods and Kings*. Director Ridley Scott said, "I can't mount a film of this budget, where I have to rely on tax rebates in Spain, and say that my lead actor is Mohammad so-and-so from such-and-such. I'm just not going to get it financed."

~ In *The Social Network*, Mark Zuckerberg, a white, Jewish man, is played by a white, Jewish actor. However, Divya Narendra, a real Indian American who sued Zuckerberg, is also played by a white actor. It isn't a lead role. It's not even a supporting role. The producers could spend millions of dollars to digitally re-create Armie Hammer's face on another actor's body to have him play identical twins, but they couldn't find one Desi kid to play Narendra.

If you build it, they will come. If you give audiences quality characters and stories that are authentic and look like them, those communities will turn up, enthusiastic, and applaud, relieved and grateful to finally see themselves and to be seen by the world.

In the absence of such opportunities, I became Rage Boy.

How I Became Islamic Rage Boy

The frame is everything.

In media, framing theory says that how a subject matter is "presented to the audience influences the choices the people make about how to process that information." In other words, it tells you what to think about and how to think about it.

Whoever controls the frame has the ultimate power and can determine, shape, and distort how you, the audience, see reality.

After 9/11, mention of Muslims and Islam in the media would often be accompanied by a low-angle close-up shot of an angry, scary, bearded, brown man yelling with his hand raised high, obscuring and dominating the women, who are all behind him.

Say Assalamu Alaikum to Islamic Rage Boy. He is violent, foreign, Muslim, anti-American, anti-Western, anti-democracy, anti-Semitic, anti-deodorant, and anti-KFC. His image was so frequently used in Western media after the 9/11 terror attacks that he became popularized as a meme and even inspired a cartoon character and merchandise.

There's another image of Islamic Rage Boy that you've probably never seen. It's a warm, medium close-up shot of a smiling, bearded, brown man who is probably in the middle of telling a delightful story that amuses him. He could be anywhere in the world, maybe near his apartment complex in Philadelphia, where he'll go run the steps of the Museum of Art and stand next to the Rocky statue.

Say Assalamu Alaikum to Shakeel Ahmad Butt, a Muslim activist born in occupied Kashmir, a former militant, whose neighbors describe him as "well mannered" and "sincere," who has been arrested more than three hundred times for taking part in peaceful protests. When asked how he feels about being used as a meme, he replied, "I am not happy with people joking about me or making me into a cartoon, but I have more important things to think about. My protests are for those Muslims who cannot go out onto the streets to cry out against injustice. This is my duty and I believe Allah has decided this for me."

In one frame, you have the enduring, simplistic image of Islamic Rage Boy that captures how American media has often portrayed and flattened the lives of 1.8 billion Muslims, including myself, and 1,400 years of Islamic civilization.

In the other frame, you see a human being, a complex individual, who is someone you'd probably say hello to when you walk down the street. Or, you might call the FBI or law enforcement if you saw him in the airport because you think he looks "suspicious."

In the US media, Muslims and Arabs have almost always been portrayed as violent oddities, terrorists, individuals about to become terrorists, individuals aiding terrorists, or family members of terrorists. As a child in 1991, I sang along with Robin Williams in Disney's *Aladdin* cartoon, as he said, "Oh, I come from a land / From a faraway place / Where the caravan camels roam. / Where they cut off your ear / If they don't like your face / It's barbaric, but hey, it's home!" In 2015, a *Public Policy* poll found that 30 percent of Republican voters supported bombing Agrabah, the fictional kingdom in Aladdin. They didn't poll whether the blue genie should be waterboarded.

Muslims and the Prophet Muhammad have been demonized in the Western mind for nearly one thousand years. In 1095, Pope Urban II declared a Crusade to cleanse the Holy Lands from the Muslim infidels.

The use of religious language for the sake of political ambition, the use of propaganda to claim territory and resources—it's nothing new. Before then, Muslims didn't feature that heavily in European propaganda, but as a result of this edict, Muslims officially became the enemy, as featured in the classic poem of eleventh-century Western literature, "The Song of Roland."

This poem, revered as a "masterpiece of epic drama," depicts the Muslim slaughter of 20,000 soldiers in Charlemagne's army in medieval Spain, including the Roman emperor's nephew Roland. Vowing revenge, Charlemagne heroically defeats the Muslim army. Great story. Too bad it never happened. In the real battle, which took place in 778, the killers were not Muslims but Christian Basques "furious at Charlemagne for pillaging their city of Pamplona."

In paintings from that era, Muslims, much like Jews, were portrayed as animalistic. In an iconic image from Luttrell Psalter, Richard the Lionheart is brave, dignified, and white as he fights Saladin, the Muslim commander who took Jerusalem, who is depicted as a "purple skinned, big lipped, hook-nosed monster."

The great Christian poet of the late Middle Ages and early Renaissance, Dante Alighieri, wasn't very kind either. In his masterwork, *The Divine Comedy*, we meet the Prophet Muhammad and Caliph Ali being tortured in hell. Clearly some Enlightenment was needed.

Voltaire seemed intrigued by Islam. Oh, look, he wrote an entire five-act play! It's titled *Fanaticism, or Mahomet the Prophet*, written in 1736, and premiered in 1741. Voltaire portrayed the Prophet Muhammad as "a paragon of fanaticism: an impostor desiring self-glorification and beautiful women who is willing to lie, to kill, and even to wage war against his homeland to get what he desires." Oy.

However, not all the reviews in France were unsympathetic. Historian and nobleman Henri de Boulainvilliers defended the prophet of Islam as a "divinely inspired messenger," statesman, and legislator in his famous work *The Life of Mahomet* in which he concludes the Prophet Muhammad "seems to have adopted and embraced all that is most marvelous in Christianity itself."

Another titan of the Enlightenment, Rousseau, praises the Prophet Muhammad as "a brilliant leader" and "sage legislator who wisely fused religious and political powers" in his famous work *The Social Contract*, published in 1762.

Rousseau inspired and influenced political leaders and revolutionaries across the world, such as Thomas Jefferson, who in 1765 ordered his first copy of the Quran, which was shipped from England to Williamsburg, Virginia. In the Constitution, he used his pen to affirm the religious liberties of the "Mahamdan." As president, Jefferson also apparently held the first White House Iftar dinner during Ramadan on December 9, 1805, when he hosted Sidi Soliman Mellimelli, a Tunisian envoy. He postponed dinner until sunset to accommodate Mellimelli's fast.

Over two hundred years later, President Trump canceled the annual White House Iftar dinner tradition and enacted a Muslim Ban. But we shouldn't feel nostalgic for the past, because Jefferson and other "Founding Fathers" were also slaveholders and couldn't care less about the religious and political liberties of Black Americans. Nearly 30 percent of the enslaved were originally Muslim, which means Muslims' stories, labor, tears, pain, and dreams have fertilized this country's soil from the beginning.

Near the end of the eighteenth century, we had Goethe rejecting Voltaire's depiction and instead writing poetry praising Muhammad, whom he saw as "the archetypal prophet." (Thanks, Goethe!) He wrote *Muhammad's Song* when he was twenty-three years old in preparation of a drama about the prophet that was never published. No doubt people thought he'd sold his soul to the Devil, like his Doctor Faustus. The Prophet Muhammad also got love from Napoleon, who saw him as a "charismatic leader and military genius," but he unfortunately used that adoration to try and colonize Muslims in Egypt.

For the most part, however, Muslims were lumped into European stereotypes of the Middle East, this brown bouillabaisse of savagery and misogyny, where all the men veil their women and are incapable of making witty jokes or enjoying a piña colada. The late academic Edward Said described this phenomenon as Orientalism, which centers the "Western" world (usually that means white, European, and American) and views the East as an inferior, primitive other. This mindset creates a white man's burden to enlighten, liberate, and dominate the savages.

Fast forward to the 1970s, when Saudi Arabia and several Arab countries flexed through OPEC, the Organization of the Petroleum Exporting Countries, and imposed an embargo on the United States for helping Israel in the 1973 war. This led to a brief oil crisis and long lines at US gas pumps. In 1979, the Islamic Revolution of Iran overthrew the corrupt and oppressive regime of the shah, an ally of the United States, and kept 52 American citizens hostage for 444 days. That same year, Russia made the ill-fated decision to attack Afghanistan. Meanwhile, the United States bombed Libya in 1986, the first Palestinian intifada began in 1987, and Operation Desert Storm against Iraq was launched in 1991.

Not coincidentally, our white Hollywood heroes ended up fighting these enemies in movies like *Iron Eagle* and *Delta Force*. Even comedies like *Down and Out in Beverly Hills* found time to make jokes about an Iranian millionaire with his many wives in black niqabs. In *Reel Bad Arabs*, the late historian Jack Shaheen examined nearly 1000 Hollywood movies featuring Muslims, Arabs, and the Middle East and concluded that 936 of them were negative depictions, portraying Arabs and Muslims as brutal, violent savages who terrorize white Americans and Europeans, or as lascivious and corrupt sheiks with harems of women.

Then there was the timeless and lucrative narrative of the oppressed woman who escapes the clutches of the uncivilized misogynist Muslim man, as in the classic Orientalist wet dream of the silent movie era, Rudolph Valentino's *The Sheik*. In *The Sheik*, Valentino, an Italian actor, plays an Arab who kidnaps a white woman. She escapes and is kidnapped by another Arab who wants to rape her. (This white woman just can't win!) Valentino then transforms into a hero who rescues the woman, and it is later revealed that Valentino's character is not Arab after all. Thus he literally becomes a white savior.

When the woman in the story is brown, we have what Gayatri Spivak referred to as "white men saving brown women from brown men," a classic colonial trope used to justify intervention, war, and violence. First Lady Laura Bush rationalized the War on Terror as "the fight against terrorism is also a fight for the rights and dignity of women." Thousands of girls and women have since died in Afghanistan and Iraq, in wars that still burn. At least 37 million people have been displaced as a direct result of the US War on Terror since 2001, according to a report from Brown University's Costs of War Project.

Even *Sex and the City* wants to liberate brown women. In the movie's 2010 sequel, the four "girls" travel to Abu Dhabi for a hedonistic getaway where they encounter every Hall of Fame Orientalist trope: "viagra for Western cultural imperialists," I wrote at the time. During the climax, the sex-loving Samantha, wearing shorts and a low-cut top, accidentally spills dozens of condoms from her purse in the middle of a crowded market. This act of overt female sexuality apparently triggers all the Muslim men, who surround Samantha, yell at her, and start chasing her through the crowd. The girls are thankfully saved by a few veiled women, who invite them in and take off their niqabs, revealing that, underneath, these Muslim women are just like white American girls: billboards for materialism, fans of expensive designer shoes and clothes inaccessible to most women around the world.

In America, we often forget that the world loves our pop culture and pays attention to our stories. According to a Gallup study of over one billion Muslims in 2009, their number one grievance against the United States was our "lack of respect" toward them, which includes our inaccurate and disrespectful media representation of Islam and Muslims. (Among their areas of admiration were for our democracy and rule of law. So much for the narrative that they "hate our freedoms.")

The *New York Times* portrayed Islam and Muslims more negatively than they portrayed cancer, cocaine, and alcohol, according to a study that examined the paper's headlines from 1990 to 2014. Even cancer, a universally reviled disease, had better press than us. *Cancer.*

Even though white supremacists are the number one domestic terror threat in America, Muslims accused of plotting violence received seven times more media attention and four times longer criminal sentences. I appreciate all the lavish attention.

Numerous studies reveal that negative depictions in film and media have created and perpetuated stereotypes that associate people of color, especially Black men, with violence and criminality. The repeated association of violence with brown and black skin literally dehumanizes us. In order to protect the suburbs and deal with these fictional super-predators, rapists, criminals, and invaders, America imagines it needs border walls, mass deportations, a Muslim Ban, and a "tough on crime" policing.

What we really need is to flood the market with our stories, populated not by Rage Boy but by characters that accurately depict our lived experiences and our community's legacies.

To cite the debut album of Public Enemy, you have to bum rush the show.

But before I could make my Hollywood premiere and Broadway debut, I had to cut my teeth on the streets of Fremont.

Scorsese, Fellini, Ali

My mother met Kashif's mom, Shaheen aunty, when they were the only two Pakistani immigrants working in a computer manufacturing factory in Milpitas. When you're starved for representation, you gravitate to whoever looks like you. They hit it off and our families became friends. Kashif and I were both dorks who were not invited to parties and social events, and even if we were, our parents would have never allowed us to attend. Pakistani immigrant parents from that generation didn't appreciate the concept of "sleepovers" or "going over to friends' houses" or "locked doors" in the home or, basically, any semblance of "privacy." My parents were fine with the entire world coming over to our house, but I could never go anywhere except Kashif's house. (They also knew they could track us easily and drive over in ten minutes if needed.) Our parents believed we were special. They were convinced that every local kidnapper and child molester would specifically target us and only us at the mall, concert, and Great America amusement park and whisk us away if we were left without adult supervision.

We spent weekends going to theaters and sneaking into movies with my cousins or with Kashif and his younger brother Atif. We used to plot our movie hopping like we were stealing a painting from the Louvre, checking the newspaper for movie listings and then choosing the theater that had at least two movies we wanted to see. We scoped out all the exits and entrances as we kept an eye out for the heat around the corner, usually a pimpled teenage employee who couldn't care less. (You could hide in the arcade at Cinedome 8 East, and when the coast was clear, cross to the opposite side of the theater to sneak into another movie.)

One day when I was about ten and Kashif about fourteen, lazing around his home, we decided to pick up his father's VHS camera and take it for a spin. We didn't ask Syed uncle for his permission. This was 1990 when video cameras weighed fifteen pounds and you had to rest them on your shoulder and pray you wouldn't become paralyzed after a few hours.

For our first movie, Kashif was the hero who had to retrieve his Air Jordans that were conveniently stolen by the villain, yours truly, hamming up the screen with gleeful melodrama. We had a hero, an antagonist, a goal, and some semblance of a plot. It was a start. Kashif was more technically savvy and enjoyed the camera angles and editing. I was better with dialogue and character development.

We created cinematic masterpieces over the next years, including *The Formula Trilogy* where I was an evil scientist who created a world-ending poison and Kashif was the heroic scientist/detective determined to stop my dastardly plot at all costs. We also made *The Bane Trilogy* where I was an exhausted, grizzled cop who drank several cups of coffee a day and wore sunglasses inside the house, always on the hunt for his nemesis Bane, a sophisticated criminal who wore a jacket and had a wisp of white hair. We used to huddle before filming, go over a broad outline of the plot, create characters, and then shoot scenes making sure we had enough exposition and action to make it entertaining for a fifteen-to-twenty-minute movie. Over time, we started exploring different camera angles, squibs for bullet wounds, sound effects editing, and creative transition shots.

Our loyal schlep, sidekick, and henchman was Atif, Kashif's younger brother, who was around five when we started making these movies. His mother said we had to include him. Our only condition was that he would die in every movie. As he got older, he gave some epic near-death speeches before taking his final breath.

Their sister Huma refused to participate but eagerly saw the premiere of each movie. Our families were our only audiences. Looking forward to our latest installment, they all sat down in the family room with chai and laughed their asses off. If we had had access to a budget and Sundance, who knows, maybe we could've done something, but for then it was a great way to pass the time and live out our creative dreams in the sleepy suburbs of Fremont, California.

My parents encouraged the budding cinephile in me, and by age eleven I was trusted to rent the movie of the week for the family. I brought home everything from *The Godfather* and *Ran* to *Tommy Boy* and *Pulp Fiction*.

At Bellarmine high school, most of my friends and their parents were convinced I would grow up to be a stand-up comedian or a film director. I was known to be a wiseass in the classroom, making my teachers and friends laugh. I could hold court for an hour if needed and be vocal and quick in classroom debates. Every year, I auditioned for the plays produced by our theater department. I walked up to the call list posted outside Benson Theater and never saw my name in the cast. I kept being rejected. My auditions sucked. I made peace with the fact I'd never get cast in a play, but I felt I could still make our school's improv comedy troupe, Sanguine Humours. This was an elite group of only a dozen or so kids that held auditions once a year for two or three open slots.

Improv is like walking on a tightrope without a safety net while making sure your partner, who's also balancing on the rope, doesn't fall off as the audience is constantly yelling and heckling you and expecting you to make them laugh. When you can pull it off, it's an orgasmic high, a beautiful symphony held together by wit, attention, trust, playfulness, and confidence. On the flip side, there's nothing worse than bombing on stage. You pray to a deity to end your suffering; you hope the stage swallows you whole. A minute while bombing can seem like an eternal rectal exam.

I tried for two years in a row and just flopped during each audition for Sanguine Humours. I was unwilling to go all out and commit to the scene. I was terrified when I needed to be fearless. Senior year was my final chance. I promised myself that this time I wouldn't hold back; I would put it all out there on the stage and at least make my Bellarmine exit without regrets.

I crushed it. A few days later, I walked up to the call list taped on the outside of Benson Theater for the Sanguine Humours Improv Troupe, and right there at the top I could see it: Wajahat Ali.

We practiced every Friday after school for two hours. A few squad members decided to put on a free show at the local mall, which caught the attention of a *San Jose Mercury* writer. Her feature on us was on the front page of the Eye, the weekend entertainment section of the newspaper.

There was me, the awkward guy, in the local paper. I didn't tell my parents until after the performances. I kept this side of my life "hidden." At age seventeen, I wasn't ready, comfortable, or secure enough to share this part of my identity.

"What will people say?"

There was a sense of freedom on that stage. For a kid who had spent his life being laughed at, it was so rewarding and fulfilling to know that people were laughing with me. I was the conductor and composer of the laugh track. I could be the Wajahat freed from the conformity and restraints of Pakistani and Islamic respectability. I was away from any judging eye or preemptive condescension that could extinguish the small spark that blazed inside me. I assumed that if they found out they would only laugh at me or come to see me as a freakish curiosity.

I realized early on that Allah is forgiving but Muslims are not. You can swap Muslims with any other religious group and that point still sticks. Often, in a religious environment with high standards of moral conduct, piety is understood as being unforgiving and judgmental. The irony is that most in those religious communities desperately crave catharsis through entertainment and art. It's impossible to pretend to be pious and perfect, and the act eventually becomes unbearable. We are, after all, flawed, eccentric, conflicted creatures who make mistakes. We just want to exhale. That happens with laughter. That also happens when you feel seen. Instead of shame, most Muslims felt pride and were pleasantly surprised by this "talent" I was hiding.

A few years later, at UC Berkeley, I was, again, the only brown and Muslim dude in our comedy troupe, which was called the GWOD Squad. My specific identities, which often excluded me from the American narrative, ended up being strengths I could draw on not only to entertain but also to educate. After the 9/11 terror attacks, we all thought long and hard about whether we should disband the troupe. Who was in the mood to laugh after a national tragedy? (It turns out everyone was, because they needed a release.)

In the end, we postponed our show by two weeks. We came up with a sketch where I played "Captain Islam," an average dude by day and a superhero by night, who wears a giant "I" on his chest and has a bath towel as a cape. Amid the backlash against Muslims, my troupe wanted to use the moment for comedy but also for healing. We had no idea if people thought it would be tacky or bad taste. Those were tense times when John Lennon's *Imagine* and the entire Rage Against the Machine catalogue were temporarily iced by Clear Channel radio stations.

"Let's do it," I said. Captain Islam suited up and made his premiere on the UC Berkeley stage a few weeks after 9/11. The audience responded with the night's biggest, thunderous applause.

A silly sketch, some humor, some storytelling—that's what connected with a diverse audience in need of solace, comfort, and understanding.

That and a brown dude with a giant "I" for Islam on his chest.

Chapter 4

Be Moderate So America Will (Maybe) Love You (Conditionally) One Day (Inshallah)

For the past twenty years, I have scoured the globe for this mythical creature known as the "moderate Muslim."

You must have heard of them by now.

After the 9/11 terror attacks, they allegedly became an endangered species. America and Europe have repeatedly asked, "Where are the moderate Muslims and how come they haven't condemned extremism?"

This elusive tribe was once part of the "Muslim world," another amazing destination I have yet to encounter in all my travels around Earth. What passport is needed to visit the Muslim world? Do the "moderate Muslims" live there? Are they real or are they a myth like Bigfoot? Do they ban alcohol, or are they currently taking vodka shots with Elvis and Tupac in Agrabah?

These questions burn my soul and keep me up at night, tossing and turning, moderately, in my bed. Perhaps we will never know, but still I continue my search for my Islamic Atlantis. There is a yearning to be with these lost people, my people, the moderate people, as I perilously hover in limbo, a man torn, moderately, between my radical and my mild tendencies—among the nearly four million Muslim Americans who, according to study after study, overwhelmingly reject violence against civilians, oppose terrorism, remain optimistic about America, advocate for racial equality, and help law enforcement. Muslim

American women are the most highly educated women of any religious community except Jewish women. That all sounds pretty moderate to me.

Regardless, we are still lumped into a box with different flavors of extremism. The War on Terror doesn't allow the time or luxury for truthful nuance.

For years, I've sincerely been asking if someone could just mass email Muslims a simple checklist on how we can finally be "moderate" enough for America to accept us after our having been in this country for over four hundred years. (Please use the bcc option to avoid an endless email thread. Thank you.)

Allah heard my prayers.

Fifteen years after the 9/11 terror attacks, on July 27, 2016, he sent us President Bill Clinton who said, at the Democratic National Convention, "If you're a Muslim and you love America and freedom and you hate terror, stay here and help us win and make a future together. We want you."

That's it? Phew. Lovely. I counted five "ands" in that statement. I must admit I lost track after the third "and."

Let's break down the six-part conditional contract to be a "moderate Muslim" and see if I pass the test, shall we?

1. **"If you're a Muslim . . ."** ✔ Got that one. So far so good.
2. **"And you love America . . ."** ✔ OK! 2 for 2.
3. **"And freedom . . ."** ✔ Who doesn't love freedom? I'm all about freedom! Hat trick!
4. **"And you hate terror . . ."** ✔ Boo to terror! It's only allowed on Halloween and at awkward family gatherings, but other than that, boo terror!
5. **"Stay here and help us win . . ."** ✔ ? OK, I'm cool with the staying here part, but "help us win"? Help "who" win "what" exactly? Everything was going so well, but now I'm lost. Who are "we" playing against? What's my position?

Who's on my squad? I warn you all that I can only dunk in NBA 2K.

6. **"And make a future together." ?** Together with who? With "us"? Who are we fighting? Did I just get drafted against my will? I'm overweight and have messed-up feet. Can I just stay home and support you all as you fight by using color emojis and hashtags on social media? Good luck to all of you against whomever you're playing or fighting. Thoughts and prayers.

It would be one thing if moderate Christians, Jews, and Hindus were also asked and required to root out the extremists in their ranks. But no, this one-sided contract was reserved just for Muslims. This came from the Democrats, our alleged allies. Republicans were running on a Muslim Ban.

President Clinton spoke two days before Khizr and Ghazala Khan, Muslim immigrants from Pakistan, commanded the stage and the nation's attention as Gold Star parents of Captain Humayun Khan, who was killed in Iraq in 2004. I always wondered if Bill Clinton would have changed his statement about Muslims if he had heard their speech first. Khizr uncle took out his worn copy of the Constitution and publicly asked Trump, "Have you ever read the Constitution?" He finished his moral beatdown by telling him, "You have sacrificed nothing—and no one."

Even before 9/11, America had long been guilty of voluntarily sacrificing many of its innocent residents and cherished freedoms for the feeling of safety, for political ideology, for wars, for profit, for revenge, for hate.

What's so painful and destructive about the "moderate Muslim" trope is that it assumes nonviolent Muslims are the magical exceptions, the unicorns, and not the norm. Implicit in the question is the assumption that a majority of us somehow condone terrorism or are sympathetic to violent extremists unless we explicitly denounce each and every occurrence of violence.

Ever since 9/11, this double standard colors every aspect of America's interaction with this thing called "Islam" and "Muslims."

However, it wasn't always like this for some of us.

Once Upon a Time . . . When We Thought We Were White and Moderate

Many Muslims from my father's generation, who came to this country after the 1965 Immigration and Nationality Act, chased Whiteness, which was part and parcel of the Amreekan dream.

They will deny it if you ask them, because they will say they came here just to make a better life for themselves and their families. In fact, I'll bet all my limited money they will be unable to articulate or even define Whiteness.

But, Whiteness they chased nonetheless, even though they knew they would never fully grasp it, or be accepted in its privileged country clubs, or walk through its gilded doors to executive boardrooms, or be elected to its political positions, or read its script as the protagonists of a TV drama, or receive its blessings when they asked for Suzy's hand in marriage. Still, it was enough to be adjacent to its acceptance, to be asymptotic to its power, to retreat into its warm, protective embrace, preferably in a safe, good, gated, suburban community.

They were like Icarus, who thought their wings—made of money, wax, and upward social mobility—would let them escape their brownness, their Muslimy-ness, their accented English, their multisyllabic names, their turmeric-infused fingernails.

They flew with their eyes arrogantly above the ground, oblivious to the majority of Americans, their natural allies—Black, brown, immigrant, low-income workers, the poor—who toiled below.

They kept soaring, thanks to their exceptionalism, hard work, luck, grit, kismet, and God's divine favor, or so they told themselves. If only the Blacks and the Mexicans and the other poor, lazy people pulled themselves up by their bootstraps, stopped asking for handouts, and followed their checklist, they too could fly in the clouds. They too could bask in the beauty of the Amreekan dream.

"Look at us! Started from the bottom and now we're here, flying, almost reaching the Sun!" they thought, thankful and excited to settle into the final arc of success after a long, difficult journey.

And then the heat of September 11, 2001, melted their wings of wax.

As they violently hurled down toward Earth, they kept saying, "This wasn't supposed to happen to us."

This affected Muslims of color who assumed they were white. The Fair & Lovely cream washed off. We were finally able to look at ourselves in America's mirror as we truly are, as we always were.

Dark & Lovely.

Supermodel Minorities Deserve Their Own Box

- ☐ White
- ☐ Black
- ☐ Asian
- ☐ American Indian
- ☐ Pacific Islander

Which box should I check?

This is the age-old question that many Muslims, people of color, and immigrants of color have had to face in America. Growing up, I used to check "Asian" or "Other." I never saw an option for South Asian/ Pakistani. Still, my friends and I assumed Asian really referred to those who were Chinese, Korean, Vietnamese, or Japanese. I never thought it included Pakistanis, but it was close enough so I checked it.

"Other" was a nice, easy catchall that basically was the receptacle for the lost souls of America to be given a home, the hot dog of the census, all the miscellaneous parts ground up into something whole and tasty.

Still, the questions remained: What box includes us? What box will accept us? What happens if none of the boxes look familiar, which one should we choose? These questions have inspired absurd events that reflect this country's desperate and ridiculous attempts to maintain citizenship solely for "white" people.

In 1919, Indian Sikh American Bhagat Singh Thind chose white. He argued he was a descendant of Aryans, who migrated from Europe to India, and was a "high caste Hindu of full Indian blood" and had a rightful claim to US naturalization, which at the time was reserved only for "free white people" and "aliens of African nativity and persons of African descent." In *Takao Ozawa v. United States*, the Supreme Court in 1922 denied citizenship to Ozawa, a Japanese-American man, claiming that Japanese people did not fit the definition of Caucasian, the race to which "white people" belong, and instead he was actually "Mongolian."

Thind, a veteran of World War I who had fought for the U.S. Army and earned his PhD from UC Berkeley, used the Supreme Court's own ruling and analysis in *Ozawa* to allege that he, a man of Indian origin, was actually included in the category of Caucasian at the time and thus should be granted citizenship. The Whiteness wasn't having it. The Supreme Court not only unanimously decided against him in 1923 but also retroactively denied all Indian Americans the right to obtain US citizenship.

Despite this failed attempt, historically, many South Asians, Arabs, and Latinos still chose white. First, it's because we didn't have an option that represented our identity. Second, it was the strategically smart move to make. You align yourself with the winning team, the one that holds all the power. You can't be white but you can have aspirational Whiteness, claiming it with a simple stroke of a pen. Proximity to Whiteness can help immigrants and people of color literally survive in this country. Your othering will be minimized, and if you're lucky, you can be spared from discrimination, profiling, and ending up on the wrong registries. The census, after all, was used to round up innocent Japanese Americans during the 1940s and place them in internment camps.

The lumping of all these beautiful, diverse ethnicities into Whiteness and "Other" creates amusing and absurd realities. For example, "Middle Eastern" has historically been defined in America as "white." Little did Donald Trump, Stephen Miller, and white nationalists know they were weakening the white race by implementing the Muslim Ban and restricting refugees from Middle Eastern countries. What a sad, self-inflicted wound!

A 2015 U.S. Census Bureau study found that when given the Middle Eastern and North African (MENA) option, those who identified as white dropped from nearly 86 percent to 20 percent. If you build a box, they will check it.

Many will still opt for Whiteness, in the form of either a census box, a state of mind, or an aspirational identity. For South Asian immigrants, our experience with Whiteness runs deep, coming down through generations thanks to the trauma of British colonialism. The British Raj ruled the subcontinent from 1858 to 1947, until the Partition created India and Pakistan as separate, independent nation-states. Even though South Asians eventually achieved their freedom, Whiteness, like herpes, lingers forever. If you travel across South Asia, for example, you'll look at all the ads promoting beauty products and ask yourself why everyone looks like a white person from New Jersey with a summer tan. In fact, beauty is still often measured by saaf rang, or clean skin color, which refers to "light skin tone." Fair & Lovely cream sells like hotcakes all around South Asia, even though everyone knows it's bullshit and doesn't help make you either "fair" or "lovely." You can never wipe off the brown no matter how hard you try, no matter how hard you pray, but, still, people aspire and hope maybe, one day, one bottle will contain a magical elixir that takes them to Whiteness.

Another reason to strategically choose Whiteness is to move as far away from Blackness as possible. Bad news travels fast. When I visit countries around the world, I'm usually asked the same four questions about America:

1. Why do you all love guns so much?
2. Why doesn't your government give you free health care?
3. Why did you vote for Trump?
4. Why does America hate Black people so much?

I assure them I don't own a gun, I'm all for the government providing affordable health care, I didn't vote for Trump, and the country has a diseased history of racism and anti-Blackness that it has yet to truly confront and acknowledge.

My Khala Bibi one time visited the Bay Area. She was my mother's aunt who passed away in 2020 from COVID-19. She was a lovely, generous woman who made me this killer aloo bhujia and lived most of her life in Karachi, Pakistan. I took her to Fentons Ice Creamery in Oakland to indulge her in American gluttony. Afterwards, we took a tour of UC Berkeley, my alma mater. It got late, and as we were ready to drive home, I stopped at a gas station. A Black man approached my car, and Khala Bibi reacted as if a horde of zombies were about to overwhelm us. She panicked and begged, "Beta, lock the doors! Lock the doors!"

I was amused by her hysteria and replied, "Wait, why? Because of him? He's just standing there. Look."

"Beta, please! You never know. Just lock the door," she said, still flustered and nervous.

I refused to indulge her fear and within a few seconds she realized there was no threat and calmed down.

I was fascinated by what had happened. During the car ride home, I asked her why she reacted the way she did, especially when she literally has no interaction with Black people in Karachi.

I never forgot what she said.

"Beta, we see Blacks on TV shows and news in Pakistan. They always show them as ghundas (criminals)."

My father's generation of Asian and South Asian immigrants were rarely portrayed as ghundas trying to unsuccessfully outrun the police in the hit show *Cops*, which ran for thirty years before being canceled due to long-standing allegations of promoting racist, anti-Black stereotypes.

No, sir. We were the "model minority."

We take our shoes off at the door. We are polite, timid, law-abiding, and educated. We study hard, work hard, pay our taxes, and are grateful to America for all of its opportunities. We don't whine, complain, make excuses for our lot in life, raise our voice, or critique power. We don't rock the boat, we row the boat. Like sugar, we dissolve and assimilate, leaving a sweet, nonthreatening aftertaste.

Our reward? The American dream!

The "model minority" myth is a dangerous drug manufactured and promoted by the Whiteness. It ignores all of our diverse experiences and narratives, eliminates all nuances, and lumps us with a convenient stereotype that always renders us as foreigners. It overlooks the discrimination, bias, and hate experienced by our communities and, perhaps worst of all, uses us, Asian and South Asian immigrants in particular, to launder systemic racism and discrimination against poor Black and Latino communities. Why can't they be "models" like us? Because they are lazy freeloaders who don't take personal responsibility, whine about racism, and refuse to pull themselves up by their bootstraps! The system turns us into enforcers and defenders of Whiteness, promising success and safety in exchange for loyalty and obedience. But it's an abusive, toxic relationship, in which the system has always betrayed us on a whim, without remorse or hesitation. Being a "model minority" doesn't live up to the hype. In fact, we're the only models valued for being invisible. In a 2021 survey, 42 percent of Americans couldn't name a single prominent Asian American. (I'll give you three: Vice President Kamala Harris, actor and activist George Takei, and David Chang, the founder of Momofuku restaurants. You're welcome.)

Being a "model" doesn't seem to be helping us succeed in business either. Asian Americans are the least likely group in the U.S. to be promoted to management. Being a "model" didn't protect eighty-four-year-old Vicha Ratanapakdee, an immigrant from Thailand, who was taking his usual stroll in San Francisco when he was fatally pushed to the ground in an unprovoked attack his family said was fueled by anti-Asian racism. Being a "model" didn't save Bawi Cung, an immigrant from Myanmar, and his two children—ages two and six—from receiving stitches and scars when they were nearly stabbed to death inside a grocery store in Texas because the attacker thought they were "Chinese and infecting people with coronavirus." From March 2020 to early 2021, Stop Asian American Pacific Islander Hate recorded over 3,000 incidents of hate, racism, and assault directed toward Asian Americans after President Trump and the right-wing ecosystem decided to call coronavirus "the Chinese Virus" and "Kung Flu." Asian Americans were told to "go back to Wuhan," spit upon, shoved, shunned, yelled at, and even killed. Again, bigots aren't the most nuanced bunch. Also, coronavirus does not have an ethnicity, race, religion, or zip code. It could not be reached for comment.

My father's generation had no idea they were being used to promote this fickle, volatile mistress known as Whiteness. Pakistani Muslims who came here after the 1965 Immigration and Nationality Act and achieved success bought into the myth of the American dream: if they made it in America with just a handful of dollars, anyone could make it.

They didn't realize the doors opened for them only after they were closed for Mexican workers. Everything is conditional in America, even the right to the American dream.

The 1965 Immigration and Nationality Act abolished the discriminatory national origin quotas that were imposed in 1924 to keep out previously despised immigrants like Jews, Italians, and Asians. However, this inclusion came at a cost as new immigration restrictions were put in place. As Erika Lee explains in her excellent book *America for Americans: A History of Xenophobia in the United States*, "despite its intent to treat all immigrant groups fairly and equally, the 1965 Immigration Act also ended up reinforcing inclusion for some and exclusion for others."

With the passage of the Civil Rights Act in 1964 and the Voting Rights Act in 1965, lawmakers were more comfortable with the premise of civil rights and equality, but both Republicans and Democrats still had anxiety and fear of a "population explosion" from Asian, African, and Latin American countries that would "alter the current ethnic and racial balance of American society." Anti-immigrant and nativist groups like the American Coalition of Patriotic Societies warned fellow racists that President Johnson's policies would bring "swarms of Asiatics and Africans" to America and "allow the Trojan Horse at our gate . . . from whose dark bowels can emerge into our midst a million alien misfits a year."

Racists read from the same script, regardless of the decade.

Congressman Michael Feighan, a Democrat from Ohio, was adamant that the racial and ethnic composition of the US population stay predominantly white. So, for the first time ever, the INA put a numerical cap on immigration from the Western Hemisphere that was "driven by racist and xenophobic fears" and "intentionally designed to restrict immigration from Latin America." The INA also established a preference for professional and skilled workers, which negatively affected uneducated and low-skilled migrants from Mexico as global demand for labor was actually increasing. The United States terminated the Bracero (manual laborers from Mexico) Program in 1964, implemented quotas after the 1965 INA, and added a labor certification system—all of which drastically reduced the number of Mexican laborers legally coming into America from more than 200,000 a year to a quota of only 20,000 by 1976. This in turn led to a dramatic increase in undocumented immigration.

Congressman Feighan also negotiated with President Johnson for the INA to give preference to family reunification (now known as "chain migration") ahead of immigrants with professional skills and training "advantageous" to the United States when handing out new immigrant visas. Due to the higher number of European Americans in the United States, he believed this would bring more European relatives here to protect and strengthen the white majority. Instead, the number of immigrants from Europe fell, and Asian and Latin countries ended up accounting for nearly 85 percent of all admitted immigrants. My family was one of the many unintended beneficiaries of Congressman Feighan's racism. Abu was able to bring Dadi, Dada, Yasmeen Phuppo, his siblings, and finally Ami, which led to me being born in California as a US citizen. (Thank you, Congressman Feighan!)

The INA, which helped my father's generation of Pakistani students come to Amreeka, was "more sophisticated" in its racial discrimination than the national origins quota system. According to Lee, these new restrictions and quotas "effectively eliminated most avenues for legal immigration for most Mexican immigrants and compromised the promise of equality that the 1965 Immigration and Nationality Act was supposed to embody." This is probably why Chad asked the only Mexican kid from first grade to punch me in the stomach at James Leitch Elementary School. The universe found a way to make amends.

Muslims Love Bush

In 2000, I was a twenty-year-old college student in California excited to vote in my first election. Like most Americans, I cast the vote for Al Gore, who had the personality of an inanimate carbon rod, but whose platform, experience, and intellect were far more impressive than George W. Bush, whose trouble with the English language and elementary political analysis became known as "Bushisms." My favorite Bushism has to be this gem from January 11, 2000: "Rarely is the question asked: Is our children learning?"

I assumed most Muslims would consider this a no-brainer vote. At the time, we were evolving from the idiotic debates about whether voting in US elections was haram (forbidden) or not. (Yes, there were actual conversations about this, and no, it is not haram.)

I was convinced they would not side with an increasingly regressive and racist Republican Party that was appealing to Christian nationalism and fear. My parents, who in 1988 and 1992 had voted for the elder Bush, had come around to realizing the Republican Party talked a big game of family values, morality, and deficit cuts, but offered up a dose of hypocrisy, cruelty, and greed. They voted Democrat in 1996 and never turned back.

Most African American Muslims knew the score, having endured a history of being on the wrong side of oppression. They went blue.

However, many Arab and South Asian immigrant voters, in particular from my father's generation, decided to flex their voting power for once and vote as a "bloc" for . . . Bush.

"Beta, we are all going to vote as a Muslim bloc for once and vote for Bush," Rafia aunty explained to me during one of her visits to my parents' home in Fremont.

"Aunty, respectfully, this is the most foolish thing I've ever heard," I recall telling her. "Please, please don't do this. Bush is going to be terrible for Muslims and the country," I pleaded with her, still trying to wrap my head around the insanity I had just heard.

"Neyhee, beta, Bush will be good for Muslims. He met Muslims, and also this Lieberman is a Jew who is going to be totally pro-Israel," she countered.

Unlike Democrats, Bush actively courted the Muslim-American vote thanks to advice from Grover Norquist, the longtime conservative activist and anti-tax zealot, who once famously said, "I'm not in favor of abolishing the government. I just want to shrink it down to the size where we can drown it in the bathtub."

Norquist was on to something. He knew that many Muslims believed in God, took their religious values seriously, were socially conservative, and favored business-friendly policies that promoted lower taxes and small-time business owners. Like many other voters in the nation, they were also taken by Bush's promise to "restore honor and dignity" to the White House after we endured the sordid details and impeachment scandal of President Clinton's affair with Monica Lewinsky.

As a candidate, Bush actually met with Muslims, and he visited a mosque after the 9/11 attacks. He also spoke out against racial profiling and promised to repeal the Secret Evidence Act, which was used almost exclusively to detain Muslim and Arab immigrants. If you've never been invited to the prom and have often been treated like social kryptonite, any attention, especially from the cool kid with the rich dad and the big house, makes your heart flutter and wins over your loyalty.

Bush's investment paid off. According to one estimate, up to 90 percent of Florida's 60,000 Muslim votes went for Bush, a state he won by only 537 votes. "George W. Bush was elected President of the United States of America because of the Muslim vote," Norquist later crowed.

In 2004, Norquist married Samah Norquist, a Palestinian Muslim woman from Kuwait, and has since endured endless conspiracy theories insinuating that he is a closet Muslim and part of the radical Muslim Brotherhood. I met Norquist in his Americans for Tax Reform office in Washington, DC, a few years back to talk about our shared concern about the growing Islamophobia in the Republican Party. He told me I was supposed to wear a collared shirt, jacket, and tie. I refused to wear a tie, but he still allowed me inside for a chat. He assured me he is not Muslim. I can in turn assure all of you that you cannot magically become Muslim through osmosis or by marrying someone who is Muslim. Norquist is, however, still a Republican.

If George W. Bush were to run for president in 2024 as a Republican, his own party would reject him as a Muslim lover.

You'll Be Moderate but You'll Never Be Moderate Enough

My roommate Ahsan knocked on my door and woke me up. "You have to see this. Now," he said, with a rare urgency in his voice. I rubbed my eyes and lumbered toward the living room of the apartment we lived in during our UC Berkeley years.

One of the towers in NYC was burning. They kept showing a video of a plane that flew right into it. At the time, we were hoping it was just a tragic accident.

"Astaghfirullah. May Allah protect these innocent people," I muttered under my breath, reciting prayers. We were transfixed by the ensuing horror and tragedy. Then the news anchors said this was a potential terror attack by Al Qaeda and Osama bin Laden.

Twenty years later, my Muslim friends still recite the "Muslim Prayer."

Whenever there is news of a terror attack, shooting, violence, or cringe-worthy scandal that could debase entire communities, we pray that the culprit is a white dude. Whether it's the 1993 World Trade Center attack, the 1995 Oklahoma City bombing, or the 2021 attack on the U.S. Capitol, we all pray. It's not because we wish ill will on whites. (Remember, we love whites. Some of our best friends are whites. Some of us want to be white.) Rather, it's a realization that whenever the culprit is a white man or a white woman, America will demonize only that specific individual. Their communities will not be tarred and feathered and their entire race, ethnicity, and tribe will not be asked to apologize for someone else's criminal acts. The whites will not have to spend the week defending their moderation and loyalty in front of news cameras, a Senate committee, or a jury of their peers. They can just amble on with their lives and eat mashed potatoes and listen to Steely Dan.

"Why couldn't it have been a white dude? Why was it Muslims?" we later asked, exasperated.

As the two towers fell, I was standing in my pajamas, staring at the TV, and I realized our lives had forever changed. There was a permanent fork in the road for my generation. A disruption in the timeline. A disturbance in the Force. For us, there would always be a pre–9/11 and a post–9/11 world. A few hours earlier, I had been a twenty-year-old senior still trying to figure out his major and serve as a board member of the Muslim Student Association of UC Berkeley. Instantly, I was transformed into an accidental activist, a global representative of 1.8 billion Muslims worldwide and a walking Wikipedia of 1,400 years of all things Islam.

I have to be perfect, because any flaw, mistake, errant word, or quote can and will be used against me and all my people in the court of public opinion. On the drop of a dime, I have to be an expert on the following topics: Islam, Quran, the Prophet Muhammad, Sharia, Iran, Iraq, Pakistan, India, Hamas, Hummus, Hezbollah, Arabic, Agrabah, Afghanistan, Al Qaeda, Al Aqsa, Aladdin, Salman Khan the Bollywood Actor, Salman Khan of the Khan Academy, and everything in between. I have to be able to explain them to a skeptical national audience, being sure not to say anything too radical or extreme, because that one mistake will be emblazoned on me like a scarlet letter and be used to beat up this thing called the "Muslim world."

As the towers were falling, I closed my eyes and the next ten years flashed before me. I saw it all clearly. The wrath of the entire country would descend on Muslims and those who looked Muslim-y. We would be scrutinized under the microscope, defined and judged through the lens of national security. There would be blood, and there would be a reckoning. That violent lust for vengeance and restitution would claim many innocent lives and communities. We had to steel ourselves for a bruising, but also dig down deep and commit to working for a better future.

Of the many images, thoughts, and fears that passed before me, I recall zeroing in on one inescapable regret: "Why the hell didn't I join the Indian Student Association instead?" Life would have been easier. I could have learned how to do bhangra, met some cute girls, and participated in their awesome, annual talent show. But, no, I joined the Muslim Student Association. FML, as the kids say.

When I started college, I was thrilled to finally not be the token practicing Muslim at school or work. I met and befriended Muslims who prayed, Muslims who drank alcohol, Muslims who wore hijab, Muslims who took off their hijab, Muslims who fasted during Ramadan, Muslims who went to Jummah prayer, Muslims who partied, and Muslims who were losers like me and played PS2 and Dreamcast. In my final year, the Muslim students elected me and four others to the board. Ahsan made us a free website and put my name and email for media outreach. Guess who got all the lovely hate mails, death threats, vile anti-Muslim filth, demands to fornicate with animals, and media requests? Yours truly.

Awesome.

The board called an emergency meeting. All of us knew that shit was going to go down in America. The fear of hate crimes and blowback was palpable. Muslim women who wore hijab were concerned about their safety after receiving ugly hate mail and hearing incidents of assaults. Those who looked Muslim also bore the brunt of the attacks. In fact, the first post 9/11 hate crime was the murder of Balbir Singh Sodhi, a Sikh gas station owner in Mesa, Arizona, who was shot and killed on September 15th as retaliation for the terror attacks. His murderer told his friends he was going to "go out and shoot some towel heads."

We decided to create an escort service for Muslim women so they could feel safe walking from their apartment to classes. There was a list of about ten Muslim men they could call. Surprisingly, Faiz, the best-looking of us, got *all* the calls, especially late at night. A chivalrous, decent guy, he did what he could but then had to outsource the rest of the requests. I was called twice, so at least it wasn't a total shutout.

At first, many Muslims didn't think Al Qaeda could have done it. We simply didn't think Muslims, especially suicidal terrorists who usually weren't that brilliant, were capable of executing such a sophisticated terror plot. For a few days, we sincerely doubted that Muslims would be able to bypass US security and law enforcement, hijack several planes, and then coordinate a plan to crash them into the Twin Towers and the Pentagon. It just seemed like an implausible plot out of a terrible movie.

Also, contrary to hateful and false conspiracy theories promoted by Donald Trump, no Muslims in New Jersey celebrated the deaths of the 3,000 innocent civilians killed on September 11, 2001. He claims to have seen a video that doesn't exist. The civilians killed in that terror attack included Muslims.

Muslims were also among the heroes, like Mohammad Salman Hamdani, a twenty-three-year-old first responder who was working on his medical school applications the night before. Mohammad came here from Karachi at the age of thirteen, learned English, and dreamed of becoming a doctor. According to his mom, Talat Hamdani, he always wanted to help people. He was a part-time emergency medical technician and had joined the NYPD's cadet program. When he saw the smoke from the buildings, he rushed in to save people as others rushed out. For the next forty-five days, he wasn't remembered or praised as a hero. Instead, he was a suspect. Based on what evidence? His religion.

As his parents wept, searching for answers, awake for sleepless nights, wondering if their missing son was still alive, Hamdani was being investigated. The *New York Post* published a piece with the headline: "Missing—or Hiding?—Mystery of NYPD Cadet from Pakistan." His body was finally found in thirty-four pieces by the North Tower. Twenty years after he died trying to save lives during the terror attacks, his mother is still trying to have him recognized as a first responder and named alongside other heroes at the North Pool of the 9/11 memorial. Currently, his name is at the South Pool memorial. "I want to see it in my lifetime," his mother said. "It's a very—it's so intense pain that is indescribable." Eventually, Congress referred to him as a "hero." But not before America saw him as a potential terrorist.

One's moderation as a Muslim was now so suspect that even if you became an EMT, helped the NYPD, and ran into a burning building to save civilians, you were still a potential threat.

What hope did the rest of us have?

*   *   *   *

Back home, we received a call that UC Berkeley's chancellor Robert Berdahl wanted to have a private, off-the-record meeting with just the five of us Muslim Student Association board members. I remember walking into a large room with very tall ceilings lit only by the sunlight coming through the windows. It was just us, the chancellor, and the president of the university.

Their first question was to see if we were experiencing any backlash and hate, and what they could do to help us. Their second question was a very diplomatic means of asking if we were going to cause any trouble or ruckus. If they should "expect" anything from our group.

Aside from standing outside on Sproul Plaza and passing out pamphlets or eating halal meat at Julie's Restaurant after Friday prayers, we were pretty square. Some of us participated in pro-Palestine rallies during the second intifada, with students and activists marching, chanting, holding signs, and clapping, but other than a misplaced keffiyeh or two, those were always peaceful and harmless with the occasional swear words thrown in, both foreign and domestic.

My most "radical" act was dancing with other brown men in the middle of Sproul Plaza to a dance I choreographed for the independent political party I created: the Goatmilk Party. During election season, we premiered a new dance every few days and then passed out fliers with our platform. I didn't win when I ran during my freshman year, but the Goatmilk Party successfully elected senators to the Associated Students of the University of California Senate during my junior and senior years. One of the elected members, Sajid Khan, successfully made a motion to name the clock in the ASUC chamber after me.

This was the kind of dumb stuff a bunch of horny Muslim kids who didn't drink alcohol or smoke weed did for fun during college. We also prayed a lot and played basketball and talked about girls we wanted to date but didn't even muster the courage to talk to. Nowhere in our daily itinerary were there plots to overthrow the USA, implement Sharia, practice violent jihad, or convert infidels to Islam.

Instead, we should have been interrogated for being dorks, a sausage factory of dudes who spent their nights in my apartment drinking chai, playing video games, talking shit, and eating brownies—without weed.

Regardless, present throughout that one-hour meeting with the chancellor was an unspoken tension, a palpable feeling that our moderation was being monitored. But why waste an opportunity? We used that meeting to have the university commit to helping us coordinate proactive, educational forums and activities that could help bridge divides with our local community. We asked for space, advertising, and resources, and they got on board. The first event we did was an Open Jummah where we hosted our Friday prayers for the entire UC Berkeley community just three days after 9/11. Over 1,000 people showed up.

Throughout the year, we built alliances with other student groups and brought speakers, including Professor Noam Chomsky, to talk about human rights, social justice, and foreign policy and to warn about the disastrous War on Terror that was about to be unleashed on the world.

This was my initial political awakening, and little did I know that my experiences over the next year were a training ground, an X-Men danger room simulation, that would prepare me for the rest of my life.

I even had my first awkward encounter with right-wing media, which would eventually blossom into a beautiful, enduring friendship. UC Berkeley took pride in its legacy and reputation of protests. After all, we led the Free Speech Movement in the 1960s, right there on Sproul Plaza. About two weeks after the terror attacks, there was going to be a massive anti-war rally. Some firefighters in Berkeley were ordered to preemptively take the American flags off their truck because they assumed some protestors might try to rip them off and compromise the safety of the firefighters. I assure you none of us sat there at night and plotted how to climb up the fire truck, remove and destroy a flag, and then beat up firefighters. We were just worried about the madness that was engulfing the country and fearing for the world's safety. White people would even turn on the Dixie Chicks, three of the most moderate, popular, beloved white women at the time. In 2003, during their Top of the World tour, lead singer Natalie Maines addressed the London crowd and said, "We do not want this war, this violence, and we're ashamed that the president of the United States is from Texas." For that unforgivable crime, people in America boycotted the Chicks, made them public enemy number one, branded them as anti-American radicals, burned their CDs, and destroyed their albums with tractors.

If this is what America did to three cute, talented, fun-loving, white women, what the hell would they do to brown-skinned Muslims with immigrant parents from Pakistan?

My moderation didn't last long. I became a "radical" a few days later.

After 9/11, the school paper, the *Daily Californian*, published an inflammatory cartoon by Darrin Bell that showed two men with beards and turbans standing in the giant hand of Satan surrounded by the flames of hellfire. One of them says, "We made it to paradise! Now we will meet Allah, and be fed grapes, and be serviced by 70 virgin women." The other man has a book with the title "Flight Manual." Reflecting on his cartoon ten years later, Bell said, "The evening of 9/11, I turned to my wife and said, 'It's a good thing Gore didn't win,' because I wanted blood and I knew Bush would give it to me." (Like many in America, he eventually regretted America's brutal and catastrophic response, but not before getting his belly's full of blood.)

I thought I'd walk over to the newspaper office in Eshleman Hall and have a chat with the editor and explain why so many students were hurt, and the conversation could open up a dialogue and relationship for the future. I waited. No one came. One hour later, I was still waiting. By nighttime, over a hundred students had shown up and demanded that the editors address them. Next thing I know, I am speaking into a microphone and rallying a massive, energetic crowd of students and protestors, giving them encouraging words.

Apparently, I also said, "They have to be held accountable," and accused the cartoon of dehumanizing Muslims and Arabs. For this quote, I made my inaugural appearance on Fox News. I was told by friends that I was cited by Bill O'Reilly, who back then was their most influential host and is now most well known for being a serial sexual harasser.

I also got on the radar of Michelle Malkin, who was then an emerging firebrand pundit of the conspiratorial fringe but is now an established pundit of the right-wing mainstream media. She's the daughter of Filipino immigrants whose first book was a subtle polemic known as *Invasion: How America Still Welcomes Terrorists, Criminals, and Other Foreign Menaces.* Her second book was in defense of the internment of Japanese Americans and racial profiling. Since then, she's supported Holocaust deniers and kept company with white nationalists and neo-Nazis, becoming an extremist version of the "model minority" stereotype. According to Malkin, who supported internment of Muslims, *I* was the radical. She published a column titled "Berkeley: Some Kind of Foreign Country," in which she wrote, "Only in America do we tolerate this radical indoctrination of self-loathing in government-run schools."

In a way, we were insulated and protected in Berkeley. There was a political and social culture that understood how America used propaganda and fear to fuel the engines of war. We anticipated and predicted that disaster would result from Bush's War on Terror. Our congresswoman Barbara Lee was the only one to vote against the authorization of the use of military force after 9/11. Ridiculed and attacked at the time, history has honored her brave vote as the sole voice of sanity and courage.

The first two groups that reached out to us after the attacks were the local Japanese-American community and Catholics. Their leaders told me their communities had endured this hazing in the past, and if we needed any help and allyship, they'd be in our corner.

This was the America I believed in. This was the America I knew we could be.

Before the 9/11 attacks, my Muslim friends and I used to pray openly, in public, without a fear in the world. When it was time to drop down and face Mecca, a few of us chose a quiet spot, away from people, and prayed without a worry. I've kept a running tally of all the public spots I've prayed at, and here are some highlights:

~ Alcatraz Island
~ The Empire State Building
~ Cordoba Mosque in Spain
~ The BART station
~ The NYC subway
~ Toys 'R' Us
~ Most movie theaters in the Bay Area
~ The parking lot of nearly every major fast-food franchise
~ The Kennedy Center
~ The State Department
~ The White House
~ Candlestick Park
~ The Oakland Coliseum
~ Pac Bell Park, now known as Oracle Park
~ A Cirque du Soleil concert
~ A Pearl Jam concert at the Mountain View Shoreline
~ Disneyland
~ Disneyworld
~ Gap stalls

Since 9/11, I regret to admit that I, and many other Muslims I know, hesitate to pray in public. It's not because we are ashamed of our faith, but rather we feel a warning, a tension in the air, a threat, a hint of hostility that didn't exist before 9/11. Why add any more unnecessary stress to your life? Who wants to be stared at, especially with fear? Trust me, it's not pleasant. You might as well just pray in the parked car or in your home or at a friendly Muslim restaurant and establishment.

In February 2002, I was traveling with my mother to Raleigh, North Carolina, to attend Fayez Mamoo's wedding. Many of us by that time had heard stories of the dreaded SSSS mark on our boarding pass that would subject us to extra scrutiny. "Flying While Brown" became a thing. We all have a story or two.

This was my first time flying after the terror attacks. I passed through security and was deemed safe and moderate. My section was called and I was about to board the plane. An airport security man pulled me out of the line right before I was about to enter the connecting bridge. Everyone else went in and saw me, the only brown guy on the plane, being thoroughly reexamined. I ended up being the last person to board. As I walked to my seat—which, of course, was all the way at the back of the packed plane—I could read the darting eyes, see the tightened jaws, and observe the nervous, blushed skin. The other passengers were terrified of me. I tried to break the tension. I smiled and nodded as I kept walking by, but that only made them more afraid.

"Great, a happy terrorist!" they probably thought to themselves.

I was tech support. I was the cab driver. I was the goofy engineer with the funny accent. I won the spelling bee competition. I was the model minority who aced his honors classes. I was the silly brown kid. That was my stereotype. We were never feared.

All I wanted to do was tell them, "Hey, all, I'm good. I'm just going to a wedding. Nothing to worry about!"

But it didn't matter. In a duel between logic and fear, fear wins eight times out of ten.

And as a result, I became a suspect.

Be a Patriot

If you heard President Bush's remarks to the country after the 9/11 terror attacks, you'd assume America embraced its Muslim American citizens in a monster bear hug, fed us a warm, gooey, apple pie, and invited us to dance in the local hoedown to celebrate hummus, equality, and mutual respect. On September 17, 2001, at the Islamic Center in Washington, DC, surrounded by Muslims, President Bush said the following:

> *The face of terrorism is not the true face of Islam. That's not what Islam is all about. Islam is peace. These terrorists don't represent peace, they represent evil and war. . . . When we think of Islam, we think of a faith that brings comfort to a billion people around the world . . . and that's made brothers and sisters out of every race.*
>
> *. . . I've been told that some fear to leave home; some don't want to go shopping for their families; some don't want to go about their ordinary daily routines because, by wearing cover, they're afraid they'll be intimidated. That should not and that will not stand in America.*

On September 11, 2020, the nineteenth anniversary of the terror attacks, *New York Times* columnist and famed liberal Paul Krugman tweeted, "Overall, Americans took 9/11 pretty calmly. Notably, there wasn't a mass outbreak of anti-Muslim sentiment and violence, which could all too easily have happened. And while GW Bush was a terrible president, to his credit he tried to calm prejudice, not feed it."

In the haze of privileged nostalgia, Krugman must have forgotten the 481 hate crimes recorded in the year after the attacks, and the real figure was likely much higher considering that most cases are not reported or documented. On October 26th, a month after his speech, President Bush signed into law the USA PATRIOT Act, a jingoistic and catchy acronym for "Uniting and Strengthening America by Providing Appropriate Tools Required to Intercept and Obstruct Terrorism." Those tools happened to be used predominantly against Muslims. According to one former senior FBI counterterrorism official, the FBI conducted "voluntary" interviews of nearly 500,000 Muslim and Arab men from 2001 to 2005. A family friend told us how the FBI showed up at their house and demanded to speak to her son, who at the time was in high school. Terrified, she let the FBI in, offered them water, and the boy answered every question. About fifteen minutes into the conversation, they realized they had visited the wrong individual who simply shared the first name, religion, and skin tone, and they left.

Most of my Muslim friends have a similar story or one degree of separation from a family member or friend with the same experience. These experiences won't appear in stats, data, or charts, but that doesn't mean they didn't happen or cause emotional scars.

The Patriot Act vastly expanded our domestic security apparatus and allowed the government to surveil Americans under the guise of combating terrorism. Americans are historically fine with castrating their own civil liberties, because we'd rather feel safe than actually be free, especially when our illusory feelings of safety can come at the expense of people of color, immigrants, and Muslims—you know, "them."

The Patriot Act also expanded money-laundering "unlawful activities" to include providing "material support or resources to designated foreign terrorist organizations." If a charity you supported, for example, was now deemed a terrorist group by the US government, you potentially could be indicted as well. This included the Holy Land Foundation, the largest Muslim American charity at the time, which was declared a terrorist organization in 2001 and accused of laundering money to help Hamas. Terrified Muslims no longer felt free to donate to and support Muslim organizations.

In 2003, FBI director Robert Mueller, more active and productive than he was during the investigation into Russia interfering with the 2016 election, "directed each of the FBI's 56 field offices to count the number of Muslims, mosques and Muslim-run charities in their regions."

Then President George W. Bush unleashed an illegal, preemptive War on Terror. Muslim immigrants tried their best to prove their moderation. If you drove down "Little Kabul" in Fremont after 9/11, you'd see the Afghan restaurants and grocery stores plastered with US flags, big and small. You'd think they were preparing for a military parade honoring World War II veterans. "Little Kabul" is the name affectionately given to a few blocks on Fremont Boulevard in honor of the large, thriving Afghan population that resettled there as refugees in the early 1980s, escaping the Soviet Union invasion of Afghanistan. Local news stations and papers swarmed on owners and patrons, asking them how they felt about the terror attacks, Bush's response, the War on Terror, and America.

I always felt bad watching these Afghan uncles and aunties being scrutinized and asked to perform for the cameras. In the weeks after 9/11, if you had asked some Muslims to dress up like Uncle Sam, wave two flags, hold a red, white, and blue firecracker in their mouth, and sing and dance to "Yankee Doodle Dandy," they would have done that and given you a free performance of Britney Spears's "Hit Me Baby One More Time" just to prove their love for America, and freedom, and democracy, and Western values, and capitalism, and Rambo, and American culture.

Over time, Muslims began to gain a good grasp of what traits and activities helped make us appear moderate versus those that made us look shady.

First, don't be a noncitizen. Citizenship tempers the threat. Allahu Akbar! Thank you, Allah! That's good for me and my family.

However, if you were a Muslim foreign national, it sucked to be you. We didn't need a modern Muslim registry, because we already had one in 2002 called NSEERS (the National Security Entry-Exit Registration System), which was implemented to register certain noncitizens from 25 countries, 24 of which were Muslim majority. America ended up deporting 13,153 individuals, overwhelmingly Muslim immigrants, shattering families and replacing their Amreekan dream with an American nightmare. Of the 93,000 cases it created, NSEERS produced 0 terrorism-related convictions. It was disbanded by President Obama in 2016.

Second, you are moderate if you don't speak Arabic out loud.

I take back that "Allahu Akbar!" from earlier.

This one is tricky because, although I don't speak Arabic, I do read it whenever I pick up the Quran or try to pray five times a day. I guess I'm safe because I could do that quietly when no one was looking. The trick is never to speak it out loud, especially while on an airplane. Also, never talk about how you're taking flight classes and studying to be a pilot.

Since 9/11, there's usually one story a year about how some student, family, or adult passenger is removed from a flight because their use of Arabic triggered a fellow passenger who assumed a language spoken by over 400 million people was evidence of a nefarious, violent plot.

In 2016, an Iraqi-American college student said he was removed from a flight after a passenger was terrified hearing him end a conversation with the Arabic word "inshallah." I say "inshallah" like fifty-seven times a day. It means "God willing" but is often used as "hopefully." Such as, "Inshallah, people won't be terrified by a foreign language that they use when ordering Mediterranean food at their favorite restaurant." Inshallah is a beautiful, versatile, Swiss army knife of a word. Consider it the Arabic version of "fuggedaboutit." Depending on the tone and context, it can be used for many things.

For example, inshallah is often used sarcastically to mean "it'll never happen." Imagine you're high school Wajahat and interested in talking to a beautiful girl. You muster the courage to approach her and offer your number. You ask her if she'll ever call you, and she replies, "Yeah, inshallah."

See? Harmless. Yet Arabic was so frightening after the terror attacks that it united anti-Muslim bigots to temporarily block the opening of the Khalil Gibran International Academy in Brooklyn, New York, a secular public Arabic-English school that opened in 2007. They accused the school of peddling "soft jihad" and promoting "radical Islam." Khalil Gibran was not a Muslim, but instead a Lebanese Christian who wrote *The Prophet*, which was Elvis Presley's favorite book. (Elvis was also not a Muslim, but with those killer hip thrusts, some Arabs might claim him as their own.)

One of the activists, Pamela Geller, wrote, "Arabic is not just another language like French or Italian, it is the spearhead of an ideological project that is deeply opposed to the United States." Arabic is so opposed to the United States that 56 percent of Americans in a survey believe that the Arabic numerical system they learned in school, and that was introduced to Europe around the twelfth century, should not be taught in schools.

They just got a 0 (an Arabic numeral) on that test.

The anti-Muslim hysteria unfortunately was so great at the time that this nonsense campaign succeeded in pressuring the NYC mayor's office to ask for the resignation of the academy's founding principal, Debbie Almontaser, a Muslim American of Yemeni descent.

So, here's a friendly recap if you're overwhelmed: Don't be a Muslim immigrant. Don't speak Arabic. Don't teach at or open a secular school that teaches Arabic. Don't wear hijab.

If you are moderate, don't hang out at Muslim grocery stores. Better yet, don't hang out at Muslim restaurants. Actually, just stay away from mosques too. Actually, to be totally 100 percent kosher, you have to avoid Muslim student groups and Muslim communities altogether.

They finally got me. I'm screwed. I've purchased halal meat at Muslim butchers. I've bought "ethnic condiments" from Muslim "ethnic" stores. I eat halal, so you'll see me picking up kabobs from Muslim-owned restaurants all the time. I go to Friday prayers, so I guess you can say I visit the mosque. Finally, I was a member of the Muslim Student Association at UC Berkeley, so I'm branded for life.

All of these innocuous activities would have been enough to get me profiled and surveilled by the New York Police Department and its Intelligence Division if I had lived in New York.

They claimed to identify a "radicalization process" of Muslims by which unassuming, regular folks turn into terrorists. Some of the indicators included "wearing traditional Islamic clothing," growing a beard, abstaining from alcohol, and "becoming involved in social activism." That basically described me and all my Muslim friends during college. Most of us are now lawyers, doctors, engineers, businessmen, parents, teachers, politicians, and overweight middle-aged nerds. Shockingly, not a single one of us turned out to be an extremist who flirted with the violent jihad phase only to outgrow it and love gluten-free baking and emojis instead.

The NYPD mapped Muslim communities in New York and neighboring states. They surveilled them and infiltrated their mosques and social circles with informants who were called "mosque rakers," law enforcement who posed as Muslims to scope out extremists. There were also plain-clothed "community rakers" who attended local events, took notes, identified "hot spots" (basically any place where Muslims congregated and did Muslim-y things), and compiled information on community members.

For about fifteen years after 9/11, an ongoing joke for Muslim speakers was to greet all the hidden FBI agents in the audience: "And a special Assalamu Alaikum to anyone from the FBI in the house tonight! Please stay for dessert."

The NYPD spent years spying on innocent communities that were seen as a threat simply due to their religion and ethnicity. They uncovered zero terrorism plots. Instead, a study found "that mosques and religiosity are actually associated with high levels of civic engagement and support for the American political system." The chairman of the 9/11 Commission eventually admitted that racial and religious profiling is inherently dangerous and ineffective counterterrorism policy.

For over a decade, Muslims were used as canaries in the post-9/11 coal mine while white-supremacist talking points, conspiracy theories, and sympathizers became mainstreamed to the point that thousands of Trump supporters engaged in a violent insurrection on January 6, 2021, took over the United States Capitol, and failed to overturn a free and fair democratic election. Five people, including a police officer, were killed to satiate the "economic anxiety" of individuals who brought nooses, weapons, and zip ties, some hoping to assassinate elected officials, such as Vice President Mike Pence and Speaker of the House Nancy Pelosi. Imagine if all these white, violent extremists, criminals, and insurrectionists were practicing Muslims who fast during Ramadan, have a beard, and say "Allahu Akbar." Or, imagine what would happen if I organized a march of 500 bearded Muslim men to assemble peacefully in front of the U.S. Capitol and speak in Arabic, Urdu, Farsi, and Turkish denouncing gun violence?

I have an active imagination, and all I see are dead people and chalk lines on the ground. We don't need to imagine what would happen to peaceful Black Lives Matter protestors. On June 1, 2020, President Trump unleashed tear gas, rubber bullets, and flash-bang shells to disperse the crowd assembled in front of the White House to protest the murder of George Floyd so he could visit the nearby church for a photo-op.

For white America, there's no widespread surveillance, no spying, no mapping program, no registry, no targeting of their financing and charities, no "voluntary interviews," and no demonization. And that's exactly how it should be. Blanket profiling and stereotyping are harmful, counterproductive, and cruel.

If only the rest of us could be accepted without conditions and seen as moderates one day.

A Moderate Muslim Checklist

To quote the French playwright Charles-Guillaume Étienne: "If you want something done, you have to do it yourself." Never say I never did anything for you, America. I went ahead and made a "Moderate Muslim Checklist."

Consider it the Voight-Kampff test for Muslim moderation. You will be able to easily spot and eliminate replicants after administering it.

It's a three-step test.

1. Read the thirty prompts and check the boxes if they apply to you.
2. At the end, tally up the number of boxes you checked.
3. Depending on the number of boxes you checked, you will be assigned a number (from 1 to 5) on the moderation scale. For example, 1 is an ISIS cheerleader, and 5 is Dr. Oz.

Only one test per person. Please do not talk to anyone else or consult any resources before or during the test. Remember, Allah is watching, so don't lie or cheat, or else you'll burn in hellfire forever.

Check the box if you believe that:

1. "Allah is watching, so don't lie or cheat, or else you'll burn in hellfire forever." ☐

Congratulations, the test has already begun!
Check the following boxes if:

2. You apologize in advance for every terrorist act done by Muslim extremists you have never met in countries you've never visited. ☐
3. You read Rumi in the original Farsi and think the English translations are lightweight, whitewashed fluff that are great for social media quotes and scoring on first dates. ☐
4. You yell "Allahu Akbar!" out loud several times a week, in prayer, while watching a sporting game, or even at times after relieving yourself in the bathroom. ☐
5. You volunteer to be racially profiled at airports and think it's a great way to make new friends. ☐
6. You see something, and you always say something. ☐
7. You have a worn-out copy of an Al-Kitaab textbook for learning Arabic. ☐
8. Your favorite Salman Rushdie novel is *Satanic Verses*. ☐
9. You support religious freedoms and women's rights but believe the hijab and niqab should be banned. ☐
10. You eat with your hands and only bring out utensils for guests. ☐
11. You wear hijab only on bad-hair days. ☐
12. You think the Muslim Brotherhood is a powerful union. ☐
13. You love democracy and socialism and especially Democratic socialism. ☐
14. You know the difference between a dry and a wet martini. ☐
15. You prefer peaceful MLK to radical Malcolm X. ☐
16. You draw offensive cartoons of the Prophet Muhammad in

between taking bites of a delicious BLT sandwich with extra bacon. ◯

17. You use a bidet or pour water from a receptacle, known as a lota, to clean your behind. ◯

18. You have a worn-out VHS copy of *The Message* starring Anthony Quinn as the uncle of the Prophet Muhammad. ◯

19. You are able to immediately identify the pungent smells of a mosque carpet or an uncle's feet. ◯

20. You think pigs in a blanket refers to cute farm animals. ◯

21. You only bow during the downward dog. ◯

22. You voluntarily fast during Ramadan because it's a great weight loss and cleanse. ◯

23. You fast during Ramadan because you believe it is one of the five pillars of Islam. ◯

24. You want more prayer in school and government, but you fear Sharia. ◯

25. You would support US troops bringing democracy to Agrabah. ◯

26. The Israel-Palestine Section:

    a) You support a two-state solution in the Middle East. ◯
    b) You support a one-state solution in the Middle East. ◯
    c) You believe Israel occupies the West Bank, Gaza, East Jerusalem, and the Golan Heights. ◯
    d) You believe Palestinians deserve self-determination and a homeland. ◯
    e) You believe it's a really complex conflict that has gone on for thousands of years and both sides are to blame and Palestinians and Jews hate each other and there's no political solution so we should instead just forget about it and eat hummus. ◯

27. You think the Obamas are a very fine, well-spoken, Muslim family. ◯

28.　You have a thick, bushy, well-groomed hipster beard. ○
29.　You think Allah and God are the same thing. ○
30.　You know the lyrics to Lee Greenwood's "God Bless the
　　　U.S.A." and you gladly stand up and sing along whenever
　　　and wherever you hear it playing. ○

Now count up how many boxes you checked.

If you checked up to 5 boxes, please give yourself a 5.
If you checked 6 to 15 boxes, please give yourself a 4.
If you checked 16 to 20 boxes, please gives yourself a 3.
If you checked 21 to 25 boxes, please give yourself a 2.
If you checked more than 25 boxes, please give yourself 1.

The Official Scale for Muslim Moderation

5. You are Dr. Oz: You are moderate, safe, and thoroughly sanitized for mass media consumption. White, Midwestern moms find your ethnic background and spiritual practices to be "enlightening" and "interesting." You are safe to wear a doctor's coat and say whatever you want, and Americans will believe you.

4. You are Fareed Zakaria: You are mostly moderate, civilized, and presentable to international audiences. White audiences with a college education find your opinions to be informed and edifying. However, your occasional critiques and accented English keep many others on the fence, skeptical about your motivations.

3. You are a sketchy Uber driver: You are trusted enough to be allowed to drive us, but that's only because it's late, we're drunk, and we left our car at home because we didn't want to drive in the city. We appreciate you giving us a mint but that doesn't mean we're inviting you over for a barbeque. We're watching you. You'll only get four stars from us.

2. You are Congresswoman Ilhan Omar: You are terrifying. Everything about you is foreign, ethnic, disturbing, and triggering. However, you speak English and enough people seem to like you, so that means you're crafty and cunning, able to hide your radical ways through charm and subterfuge. We know you will mess up one day and reveal your plot, and we'll be there, waiting, vigilant, and then we'll pounce and gloat, "Aha! We warned y'all, but you didn't believe us!" But by then it'll be too late, because we'll be slaves of Sharia in your caliphate of cruelty.

1. You are an ISIS cheerleader: You're so radical you piss terror. If you were a cheerleader, you would ask students to give you a "J" for jihad. You were disappointed your parents didn't get you scimitars and Kalashnikovs for your War on Christmas—a holiday you don't celebrate! You dream of breakdancing to the screams of infidels. You say "Allahu Akbar" five times a day and you wear ethnic clothing and hang out with practicing Muslims who do the same in mosques. You eat halal meat, fast during Ramadan, and believe in the moon god known as Allah. Your name most likely has more than two syllables. You are a radical Muslim, and you must go back to where you came from!

On second thought, screw this checklist.

Tear it all up.

I just realized we will never, ever be "moderate" enough. Because no matter how many times we've played the "condemnation game," condemning every violent act ever done by a Muslim, and no matter how many times we've proven our loyalty, and no matter how many times we've smiled with our white teeth, and paid our taxes, and abided by the law, and done everything right, we are still seen as suspects and not as complex, diverse, strange, funny, hypocritical human beings among the 1.8 billion who happen to be Muslim.

I'm done playing this game.

Chapter 5

Die Hard in Amreeka

Every journey has its perils. If you are what they call a "person of color," it seems your path will be beset with more challenges, setbacks, and villains than the rest. In addition to climate change, cancer, heart attacks, diabetes, and hypertension, this thing called racism—which some claim no longer exists—apparently also kills. Men of color, especially Black men and especially those who are poor, die younger than the rest.

May the odds be ever in your favor.

But it's too early for morbidity and cynicism, and we have just begun our journey to making you a full-blooded Amreekan!

For example, I never thought I'd live to the age of forty.

And yet here I am, a man who reached that milestone last year, pleasantly surprised to be having this conversation with you, dear reader. I'm also grateful to still have hair on my head. This makes me a unicorn among South Asian men. Most of us become human Chia Pets in our late thirties and end up losing all the hair from the right places and gaining it in all the wrong places.

But having the gift of breath and life is more important than the trivial concerns of male-pattern baldness.

By my count, I have survived about four near-death experiences by now. I was that kid who used to always get hit with the errant ball when the kids yelled "Heads up!" during recess. I remember looking up and saying "What?" right before the football/basketball/baseball/soccer ball landed on my face.

I was that kid who knew the school nurse by name and had a doctor's note in my back pocket to get out of nearly every school activity. I was the sick kid, who had pneumonia, malaria, and a heart disorder, got hit by a motorcycle, and inherited an anxiety disorder.

It's not the only gift I inherited. For most of my life, I was convinced we were plagued with what I called "the Ali Family Curse." This was how my imaginative mind made sense of the seemingly chaotic and tragic events that befell our family like seasonal monsoons. A brief moment of worldly success and emotional calm would always be disrupted with an unforeseen tragedy, a brief flirtation with the Angel of Death, or a great "undoing," a complete inversion resulting in near economic and emotional annihilation. Then, on the edge of ruin, at the last second, a deus ex machina, a hand of God, would come out of nowhere and "save" us and we'd recover and rehabilitate and succeed.

Then the cycle would start all over again.

You can decide whether the following events described are due to a supernatural force, an act of God, or an interfering malevolent hand. Or, simply kismet, fate, tough luck, random occurrences, or, as the school of hard knocks teaches us, "tough shit."

The Bad, Bad Case of Jadu or Just Some Tough Shit. Either Way, Survive It

In Islam, there's a concept of sihr, or dark magic. In South Asia, we call it kala jadu, which literally translates to "black magic." A person who seeks to inflict harm on someone usually seeks out this practitioner of the dark art. It's an element of the ghayb, or the unseen world, that has detrimental effects in our reality.

A supernatural curse or hex often allows an otherworldly explanation for ordinary people being afflicted with overwhelming, inexplicable bad luck and hardship. It's called "fuku" in Junot Díaz's *The Brief Won-*

drous Life of Oscar Wao, a curse the protagonist believes was unleashed by colonizers and has haunted the Dominican Republic for centuries and has followed his family all the way to the United States.

In Islam, there's a concept of nazr, otherwise known as "the evil eye." If you ever visit Turkey, you'll see an eyeball shaped like a teardrop embedded in a blue pendant everywhere you go. This symbolically protects you from nazr, which manifests from the envious eye and jealous heart of others. It shoots out like an arrow that can wound another person. There are traditions that describe its power as being able to crack a rock in half or wilt a blooming flower. There is a verse in the Quran, Chapter 113: Verse 5, that is specifically cited to protect oneself from nazr: "And [May Allah protect] from the evil of the envier when he envies."

There are many "nazr traps." Instagram is the biggest one. Example: Imagine if you just got married, and you look like a doorknob but somehow you scored a partner who is a 9, and you're posting pics of your glorious honeymoon, sipping from the same fruity, coconut drink with the umbrella, looking at each other with ogling eyes.

That's gonna get nazr!

Suppose you just posted a photo of your new, spacious home. You've left the apartment life and now you're a homeowner, and you even have space for a garage and a lawn where you can plant your own mint garden.

That's gonna get nazr!

Say you're a happily married couple who get along and you're able to live with your in-laws, which is a recipe for homicide in most households, and you were able to buy one of the "big houses" before your immigrant community members, and you have a Mercedes in the driveway.

That's going to get hella nazr and describes my childhood.

Even if you don't believe in the supernatural cause and effect of nazr, the consequences of envy and a deviant whisper have been written about since forever. One need only look at Othello's downfall because of Iago, his best friend, who was so beset with jealousy that he brought about tragedy with just a few lies. Even Shakespeare warned us!

These afflictions usually have supernatural remedies, which in the case of Islam means reciting specific verses of the Quran or seeking the counsel of men and women who are one with the Force and able to undo the damage. Or, you can just be a decent human being who takes joy in the success of others instead of talking massive smack and being a bitter, resentful hater.

I happened to inherit my own "interesting" experiences and flirtations with death and sickness thanks to my father.

Hereditary Nazr

My father didn't know he would fall into a tub of scalding water when he decided to go out to the courtyard to play with his five-year-old brother Sultan. Before moving to Karachi, Pakistan, as Muhajirs (Muslim immigrants after the Partition), my father's family lived in Hyderabad Deccan, India, which was once ruled by the Muslim Nizam as a princely state. A tradition during that time according to my father dictated that a woman who had just given birth was to be cleansed in a tub filled with neem leaves. They'd pour scalding hot water into the tub and let it cool until it became warm and soothing. Well, no one told my father, who was four years old at the time, and somehow he found himself in the tub of boiling hot water, screaming for his life.

He didn't fall headfirst or else he'd be dead. In fact, the water never touched his head or his face or most of his neck. My grandmother told us this story and always used to thank Allah for that miracle. Yes, he received third-degree burns all over the rest of his body, but at least he was alive. That was my grandmother's optimistic outlook on life. We inherited that as well.

In 2000, my father went to Pakistan to visit family and do some business. He went to the bathroom to wash his hands and brush his teeth. He turned on the water in the sink, and then he woke up and saw the flesh melting off his left hand. Right after turning on the water, he had passed out and instead of falling directly into the sink or on the floor, he slumped forward, hit his head on the mirror, and only his left hand got caught under the scalding water. How and why was the water this hot? Nobody knows. But he was able to add a new body part to his collection of third-degree burns. After several surgeries and skin grafts, his hand has healed enough to resemble a mashed pepperoni pizza.

In 1971, my father was a twenty-three-year-old student with bell-bottoms and shoulder-length hair in the United States. All was going well until a routine checkup revealed he had Hodgkin's lymphoma, a blood cancer. There were concerns that it could be fatal. My Dadi, who was in Pakistan, made arrangements to travel to the United States to be with him during his recovery. Before leaving, she had a chance encounter with a spiritually elevated person who said he was from the family of Shaikh Abdul Qadir Jilani, a revered Sufi saint and jurist who lived in Iraq during the twelfth century and was the founder of the Qadiriyya tariqah, or Sufi order, to which both my maternal and my paternal families belong. If there is a yin to the yang, a Force to the Dark Side, then consider this person she met one of the good practitioners of the spiritual arts. With whatever foresight, insight, clairvoyance, or third eye he possessed, he confidently told my Dadi not to worry, that Abu's health would be better soon. My grandmother, a woman of faith, remained hopeful and was comforted by the prediction. My father, meanwhile, was like, "Yeah, great, but I have Hodgkin's disease."

Six weeks later, the doctors expressed shock and relief as the tests revealed Abu had gone into auto-remission.

Some supernatural help from heaven or just plain old luck? Regardless, he survived. Others in my family didn't.

In 1978, my father's older brother and best friend, Sultan, was a successful hiring manager for GTE Lenkurt Electric Company, and a good-looking and popular bachelor. He decided to detox for a bit and take a vacation in Hawaii. He went to the lagoon in front of the hotel and decided to lounge on a floating tube. Ten minutes later, his dead body washed up on shore. The toxicology report showed no alcohol, drugs, or poison in his system. There was no foul play. It was just a freak occurrence. A healthy young man went into the water to relax and within ten minutes he was gone.

I was born in 1980, and my father's business became successful. They moved into the big triangle house in the Fremont suburbs. They got the Honda and the Mercedes. They got the big-screen TV. They had numerous religious and social functions where they entertained and fed the community. It was six years of bliss.

Then came the year of sorrow.

In 1986, my father's younger brother Wasif suddenly passed away in Dallas, Texas. He left behind a wife and three kids. A few months later, my grandfather, a relatively healthy man, went for a checkup. The doctors encouraged him to have what turned out to be an unnecessary bypass surgery. My father, deeply anxious whenever it came to anything related to health, was skeptical but convinced by the doctor's confidence. I recall visiting Dada after his surgery in the hospital and jumping in his lap despite the nurse's warnings. He fed me his spaghetti with "red sauce," and we watched cartoons on the TV. He returned home a weakened man, sitting in his La-Z-Boy chair. I left the family room to play and returned to see him lying motionless on the floor. Within two weeks, he had died of complications from the surgery. A needless invasive procedure had caused a blood clot that took a healthy man at the age of sixty-three, who walked every day and avoided alcohol and cigarettes.

I once asked my grandmother while she was alive what she believed: was it just fate or was there something foul at play? She vacillated. She was content with whatever Allah had written and was thankful and hopeful despite having buried two children and her husband. Still, she remembered a friend from Karachi, Pakistan, who once visited their home and said, "Oh, not everyone gets lucky like you and has not one, but four sons. All handsome and brilliant. I don't even have one. But look, you somehow got four!"

Nearly fifty years later, sitting in our home in Fremont, California, my Dadi remembered this conversation, reciting it with trembling lips. Her voice quaked and she held back tears. "She nazr'd my boys," Dadi said.

"She nazr'd my boys."

If Pakistan Can't Kill Me, Nothing Can

Pakistan has tried to kill me at least three times by my count, yet I keep returning. We have a twisted but endearing love affair. I am either a masochist, a daredevil, or a man of immense, optimistic faith. At the very least, I am loyal.

Both my maternal and my paternal sides of the family moved to the port city of Karachi, Pakistan, after the Partition. Karachi is one of the most densely populated cities in the world, with around 16 million people, officially, somehow finding a way to survive with limited resources, water, electricity, and space. Sri Lanka and Australia have populations of about 21 million and 25 million people, respectively, and they are both countries.

My cousin who lives there joked, "Only the strong survive in Karachi. Even then, they don't survive."

Like many immigrants who came to America after 1965, my father nursed romantic hopes of returning one day with his education and wealth to help revitalize his country, beset with so many challenges. Over the years, each attempt at starting a business in Pakistan was met with disappointment and failure. Still, he tried. Often, he brought me and my mom along, and throughout my life, I've visited numerous times, both as a child and as an adult. Whenever I land, I immediately eat the local yogurt to acclimate my stomach and make peace with the fact that I'm still going to have horrible diarrhea for at least one to two days. Nothing will stand in the way of my fresh, homemade parathas and glorious nihari made with sweat, oil, and anger on Burns Road.

My Masood Mamoo, my mother's eldest brother, who wrote the investigative report on my father's family back in the day, says Pakistanis are the most faithful people in the world. His proof was the pedestrians who walk the streets and cross the roads in Karachi traffic, which can be best described as a racing game designed by a meth addict. "Look at this person in front of us," Mamoo said, pointing to a pedestrian as we were driving home. "He is literally going against traffic confident that the cars will move for *him*. If that's not faith, then what is it?" While sitting in Karachi traffic, you will find numerous examples of human creativity, resourcefulness, and resilience. You will see a family of five, all without helmets, sitting on a scooter. You will also see people jam-packed into a colorful bus, hanging from the sides and surfing on the roof. Many of them do this every day because they have no other means. Many of them survive. Some do not.

I decided to test my faith, or try my luck depending on your perspective, with Karachi traffic. When I was four years old, I had the brilliant idea of crossing the busy road in front of my Dadi's home in Nazimabad, a suburb of Karachi, to greet our driver. I remember he always wore a khaki Bernard cap and a khaki shirt, and he dyed his mustache and hair with henna. He was always kind and I assumed we were buddies.

In America, my parents taught me to look both ways before crossing the road. Usually, the right of way goes to the pedestrian. Well, Karachi doesn't play by our rules. All I remembered before being hit by the motorcycle was waving at the driver and walking toward him.

I flew up in the air and landed with full force on my forehead, which split open like a messy grapefruit all over the road. Fortuitously, my Yasmeen Phuppo, my father's sister, was coming down the stairway at the same time. She saw me flying in the air, scooped me up off the road, and immediately drove to the nearest hospital. From the balcony of our house, my parents witnessed the entire event, and they rushed down, got in their car, and followed her.

Let's just say the local hospital was "lacking" in several resources. I remember lying on the gurney and my mother promising me that if I stayed awake she would get me comic books. I woke up with a bandage over my head and a Captain America and Spider-Man comic book at my bedside. I looked like *Darkman* (a highly underrated 1990 classic starring Liam Neeson), bruised, bloody, scratched, disfigured, but still alive. It was as though the doctors operated on me with a spork. I was grateful. Alas, kids who get hit by motorcycles in Karachi and have their foreheads split wide open can't be choosers. The doctors said if I had landed one inch to my right or to my left, I would've died on the spot. If only I had such impeccable aim in sports.

Recently, my father reminded me that he almost died around the same age, surviving third-degree burns. My daughter Nusayba endured stage 4 liver cancer at the age of three, and we initially assumed she wouldn't survive.

However, we're all still here and alive.

My family says it was the hand of God that saved us. Or, maybe it was nazr that struck us? Or, maybe it was just bad luck? Maybe I should have just checked the road or the motorcycle should have swerved? Maybe it was Karachi's subtle way of saying, "Get the F out?"

When I was nine, I returned to Karachi for a summer vacation with my mom. My dad stayed home in California and looked after the office. This time, thankfully, there were no split foreheads or motorcycle accidents. This time, an infection got me, and I developed life-threatening pneumonia. Usually, this is very treatable and Karachi has competent doctors. However, with my luck, my pneumonia was misdiagnosed for several weeks. I still remember one doctor, a family friend, telling me to rest, drink Sprite, take some Tylenol, and "eat a slice of toast" and I'd be fine. Another doctor told me I'd develop huge red lesions and bumps on my back filled with pus. That didn't sound pleasant and thankfully none emerged. Instead, I coughed, vomited, and had excessive diarrhea. I became bedridden and resembled a skeleton drained of energy. I was literally dying on the cot in my grandmother's Nazimabad home when by chance the neighbor, who was a young doctor visiting from America, was called to check on me.

He came up the stairs with a stethoscope, asked about my symptoms, and checked my breathing. I'll never forget as his eyes widened and he yelled, "Good God, this boy has pneumonia! Get him to a hospital now!"

They rushed me to the local hospital, which was, again, severely lacking in resources. I thought I saw a cat running around but I was informed it was a rat. Also, there wasn't a window but instead a net, which meant I woke up with about a dozen fresh mosquito bites every day. As soon as I entered the room, I had to use the restroom with a vengeance. (Pneumonia diarrhea waits for no man.) We opened the bathroom door and the contents that are supposed to be in the toilet were all over the walls instead.

The staff kept messing up the medicines, so my mother, who isn't a doctor, had to take over and make sure the schedule was being followed. Did you ever want to know what happens when an IV antibiotic goes inside your skin instead of your vein? The flesh in my hand swelled up like naan, as if someone were pumping it full of air. The pain was so excruciating that I remember banging my hands against the wall just to keep from passing out. Eventually, my skin deflated. I survived pneumonia, and one positive was that I lost a lot of weight. As Monty Python advised us, "Always look on the bright side of life."

My family says I should be grateful to Allah. If it wasn't for that one doctor who happened to be visiting, I could have died. Maybe it was the continuation of the Ali Family Curse, or someone's nazr, that tried to knock me out. Maybe bad shit just happens.

Pray the OCD Away

My third flirtation with death was when I contracted malaria in Pakistan during my junior year of high school. The high fever and delusions hit me as soon as I landed back in the United States. While knocked out flat on my back, dripping in sweat, I endured an endless, tormenting stream of vile and deviant sexual thoughts that would make Caligula blush. Every effort I made to stop them seemed to make them multiply. This torture lasted for a week, even after my fever broke, and I eventually recovered on my own once I immersed myself in school activities. A year and a half later, at the beginning of college, the thoughts returned. This time, I lost fifteen pounds, couldn't concentrate, and was stuck in a haze.

Ever since I was young, my mind would get "stuck." Growing up, I was unable to shake off certain thoughts or images. I felt I had to replace them or fight them, and it would just make them more resilient, bigger, angrier, like the Hulk. The endless thoughts would transform into burning questions: "What if I left the stove on?" "What if I lose control and do something violent?" "What if I become sick?"

I eventually told Abu and Ami, which is a ballsy move considering many of my Muslim and South Asian friends, married and with kids, to this day cannot fathom having a single conversation about sex or relationships with their parents.

My parents were outliers who proactively broached the subject of sex with me. During seventh grade, my father sat me down in the kitchen as my mother hovered nearby, failing at pretending not to listen to the conversation. "Beta, we have to discuss something very serious," he told me. Based on the stone-cold sobriety that suffocated the room, I assumed an elder had died. "Beta . . . there is something called a nocturnal *emission*," he told me, stressing the word. I immediately leaped out of the chair and begged to leave the awkward conversation, but my father demanded I sit down and listen about "wet dreams" because it was his obligation to teach me about "such things."

My parents also knew I put up photos of beautiful women on my wall since the age of twelve. The first time I did it I was just compelled, like a calling. Ami subscribed to *Vogue* for a year and it coincided beautifully with the onset of puberty. It was the age of supermodels, specifically Cindy Crawford, Claudia Schiffer, and Naomi Campbell. Allah had also given me Sharon Stone in *Basic Instinct*, which my friends and I all thought was the greatest movie ever made. One day, Ami came home and saw me, her innocent son, putting up these photos of scantily clad women on my bedroom wall and was livid. "This is disgusting," she said. "Wait until your father comes home!"

I assumed Abu would make me tear down the pictures. Instead he saw them and I caught a brief smile that emerged on his face before he quickly pretended to be stern and serious. "It's . . . OK, Sameena. Let him keep it," he told my mom, whose jaw dropped in shock. I emerged victorious. Years later, I realized that my father, like most spartan South Asian men, was once a horny teenage boy who had discovered women.

In hindsight, exchanges like these created an open environment where we could discuss topics of sex and sexuality that were taboo and rarely discussed in my fellow Muslim friends' homes. This allowed me finally to tell my parents about how and why I was suffering from such agonizing, stressful, and repetitive thoughts.

My parents were understanding, and they forced me to go to three psychiatrists, each of whom quickly concluded I had something called OCD, which I had understood as eccentric behaviors of quirky characters in Hollywood movies.

Obsessive-compulsive disorder is an anxiety disorder that afflicts two percent of the population. It's an electrical misfiring in the brain, causing it to overreact to disturbing thoughts, images, and ruminations that are very common and shared by most people. If you're the lucky 98 percent of the population, you naturally ignore the thought after a few seconds and move on with your life. If you have OCD like me, you become stuck, flooded with anxiety and dread. You desperately seek escape, so you engage and become addicted to absurd compulsions that give you immediate relief, such as counting up to a specific number or repeating mantras.

Dr. Steven Phillipson, an expert on the disorder, told me, "All of our brains have these naturally occurring, very edgy ideas," listing all sorts of violent, sexual acts and criminal activities. Those of us gifted with OCD become overwhelmed with a "tsunami of emotional distress," he said. Instead of seeing it as some sort of God's cruel joke, Dr. Phillipson compared it to a "best friend" who desperately wants to protect us, so it warns us about threats, even those that are illegitimate and don't exist.

I obviously need new best friends.

The first step is to forgive ourselves for having an anxiety disorder beyond our control. The second step is to stop fighting the thoughts. The best treatment so far is exposure and response prevention, a behavioral therapy that recommends confronting your terrifying anxiety, thoughts, and ruminations and delaying your compulsions. Sit with the dread and pain. Let it wash over you. Eventually, you change your brain chemistry through your behavior. Your brain learns that it doesn't need to fear the triggering thought or image, and it doesn't flood you with anxiety and dread.

The only way out of it is through it. You must confront your demons head-on.

Dear reader, I have not forgotten that this is a book meant to help *you* become American. I am writing this because, in order to become American, you must survive. The good news is that if you're a "minority," specifically a person of color, you are on average more mentally resilient to stress than white people. We don't have to cite eugenics to explain this phenomenon. Research shows that the white majority in America, historically, is not as prepared to cope with adversities compared to communities of color, who have consistently lived under economic and social pressures that have simply given them more experience.

Hooray, we get one win! One small advantage!

If you come from a religious community, you also apparently have another valuable advantage: prayers!

In many Muslim and South Asian communities, you are told to "pray it away." A strong spirit and a resolute faith in an omniscient and all-powerful God creates belief in miracles and in profound, inexplicable occurrences that defy science and magically heal physical ailments and diseases. Nothing is above Allah's will. Just pray, be more pious, read the Quran, and, inshallah, there will be shifa, a healing. When it comes to mental health, especially anxiety and depression, I grew up hearing that these things are common in privileged, spoiled Western societies where the people have too much idle time and decadence. If they only knew real hardship and had faith, they would be "resilient."

You could never dare mention "psychiatrists" because they were only for gora people. Only goras have the luxury of time to go sit on a couch and babble to idiotic doctors who steal their money and waste their time. Do we look like Woody Allen? No.

My father's generation, the one that promoted the myth of "praying the sickness away" and the belief that seeking help for mental health is for goras, probably suffers the most. The tragedy is that they often suffer in silence. My mother shares with me how her friends tell her that their husbands, now retired, are probably depressed but will never admit it or get help. They beg them to go see a doctor, but they stubbornly refuse. They ask them to take medications, but they see it as weakness. My father was eventually diagnosed with OCD as well. In fact, his is more severe than mine. Perhaps that is why he was so sympathetic and understanding when I first explained how my mind was stuck with such unrelenting thoughts and anxiety. The Ali Family Curse—or "the best friend," depending on your choice—strikes again. OCD has a genetic component, and it seems we both got it. My father, now in his seventies, goes to his therapist every two weeks. He has gotten books on cognitive behavior therapy and is trying his best to control it. When asked, he openly admits it without shame.

In our old Bay Area community, I can probably count on one hand how many elders talk about their mental health issues, anxiety, and personal challenges. It's truly a tragedy. We never know what demons they are battling. We'll never know because they'll elect to suffer in silence due to shame and fear. I always wonder how many could live happier, more fulfilling lives if they simply unburden themselves from the unbearable expectation of perfection and allow themselves to just breathe and be human, disorders, warts, and all.

I wish I could go back in time and give myself this advice at age twenty-one after my parents were both arrested.

Chapter 6

Avoid Jail

I was eating tandoori chicken at Shalimar Restaurant in the Tenderloin district of San Francisco on a school night when I received a call from Yasmeen Phuppo that my parents had been arrested.

Initially, I assumed she was calling to lament in her custom passive-aggressive fashion and guilt me, her favorite nephew, into calling her more often.

"Slalaikum Phups, what's up?" I asked, still licking the chicken boti off my lips.

"Beta, you need to come home," she replied in Urdu.

Something was off. Her tone was different—somber, restrained, worried.

"Why? What happened?"

"Your parents have been arrested. They are in jail right now, in Oakland, and your Dadi and Patata Dadi are home by themselves, so . . . I think it's best if you come home."

Earlier in the morning, a dozen armed FBI agents raided our home in Fremont, California, dragged my parents out of bed, handcuffed them while they were in their pajamas, and drove them to Oakland County Jail. There was even a helicopter circling our house. My father later described it as being treated like a captured drug kingpin.

My grandmothers were still at home and begged the FBI agents in their broken English to at least explain why they were being taken.

They didn't receive an answer. My aunt deemed it best if I, the only child, drove down and figured out what the hell was happening.

Overnight, my Amreekan dream turned into the Amreekan nightmare.

It was April 2002 and I was about to graduate from UC Berkeley and head to law school. My biggest decision was choosing between UC Davis or UC Hastings. My "model minority" narrative and sheltered life, previously disrupted by the 9/11 terror attacks a few months prior, was now permanently reconfigured.

You might be done with the Ali curse, but the Ali curse isn't done with you.

The Great Unraveling

My parents were swept up in Operation Cyberstorm, which at the time was the largest anti-piracy sweep in the FBI's history. Robert Mueller, then FBI director, even came down to San Jose for a press conference. It was a two-year undercover operation with over 27 arrests, a coup for Microsoft. The majority of the arrests were of people who were part of a highly organized criminal conspiracy involving the alleged sale and distribution of counterfeit and infringing software.

My parents actually had nothing to do with the piracy ring itself, which coincidentally was masterminded by a lady who worked in their same office complex. Instead, they were hit with thirty counts of conspiracy, mail fraud, wire fraud, and money laundering in a scheme to defraud Microsoft of millions by obtaining discounted academic software under false pretenses.

Microsoft initially alleged they lost up to $100 million, and the local newspaper ran with the number. People only see the headlines, and they don't read the fine details of a criminal indictment. Overnight, everyone knew only that my parents were scooped up in a giant, massive, anti-piracy raid. Their faces were plastered on the FBI website's front page for days, and people assumed I was somehow sitting on $100 million stashed away in domestic and foreign accounts.

Oh, how I wish it were true. I really could have used that money.

The papers called my parents "scammers." This was the feather in the cap of their midlife career transition from upper-middle-class entrepreneurs to budding "criminal masterminds."

The 1990s had been a period of immense financial success for my parents. Their company, University Systems, submitted bids to provide computers and computer accessories to the US government and colleges. My father was the CEO of the company and my mother was the president. I remember they had moved into a rather large office in Milpitas, employing dozens of people. I used to hang out there during the summers reading comic books and playing PC games. They even had a Pepsi vending machine, which to me was the pinnacle of American success. Everything was on the up and up.

My mom said that ever since she's been married to my father both success and devastation have come in cycles lasting several years. "Kismet, destiny, who knows? Bad luck," she mused when I asked her to explain why. "Also, in hindsight, there were many things we did wrong that we shouldn't have done. That's the truth."

In 1995, two employees who used to successfully submit bids for years made a mistake concerning a mouse device on a $200 million contract with the Department of Health and Human Services. The government decided to act aggressively against the false statement, and in an extreme measure they debarred both employees and my father, the CEO, even though he did not submit or sign the bid. Oddly, my mother, the president, was not debarred.

The family business for all intents and purposes was finished. Eventually, the money dried up. For the most part, my parents shielded me from all this chaos. I was in high school and still had a relatively happy and privileged life, playing LucasArts PC and PlayStation games during the weekend. But there was tension in the house. My parents were on edge. There were loud discussions and worries about finances. I caught a few threads here and there, but they didn't give me any details. I remember one time my mother admitted to me she had to borrow money from a friend visiting from Pakistan just to buy underwear at Mervyn's. She assumed she had enough in her wallet, but when she got to the store she realized she was completely and totally broke.

My parents are not the type to mope or sink into despair, so they returned to what they knew best: creative, old-school immigrant hustle. Because she wasn't debarred, my mom decided to start another company, Samtech, and she started winning government contracts again. My father went back to coming up with new business ventures. Even after being wiped out, my parents, again riding their yo-yo life, were moving back up.

In 1998, another employee made a mistake submitting a bid to the government for a contract that demanded a company have "4 to 5 years of experience." My mom's company at the time had been in existence for two years. The government came around again, but this time they accused my father of engaging in fraud, using my mother and her company as a patsy, doing business with the government even though he was debarred. My parents were unable to comprehend their shit luck and why this was happening to them. They were now stuck in quicksand, and each attempt they made to get out just made them sink faster and farther down.

"You know, it's funny," my mom said. "We initially got screwed because of some dumb mistakes done by our employees. But then one thing led to another and to another." Then to a criminal case.

Up until this point, my parents had never been arrested or spent a night in jail, either for debauchery or for civil disobedience. They had their ups and downs with business, sure, but nothing remotely approaching the plot of a Lifetime Channel criminal melodrama. My dad appealed his debarment from 1995, and he won, but my parents were both convicted of making a false statement to the government, which is a felony. They were given probation.

In 1998, we were living in a rented house in Milpitas. Due to the collapse of their company and the resulting financial struggle a few years earlier, we had to let go of the beloved, brown, triangle house in Fremont, California, the childhood home where we had Quran khatams and social events, where I watched TV on my grandfather's lap, where Kashif and I made movies in the backyard. From that time on, we moved through a few rental houses for several years, mostly ping-ponging around Fremont. During my senior year in high school, my parents found a home in nearby Milpitas.

At that house, my grandmother's health care assistant accidentally kept some oil near the stove, which somehow caught fire and burned the kitchen. I remember I was driving home from high school and a cop pulled me over for speeding. He approached the window and said, "Well, I'll let you off with a warning considering your house just got burned." That's how I found out. I immediately called my house to check up on my grandmothers, and thankfully everyone was fine. Still, the landlord was mighty pissed, had unpleasant words with my father, and decided to unleash a private investigator on my parents and sue us.

A recurring trend I've noticed both with my parents and with myself is that we have at times inspired the worst demons in otherwise rational, calm people. Their anger and bloodlust are disproportionate to whatever harm we have allegedly inflicted on them or the universe. It's like there's a phantom *waswasa* that just travels and whispers the worst narratives about us in their ears and radicalizes them against us in inexplicable ways.

This landlord, otherwise mild and friendly, was a case in point. We had to move out and rent another house—back in Fremont. As all this was happening, my father wanted to purchase and develop a piece of land in Pleasanton. He got a bank loan, and that of course eventually led to the government accusing him of bank fraud.

Don't worry, it all gets crazier.

The government made a case that my father defrauded the bank because he obtained the loan using a different name with a different

Social Security number. On the loan, he didn't disclose that he had filed for bankruptcy years before.

"He should have done that," my mom said. "I think they asked if it was under ten years," my father chimed in, trying to recollect, "but we had gone through bankruptcy over a decade ago at that point."

Now, why would my parents have different legal names and different Social Security cards? Excellent question.

"I was in India for business and a friend of mine in Saudi Arabia recommended I go see a Muslim wise man, a numerologist, for advice. We were facing so many hardships, one after another, and we were desperate for any answers. So, this man told me that 'your fate is cursed and you have to change your name,'" my father explained.

"You do realize how insane and stupid this was, right?" I asked, shaking my head.

"We were desperate and confused and under so much stress, and it was terrible advice," my father agreed. "Dumb, dumb decision," my mom seconded. "They were mistakes in hindsight," my father admitted. "We should have never gone to that goddamn numerologist for one."

So, he returned home, and my mom and dad changed their legal names and got new, legal Social Security cards under those names. I told them that from appearances all of this looks very shady considering they were already engaged in so much litigation and under so much scrutiny. "Agreed. To the common person, all these things look shady. The truth is the truth. But, we paid the price for it," my mom said. "Obviously, all mistakes," my father admitted. "But, it shouldn't have resulted in the prosecution. It might have looked shady, but it wasn't illegal."

That last line explains my father's approach and mindset during this intense time. He says he was trying to protect the family, stay alive, and keep a step ahead of this avalanche of chaos that was coming from all directions. He also was at a loss, unable to intellectually understand why all this "bad luck" was hitting them. He was also too clever for his own good, but throughout it all he actually did the research and believed it all to be legal. Still, even if you think something is legal, that doesn't make it legal. Also, if something looks or appears shady as hell to the average Jose, say a potential jury member, then perhaps err on the side of caution, especially as you have the Eye of Sauron actively hunting for you.

That's the counsel I would have given my parents, but nobody asked the advice of the only son who at the time was in college.

A few years later, in early 2002, the Ninth Circuit court ruled in favor of my father in the bank fraud case. My mom exhaled in relief. If he had lost, my father would have been in jail for several years. This case garnered only minor publicity and the tawdry details were published in the local Fremont newspaper. Obviously, the Muslim community jumped on it and it led to some scintillating water-cooler conversations at social events.

I was a senior in college, and by this time we had purchased a family home again in Fremont, in my name. A friend of mine confessed, "Hey, just to let you know, people are talking about your parents. I want you to know we didn't say anything bad, but people talked."

"Where was this? Who?" I asked.

"Well, I don't want to give names, but we were at a halaqa [religious gathering] with a bunch of the [Muslim] sisters, and right after it finished, someone from Fremont just started talking about you and your parents and all your family members, and like, she went back years and knew . . . everything. After a while, two of us were uncomfortable and said, 'You know, maybe we shouldn't backbite after just finishing a religious gathering?' and that killed it," she explained.

I appreciated the information and offered my gratitude. That was the first time I realized my family's tragedies and scandals were the fodder of halaqas. I had no idea we were the topic of conversation among Muslim college women studying the Quran, with so many taking such intense interest during chai breaks. This was unfortunately before reality-TV shows took off; otherwise, a show about our family's dysfunctions and miseries would have crushed the ratings.

Soon after my father won his Ninth Circuit appeal, my parents were arrested.

✳   ✳   ✳   ✳

"You have a collect call from . . . ," said the robotic, detached female voice. My parents were eventually able to call me from the Oakland county jail a day after their arrest. On and off over the next decade, I picked up hundreds of calls with that greeting. Now, almost twenty years later, whenever I hear a collect call recording I'm immediately transported back to the chaos of 2002.

My father initially had no idea why they were arrested. Usually, people who have knowingly committed criminal acts are always waiting, sleeping with one eye open, dreading the moment they will be caught. My parents had no hidden safe, cache of money, fake passports, or elaborate get-out-of-jail schemes. The night before their arrest, they simply did their usual, middle-aged Desi parents routine. My dad flossed. Ami was in bed watching some TV. Abu read his prayers and wazifas and they went to sleep, only to be rudely awakened and handcuffed by FBI agents pointing guns at them. After Abu heard the thirty-count indictment, he almost passed out from shock, as if the universe were still playing its cruel joke on the Alis without revealing the punch line.

"Did you do anything shady or criminal? If you did, just let me know. I have to know what I'm dealing with," I asked him calmly. Just because they were my parents didn't mean I was going to bury my head in the sand and make excuses for alleged criminal acts.

He assured me he had consulted with attorneys and assumed everything they did was legit. My mother eventually called, and I asked her the same. She was just as shocked as my dad to see their names on the indictment.

If hindsight is 20/20 and not blurred with a numerologist's Magic 8-Ball predictions, my parents should have settled the case and taken a deal. But my parents believed they were being unfairly targeted by Microsoft, and didn't want to sign their names and accept guilt over something they felt was legal.

My father told me to call and retain his lawyer, Chris Cannon, who had read about the case in the newspaper. I asked him if he thought my parents were innocent. He said my father was a good man, but he reminded him of many of his clients, who were "aggressive business-men," and "that gets them into trouble sometimes." He also asked me to send him $5,000 so he could get started on the defense.

Where would I get $5,000? So he could get started on what? How long would this last? When would my parents be released? Who was going to take care of the house, the bills, the office, the salaries of the employees? How was I going to study and take my upcoming finals? What about law school in the fall?

All of these thoughts crashed through my mind, but instead of freaking out I was overtaken with an odd sense of calm. I realized I'd just have to get to work, because I had two elderly grandmothers at home, and if I lost my shit, then everyone would lose their shit, and then we'd all be dead, bloated corpses floating in a river of shit. I couldn't afford to have a meltdown. Too many people depended on me.

I also thought this would clear itself up within a short time, and I maintained optimistic faith that, inshallah, God willing, my parents, like always, would be able to clear their names and bounce back.

I heard laughter from the heavens.

✳   ✳   ✳   ✳

I have no desire or appetite to litigate or clear my parents' name. That's their story, if they choose to tell it. My take on it after all these years is that my parents made dumb and shady business decisions, but I sincerely don't think they were Walter White from *Breaking Bad*, deliberately orchestrating a criminal plot.

Personally, I would have never done what they did. There were multiple unnecessary risks, reckless and foolish, and even if you assume you're doing something legit, if it skirts the line then you have to remember you're not Wall Street, white, connected, influential, loaded with "F You" money, and strapped with "F You" connections. At the end of the day, you're a small, brown fish in the ocean, and if the heat comes looking for you, you'll be caught and cooked.

I still marvel at the absurdity of how my parents, two Pakistani-American immigrants who had a beef with Microsoft, spent nearly five years in jail, but the Wall Street architects of the 2008 financial crisis that ruined so many Americans mostly all got wealthier and failed up in life.

To quote George Carlin, "It's a big club, and you ain't in it."

Folks like my parents also don't have a media platform. The real story, with nuance or even truth, rarely matters. The perception is what makes the final copy. An entire lifetime can be flattened and essentialized in a headline. An entire family's narrative erased and replaced with a caricature of brown, immigrant criminals who came to America to defraud the system, as they twirled their thin mustaches, laughed diabolically, and did bhangra on an enormous pile of money. If you read the complaint and all the news stories, you would walk away having this same image and perception about my parents. Honestly, if I didn't know them, I'd believe it too.

From that moment in April 2002 to now, my parents were Pakistani Muslim criminal masterminds from Fremont, California.

To me they've always been Ami and Abu.

They were the same couple who watched 20/20 with Barbara Walters and Hugh Downs on Friday nights. Abu was the same son who organized his mom's grueling regimen of medications every night into day-coded color containers. Ami was the same wife, mother, and daughter-in-law who came home from work, cooked a tasty meal for the family, did some chores, read a book, and watched late-night talk shows. Every other weekend, my father did his Costco shopping and my mother attended a social event on our family's behalf.

Now? Criminals. Branded. For life.

The old Wajahat Ali died that day as well. I was no longer Wajahat Ali, an only child of a "good" Pakistani family. I was Wajahat Ali, the son of criminal masterminds. I became both "us" and "them" within my ethnic and religious communities. The checklist of success blew up. I would never be able to attain it. Just like that—gone. "Criminal master-mind parents" isn't on the biodata or the baseball cards or the checklist of "good kids" who come from "good families." There was no recipe for this or any training given to a suburban kid who was supposed to go to a "good law school."

In America, immigrants of color were informally told we had to act white and things would be all right. We knew to never emulate the "bad" Americans: the poor, the Blacks and Latinos, the uneducated, the criminal element, and the "super predators." That wasn't supposed to be my American story, especially not my parents' story. Now? I had one foot in privileged spaces as an educated suburban kid and one foot in the Santa Rita penitentiary trying to visit my parents on the weekends.

I was a man on two separate islands divided by class and race, sharing the same real estate of two completely different Americas.

And just like that, with the snap of Thanos wearing his Infinity Gauntlet, the money was gone. The house was gone. The assets were gone. The reputation was gone. The community was gone. Our friends were gone.

My mother said it best: "Everything we touched turned to dust."

Get Your Hair Cut

I was a twenty-one-year-old young man who was supposed to go to law school and eventually become a successful writer in Hollywood or New York. Instead, I was in Fremont, California, taking care of my grand-mothers, trying to pay all the bills, retain and maintain legal counsel for my parents, and raise money for their bail.

The following Monday after their arrest, I went to my parents' office in the morning, and called the employees and told them to return to work if they were comfortable. My parents used the money from the Microsoft educational software business to start an online company. I spent the next two weeks trying to learn how to run every aspect of the business.

We had a warehouse in the back that received all the goods, which were mostly vitamins and health supplements, and we packed and shipped them to our customers. After my coworkers left, I used to stay behind and pack some boxes as a stress-relieving activity. I called all the existing vendors and told them I was temporarily filling in for my parents and would be their new contact. I had to find a way to maintain the payroll, which included the international payroll for the employees in Karachi, Pakistan, who were doing all the technical work on the back end. Khalu Baba, my mother's relative, was retired and decided to go to the Karachi office every day to keep employees calm and to give me an overview of what was going down. Masood Mamoo, my mom's brother, also kept me updated and sent me money when he could. Every employee had figured out that my parents had been arrested, but the business was still running, so most decided to stay on.

I became friendly customer service and dealt with irate customers who called, yelling, asking why their orders hadn't arrived and why the website had shut down. The government had decided to confiscate and remove the website server from the office during their initial crackdown. Without the server, there was no website. Without the website, there was no business and no revenue. We were dead in the water. I begged Cannon to get the government to return the server, and after three weeks they finally acquiesced. We were back in business, but the damage had been done. The business was set to finally mark its first month of profit in May, just a few weeks after my parents were arrested. However, I could never recover from those missed three weeks. The government claimed our properties, which were subject to criminal forfeiture because they were part of the alleged money-laundering scheme. I was unable to use the house or the land to post bail for my parents.

Thankfully, my parents had added me to their bank account. I could access the money, except there was only enough there to last us about three months. "If you have this one hundred million dollars somewhere, it would really, really help. I won't judge you, just tell me," I asked my parents on the phone, who assured me there was nothing and that whatever money they had made from that business had gone into setting up the website.

Bad luck, bad kismet, cursed fate, bad decisions, all of the above, none of the above—it didn't matter, because now I just had to live this new normal. While at the office, I had to field multiple panicked phone calls throughout the day. My father would call, and I'd have to calm him down, get information and instructions from him about finances, the business, and his lawyer, and relay information to him, and as soon as I had spent thirty minutes doing that my mother would call and I'd have to repeat the process. I also had to calm my mother's family in Pakistan, who were, naturally, terrified about their daughter being stuck in prison. I also had to take care of my two elderly grandmothers at home and keep them and my Yasmeen Phuppo in the loop.

It was the only time in my life I wish I had siblings so I could outsource some of the work and be more efficient. I was still a senior at UC Berkeley on track to graduate in May. I had to submit my senior thesis for Professor Susan Schweik's English class and I was also co-teaching a two-unit class with fifty students on Islam in America. I had to go to campus to teach the class, and I was able to pull it off without betraying my insane reality.

All that acting experience came in handy.

I also attended Professor Schweik's class to tell her about my "situation." She told me she had read about Operation Cyberstorm in the newspaper and had no idea that my parents were involved. She was very sympathetic and said she could give me an incomplete and that would let me submit my thesis by December 2002. I had to drop out of another seminar, a history class taught by Professor David Yaghoubian, who once told me I was one of his best students. I didn't give him details. I just didn't have the time or the bandwidth. I had to finish two other classes to graduate. I would have to come back in May and take the final exams.

I felt like I was fighting a war every day with new enemies. There was no time for rest, rumination, or crying. It was fight or die. It was like confronting an unrelenting horde of soldiers who just kept pouring onto shore, wave after wave, beating me down. I was Spider-Man taking on the Sinister Six, his classic all-star villains, who teamed up and attacked all at the same time.

The Avengers never came to help.

The first time I saw my parents was like a scene from the movies. Here were my parents in orange jumpsuits, looking haggard, seated across from me separated by a thick pane of glass. "I'm sorry you have to see us this way," my father said. He had grown a scruffy beard, and his eyes were bloodshot from lack of sleep. In prison, his OCD spiked and his racing mind, like his body, was trapped with no escape. This led to several episodes of him either passing out or losing large amounts of blood through random nosebleeds. Let's just say the health care system in prison is more lacking than in Karachi, Pakistan. When he was moved to Santa Rita, my father said he saw "horrible things." I've tried to get him to open up, but he just shakes his head and shrugs it off. Once he said he saw a prisoner bash another man's head against the wall, killing him, just because he wouldn't hand over the phone. That's the only horror story he ever shared. I know he has more but I don't press him.

My mother said the guards treated the women comparatively better than the men. The bar was low. That first time I saw her, she smiled and used some dark humor to alleviate the situation. "Well, who would have thought, but here we are. Always an adventure," she said, but her brave facade was brittle, and she wiped away tears.

My parents, stuck in jail and in different sections, were unable to see or communicate with each other. I couldn't make bail, which was set at seven figures. I visited them every weekend for the first few months while they were in Oakland before they were transferred to the Santa Rita penitentiary in Dublin. The entire process of visiting someone in jail takes hours. You have to appear at a certain time—early before they reach capacity—wait along with others until your section is called, head inside, and then wait some more. There was never enough time to see both of them on a single visit, so I got used to alternate visits. Eventually, I went every other week. Then it became once a month. I was just too overwhelmed and exhausted.

When a loved one is incarcerated, it's like an atom bomb falls on them, obliterating everything in an instant. Their freedom, their movement, their livelihood, gone. But the bomb's shock waves spread out and envelop close family and friends too. The prison industrial complex eats incarcerated people as the main course but also feasts on their relatives, relationships, and communities. Its appetite is voracious.

It's Galactus, the destroyer of worlds. Of generations.

My parents had to survive inside prison. I had to deal with the resulting collateral damage outside.

It was during this time I had a dream where my dead grandfather, Dada, took me to get my hair cut.

My family is big on dreams. In Islam, there is a saying that "true dreams are 1/46 prophethood." There is an adab, or etiquette, of sharing and interpreting dreams. You're supposed to initially keep them private and share them with someone who is spiritually elevated who can help you decipher them. Obviously, there's no online class or *Dream Interpretation for Dummies* available at bookstores. It's not an exact science and it's all subjective interpretation. For example, throughout my childhood, Abu conveniently had dreams that I died each time I asked his permission to do something adventurous, such as go to Yosemite with my class or attend UCLA. "Yeah, that's not God. That's just your anxiety and hyperactive imagination. This is ridiculous," I used to say, rolling my eyes, cursing under my breath.

But we rarely messed with my grandmother and Patata Dadi, both of whom were very religious and came from spiritual families. They were known to often have clear, predictive dreams. They would do istikhara, which is a religious practice to seek wisdom and guidance when making certain decisions. Istikhara means "to seek what is good." Several friends and family members over the years asked my grandmothers to pray for them as a result of their piety and also because their batting average made them Istikhara All-Stars.

In my dream, Dada drove me in the Honda to his old barber, Gene, who had since retired. He kept the red, white, and blue barber pole outside his small shop, and I loved going there as a kid because he had a bunch of comic books lying around. Dada parked the car right in front of the shop. He looked at me and said, "You're going to get your hair cut."

Then I woke up. I wouldn't appreciate the meaning of this until years later.

My grandmothers were too frazzled by the ongoing chaos, so I instead shared the dream with Maqbool Nana in London. He was my mother's father's brother, who was paralyzed from the waist down.

I had met him initially when I was a young boy while he was visiting Karachi. I asked him a question about fate and free will: "How do we have free will if everything is written? If Allah knows everything, then how can he punish us for doing bad things?" He was impressed that a nine-year-old would seek his counsel on such issues, and over the years he took a liking to me. He gave me an answer that Allah is the All-Knower, but he is also just and has given humankind agency to make individual choices. Each soul is different and has the opportunity to choose their own actions in light of their unique circumstances. Ultimately, they will be judged accordingly by a loving and merciful Creator—who knew what was up all along. I was temporarily fulfilled, but also more confused, and it only inspired more philosophical questions and sessions, placing me in the footsteps of Muslim scholars and religious students who have tried to reconcile predestination with free will for centuries while atheists continue shaking their heads, urging us to stop believing in fairy tales and instead relax with a Coke and a cookie.

A few years later, when I was in high school, Maqbool Nana decided to visit us in Fremont, California. When he visited, he kept telling me with a smile, "I came for you, my boy. I came for you." I never understood what he meant but I always knew there was more to those words. He was very close to my mother, and my father greatly respected him. He was a rare combination of being a man of the world and of the spirit, practical and grounded, intellectual, humorous, well-traveled, well-versed in poetry, but also deeply religious. Everyone in my mother's family knew that Maqbool Nana had "the shining," a spiritual talent if you will, but he kept it hidden from most.

"It's a good dream," he said. "Your grandfather, your loved one, an elder, is there with you. It is a cleansing, like the hair that is cut during Hajj. You will emerge from this."

He then said he wanted to give me a small gift. He told me to recite a verse from the Quran, Chapter 21: Verse 69: "We said, 'O Fire! Be thou cool, and a means of safety for Abraham.'"

The story goes that Abraham as a young man confronted his father and community about their idolatry. He then smashed their idols. As punishment, the elders threw him in the fire, which was suddenly cooled for him. The verse continues, "And they intended for him harm, but We made them the greatest losers."

I printed that verse, cut it out and taped it on top of my computer. I also found another verse from Chapter 47: Verse 31: "And We shall try you until We test those among you who strive their utmost and preserve in patience; and We shall try your reported mettle."

At the time, I felt it was me versus the world. These verses spoke to me. I used them to hype me up. If indeed this was all a "test," then I for sure would pass.

Initially, the government was pressuring my parents to accept a plea deal by threatening to go after me, saying, "We're going to drag in your son if you don't cooperate." Since I was officially the homeowner of the property that the government alleged my parents bought to launder their profits from the Microsoft business, they threatened to use that connection to charge me.

When my parents heard this, they were ready to sign any document the government put in front of them. I think if the government had asked for both of their kidneys, they would have given them all four. There was a brief moment where I imagined myself in an orange jumpsuit, arrested for the real and alleged sins of my parents, and stuck in prison. Perhaps it was due to exhaustion or delusion or faith, perhaps a combination of all of the above, but I made peace with whatever was meant to happen. "Well, this would make for a helluva story one day," I mused to myself.

Dark humor is always needed, especially in the darkest of times.

Cannon assured my parents to be patient and not make rash decisions. I knew I did nothing wrong, but by that time I was aware that in the United States of America, many communities, poorer and darker than ours, had been screwed far worse by the criminal justice system for far less. From jail, my father asked me to ask Maqbool Nana to do istikhara on whether I would be harmed and what they should do. Unlike my parents, Maqbool Nana was very judicious about istikhara and urged people to use their common sense first and foremost in making decisions. I called him and relayed my father's request.

"They won't touch you," he replied confidently.

"But how do you kn—"

"They won't touch you," he repeated firmly, cutting me off.

To their credit, the government tried their best to bring more charges against my parents. They poured through all their tax returns to get them on tax fraud, but they found nothing. I would like to assume they didn't want to maliciously destroy the life of a twenty-one-year-old unfortunate enough to be caught up in this sordid mess, but likely they realized they couldn't charge me with anything and just dropped it.

It was a baptism through pain and hard knocks. As encouragement, a family friend, Ahmed uncle, told me that I was strong enough to survive this and that I'd gain at least twenty years of life experience in a year. Relatives praised my ability to stay focused, calm, and balanced. "Man, if this was me right now, I'd probably go insane. I'd lose my mind," Fayez Mamoo told me. A college friend told me his father said, "They are grateful to have Wajahat as their son. He is smart and he will find a way." My college professor Ishmael Reed kept assuring me, "Suffering is seasoning. All of this will make you a better writer." Everyone I met told me I was a "good son."

Maqbool Nana gave me a final gift. It was hope in the form of an analogy. "We are Qadriyya. Our path and our tests are harder than most. Allah will take you to the absolute edge. You will be on the cliff, looking down. You will feel helpless. And right before you fall, Allah will pick you up and raise you."

In hindsight, he gave me the recurring plotline for the next decade.

At the very least, I got straight As on those finals.

The Betrayal

The most painful wounds are inflicted by emotional daggers. They bleed for years. Those are the ones that ache your soul. They burrow deep, beyond the flesh, penetrating your core. You can recover from broken bones, even a fractured spine, but a shattered trust can paralyze you for life.

A few months before the great unraveling, I randomly wondered if I'd ever miss my privilege and comfort if they were suddenly snatched away. I was twenty years old, a senior, and invested in my spiritual growth. The path meant living in the world but not being attached to the dunya, or worldly possessions, because, after all, we come from dust and return to dust. Well, that's easier said when you have food, lodging, a credit card, and a safety net. It is often a privileged comment made by people who have lived without such tests.

After my parents were arrested, we had to leave our home and move into my Yasmeen Phuppo's house nearby in Fremont. I slept in the spare room upstairs, which only had three walls and was visible to anyone from downstairs. I taped three large pieces of cardboard together and created a makeshift wall that was enough to block visibility, but every time someone opened the front door below, the air would make the cardboard squeak. My grandmother had a degenerative knee disorder and couldn't walk up the stairs, so we converted the family room on the first floor into her bedroom. My Patata Dadi slept on the couch next to her. It was not an "ideal" situation, but we needed a roof and it sufficed. I moved all my family's belongings during one weekend into the cheapest storage facility I could find. A lifetime's worth of material goods were buried in brown boxes, sealed away.

As we lost everything, I felt a sense of comfort in realizing that I didn't miss any of it. What punctured me instead was how so many lifelong friends and community members simply abandoned us overnight, and how some were outright gleeful at our misery, taking an active part in compounding it. Someone printed several copies of the newspaper announcing my parents' arrest and placed them at every mosque in Fremont and Milpitas. They went so far as to highlight my parents' names in each printed copy. An old family friend at the local mosque on Fremont Boulevard came early to Friday prayers and saw them outside. He was kind enough to throw them away before the congregation came.

Many people who ate our food, visited our home, enjoyed our social and religious gatherings, were now standing outside and throwing gasoline on the fire as we were trapped inside. The saying goes that true friends rush in to help during a problem while everyone else rushes out. Well, these were extraordinary circumstances. We're talking about the FBI arresting my parents, headline news, and a massive criminal conspiracy, so I was never expecting the cavalry to arrive.

But some? A few?

The collateral damage of the 9/11 terror attacks loomed large, reaching all the way to the Bay Area. There was a chilling effect on Muslims, especially those from Black and brown communities. A family friend, a lawyer and former classmate of my father, told me, "Beta, people are terrified. Everyone has skeletons in their closet." There are over two million incarcerated individuals in the United States, more than in any other country in the world. We love locking up people, especially Black, brown, and poor people. Eighty-four percent of incarcerated people are poor, and half have no income. Nearly 20 million people live in America with a felony record. Locking up people is great business. Statistically, it only makes sense that every family and community has people who have gone through the system. Over the years, I learned that several people in our community had been arrested, spent time in prison, declared bankruptcy, litigated cases, had nasty divorces, or faced sordid accusations, but it was always hushed up. Because, "log kya bolingay?" (What will people say?) So we never talked about it.

Rumors were spread that the FBI had parked cars outside our home and were taking down license plates and following anyone who would visit us.

At a pretrial hearing, the government's attorney seized on the anti-Muslim hysteria of the moment and tried to deny bail by mentioning the FBI had found "documents in Arabic" in our home and that my parents are Pakistani and as such they could be tied to the Taliban. Thankfully, the Judge cut him off. The documents in Arabic were actually Islamic prayers from the Quran and religious texts in Urdu, an entirely separate language.

Since the government had claimed our properties, I was unable to post bail for my parents. Initially, nobody was willing to step up and risk their property except Shaheen aunty and Syed uncle. People were told, "They're just going to flee to Pakistan. Don't help." I tried telling them my parents had gone to Pakistan and come back several times. They had a home, a family, and a community here, and they were willing to fight this case for years if necessary. Still, perceptions make truth, and those were heavily skewed against my parents.

Every time I was able to convince a family member or family friend to offer property as a bond, they'd balk the day before the hearing. I had to tell my parents the horrible news and listen to them deflate over the phone. Each time was more painful than the last. Hope can be dangerous because it means exposing yourself to the possibility of success, to allow yourself to imagine a happy ending, only to be confronted by cold, brutal disappointment.

My grandmother and my aunt spent their time going through every single contact they had, calling and asking for help. They were like stockbrokers or sports agents trying to represent a dead, rotting investment. I even had to work the phones—an utterly humiliating exercise because I knew half the people were simply using the conversation to acquire gossip or indulge their appetites for soap opera. But, desperate times called for masochistic measures.

I was not at all shocked or surprised by any of this. In fact, I begged my aunt to stop cold calling the universe and just concentrate on a few close friends and relatives. In her sincere effort to help my parents, she instead became a megaphone loudly telling the entire world about all of our private affairs. She called an emergency meeting at Chandni Restaurant. A dozen community friends were supposed to gather to offer helpful advice and strategies. I told her it was a bad idea and most would arrive just to see the tamasha (spectacle). I recommended she bring popcorn for everyone. She told me I was too cynical.

Well, they arrived. Instead of eight people, it was about forty folks who gathered around, seated in chairs. I didn't even know half of them. I sat in front of them, calmly observed the scene, and went through the motions for the sake of my parents, realizing this would be a pointless endeavor. The entire exercise was basically torture porn. I ended my spiel by saying, "Listen, I understand. I get it. This is heavy and it's scary, and I get why no one is eager to help. But, at the very least, I'd appreciate it if you all could call my Dadi. Just check up on her. Give her a ring. She's an old lady who's been through a lot. It would mean a lot to her if you could just do that."

Like I had predicted, people stayed away. For my grandmothers' sake, that both disappointed me and pissed me off. Still, I had no time or luxury to whine about it, because I had two parents in jail, a business to save, and money to raise. However, all my efforts proved futile. We were running dry, and even though some family and friends loaned and gave some money, it wasn't enough to cover the mounting expenses and debt. I extended my line of credit and assumed the business would somehow turn around and I'd be able to pay it off, but by the time all was said and done I went from having no debt to having $50,000 of it.

Cannon ended up doing many hours for free, but he said he couldn't continue without payment, even though he was very sympathetic to our situation and remained encouraging. I went up to his office in San Francisco with several valuables my mom said were in the bank's deposit box and in our storage. This included some jewelry my mother had kept with the intention of giving it to my future wife, and two beautiful, expensive carpets my parents had purchased with the hopes of displaying them in our home one day. I sat across from Cannon as he itemized and described the collateral into his recorder. He said he was going to get them valued, but I don't think he ever did. It seemed like he felt embarrassed going through this exercise, but he accepted the items and continued the work.

My parents rarely lamented losing their possessions. After we had to move from the house, I told my father on the phone and he replied, "We've lost everything, haven't we?"—an assessment less to do with the home than a reflection on our state of utter ruin. My mother's only regret to this day was losing those pieces of jewelry that she had kept for my "future bride." What she didn't give to Cannon, she had my aunt sell for money. She has apologized to my wife, Sarah, on numerous occasions, who never expected such gifts or felt remorse for not receiving them.

Family heirlooms forfeited to the curse, bad luck, and bad decisions.

In order to have some cash on hand, I sold as many of our goods as I could in weekly garage sales. I also had an impressive collection of laser discs and CDs that I was able to sell on Craigslist and eBay. (My childhood wasted on movies came in handy for once!) For our first garage sale, everything we had to offer we showcased outside on the driveway, inside the garage, and even inside the home. Almost everything was for sale. If someone had offered me money for a used bar of soap in the kitchen, I would have said, "Thank you! Here's your soap and come again!" I made signs and put them at intersections and on local trees.

There is nothing more viral and potent than a sensationalistic story. Apparently, I was sitting on top of $100 million and was just not admitting it to anyone. I wanted to ask people, "If that were true, why am I voluntarily allowing you to humiliate me by asking you for money or offering my entire home and goods in a cheap, desperate, garage sale?"

But I knew it was pointless. Once a potent narrative is framed and sinks deep into people's minds, it's exceedingly difficult to dislodge.

My aunt, again with the best of intentions, had told community members about the sale. I'll never forget how some of my parents' friends, whom I knew were loaded, came just for the tamasha. They walked around, made passive-aggressive comments, pierced us with a sarcastic jab here and there, tried to extract some juicy gossip about my parents, and then walked away without buying anything. We made for grand entertainment.

"Now *we* have the biggest house."

That line from my youth kept running in my head. We were in the great race where your worth as a minority and immigrant is measured by the checklist and "log kya bolingay": what will people say?

There is something karmic and cathartic in seeing happy, wealthy, or powerful people fall from great heights. We humans feel it is a sort of cosmic realignment, as if we have witnessed a rare moment of God's justice. "Now you know how it feels like to be at the bottom. Ha!" we think to ourselves, as we delight in others' misery. It also helps us, just for a moment, feel more powerful. When it comes to others being caught for crimes and misdemeanors, it also helps us, just for a moment, feel more righteous and noble.

Sometimes, we just need to stomp on someone to feel better. Based on the headlines, the charges, and the gossip, people were convinced my parents were a "done deal," as an uncle once told me. They didn't think they were ever coming out of prison. You're way more comfortable talking shit about someone if you know they're dead or locked up for life. After all, you're never going to see them again, so you'll never be forced into awkward confrontations at social events. This was a gheebat free-for-all. Gheebat is "backbiting," and in Islam it's considered a major sin to the point where the Quran describes it as eating the flesh of your brother or sister.

There was a community buffet and the Alis were on the menu. Shaheen aunty one time told me that our family's ongoing drama and misery were discussed at religious events, with people eager to start gossiping as soon as they opened their fast during Ramadan. The Ali family gossip was served with pakoras, samosas, and chai.

I asked a mosque board member, and a former family friend, if he could have the imam pray for my parents after Friday prayers. I even suggested, "He doesn't even have to mention them out loud, if he could just be vague or just mention our family, that would be fine."

"Beta, we can't do that. It would be a political act," the uncle replied.

"How is asking for an anonymous prayer a political act? Can you at least pray for our family? How about my grandmothers?" I asked, shocked and disgusted.

"Neyhee, sorry, beta, this would be too political for us," he affirmed.

Allah is merciful and forgiving unless you're the family of alleged criminals indicted in a fraud case against Microsoft. I missed that lesson in Sunday school.

Several of my college friends made an attempt to be helpful and encouraging, but they were in their early twenties and incapable of understanding what I was enduring. Also, a couple of friends said that some of the very same friends who came over to my apartment, ate my food, used my Dreamcast, and took my help were talking mad shit about me and my family behind my back.

Again, this was to be expected. But, I never anticipated how much people's behavior would wound me. I mean, let's be honest, you run as far away from a burning house as possible, right? However, I could never comprehend the hypocrisy. That gnawed at me for years, still does. If you indeed knew we were such terrible people, as people claimed they did, why were you at my house a week earlier eating my food? Why did you accept our presents? Why did you ask me for rides? Why did you come to our social events? I mean, if you knew we were criminal masterminds and I was the gilded son, filling my belly at the trough, then what does that say about *you*, who nonetheless indulged your appetites at your convenience?

I obviously never asked these questions to anyone out loud, but they kept spinning in my head. I also couldn't understand why so many turned so cruel so quickly.

The problem with gheebat and those who did it frequently is that there is no honor among gheebaters, a word I just made up but that should totally be used by everyone. I had people coming up to tell me, "Yeah so-and-so said *this* about your mom and dad. Is it true?" A week later, the accused person would come and betray the other person and say, "Do you know who was talking so much crap about your parents?" I had no desire whatsoever to hear any of this, but it all flowed back to me and my aunt and my grandmothers. I often asked my parents, "Be honest with me. Did you screw over so-and-so? I mean, if you did, it would explain why they hate you. Maybe you did?"

Each story was like a personal blow to the gut for my Ami and Abu, who assured me they had very little beef with anyone. As far as my father was concerned, I knew this to be true because the dude never socialized. If you told Abu he'd never have to go to another party in his life, he'd think he died and woke up in heaven. It was also one of his major mistakes in life. I kept telling him, "You have no friends. People don't know you like we do. The people you have helped over the years won't vouch for you. This is a reason why it's good to socialize sometimes, even if you have to make BS conversations."

My father is incapable of mindless chitchat and BS conversations. I think flirting for him would go something like this: "You have an aesthetically pleasing face and I find you charming. Would you like to eat food with me? By the way, my name is Zulfiqar."

My mother is a "social butterfly" according to my father. She's garrulous, makes friends easily, and enjoys meeting new people, and my father's idea of heaven is her personal hell. That being said, one of her fatal flaws in life is that she constantly befriended fake, shitty people. I recall early on in college I once said, "Ami, you do realize many of these aunties who smile and act like your friends are total frauds, right?"

"Neyhee, beta. You're too cynical. They're nice," she replied.

"Ami, *everybody* is nice, but that doesn't mean they're necessarily sincere," I said.

Even loyal and kind friends whom Ami knew for years disavowed her after this latest crisis. A very close family friend whose house we used to play at and whose kids came over since my childhood told other aunties she barely knew her and that she was just an acquaintance.

As the months wore on, I isolated myself completely from the world. People assumed I was ashamed and embarrassed, but I never hid my face or lowered my head due to my parents' arrest and the ensuing controversy. No, I balled myself up and put up a protective shield around me to guard myself. It was simply self-preservation.

The few times I tried to articulate what I was experiencing, I felt like I was talking to brick walls. Friends and elders just offered me platitudes in return. I felt like I couldn't trust anyone, even those who made sincere overtures. During nearly two years of self-imposed solitude, my OCD fueled my anxiety and fear that any mistake would result in more harm to me and my family.

I committed myself to working nonstop. After the employees left, I stayed late in the warehouse and would come home only when it was time to sleep. For relaxation, I used to go to the local Borders bookstore and Barnes & Noble, where I could lose myself for a bit in books, comic books, and the music listening stations. If I wanted to indulge, I'd go to the movies by myself to catch an interesting flick. It was a time of immense loneliness, but at least my "test" with the dunya was partially completed. I was not attached to material belongings. Wealth did not define my self-worth. Obviously, it would have made our lives much easier, but I didn't need its comforts to feel complete.

At one point in the journey, I hit rock bottom. I was surgical with my budget and calculations and updated my Excel sheet daily. I was expecting to have $73 left in my account after withdrawing Mr. Jefferson from the Wells Fargo ATM on Warm Spring and Mission. I looked at the receipt and instead it had "$00.03" as my balance. I had to pay rent, buy groceries, keep the lawyer, take care of my parents' office, and pay salaries with . . . 20 dollars and 3 pennies.

It was a beautiful, sunny day with a refreshing breeze, just a few hours before sunset. It's the kind of ideal Bay Area weather they put on brochures to get you to buy a house or invest in property. I started laughing while looking at the receipt. A few of the customers standing in line stared at me.

I decided to live dangerously and splurge. I drove across the street to Subway where I ordered a footlong tuna special with the works and two chocolate chip cookies. Then I went next door and ordered a caramel frappe with extra caramel drizzle and whipped cream.

Mr. Jefferson was now replaced with Mr. Hamilton . . . and 3 cents.

I drove to the office and told my parents' employees to take off early. I locked up and made peace with the fact we'd have to shut down everything. There was no way I could continue the business. I went home and told my aunt and my grandmothers I had done everything I could but I was now left with 10 dollars and 3 cents. We had tapped out all my resources. I had maxed out my credit. I was exhausted, and I decided to shut down the office by the end of the week.

They listened intently, and Dadi said, "Inshallah, Allah will take care of us." I had some homemade daal and chapatis. I relaxed and watched a movie on TV, and then I slept.

To this day, I recall that sleep. It was the deepest, most comforting and nurturing rest I've ever known as an adult. It was like I was protected in a womb. Floating. I've tried to re-create that experience numerous times to no avail. My only explanation is that I had either completely given up or given myself up to a Higher Power and the universe.

I just let go.

For a brief, beautiful moment, I was totally at peace.

A crisis surprises you in many ways. It reveals your character and resolve, both in all their glory and weakness, but it also invites people, especially strangers, to be kind and forgiving. Riffat aunty was an acquaintance of ours who used to attend our religious events. She was deeply spiritual and didn't socialize much. She had tremendous respect for my father and always appreciated his dua prayer, that he made at the end for everyone who attended the gathering. A few weeks after my parents were arrested, she got up in the middle of the night and blurted out, "We have to help them." She woke up her husband, Arshad, and told him she had a dream that inspired her to help our family. Coincidentally, Arshad uncle told her he had just experienced a very similar dream. They wanted to go with me and visit my father in Oakland to give him some encouragement. Over the years, they offered comfort, food, prayers, and a kind shoulder.

They weren't the only ones. After overcoming their initial hesitation and fear, some family and friends stepped up. A few community members, Muslims we had never met, offered to help just out of sympathy, or perhaps pity.

Every little piece of aid, comfort, and alliance helped. It held my brokenness together.

It was also critical because it gave me time to find a way to get my parents out of jail. My father's mental health was deteriorating. I eventually posted the bond nearly a year after my parents' arrest. Shaheen aunty and Syed uncle were the first to offer their house. Masood Mamoo asked an old college friend, who was wealthy, to put up a property as collateral for a bond. Mamoo vouched for my parents, and based on his word, this random man I'd never met came through. Shahed uncle, my father's first cousin, was successful in real estate at the time and he put up a property as well. We were able to eventually rally family members and a couple of family friends as signatories who vouched for my parents, and all of that was finally enough for the judge to grant them bail.

After nearly a year in prison, my parents were able to leave and breathe freely. They first entered a halfway house in Oakland for several weeks. I drove every day to Oakland to pick them up and then drop them off before curfew in the evening. For the first few days, they had to adjust to reentering a life that had been completely shattered. Many didn't know that my mom colored her hair. When she returned, she just let it go. She had no desire for the affectations. Always known to be trim, stylish, and well dressed, she still had her trademark optimism but she was more subdued and her hair was completely white. Most who saw her upon release did a double take and gasped.

But How Did It Affect You?

I don't believe my parents ever intended for me to be caught up in their shitstorm of chaos. As a father of three kids, I can say without hyperbole I would gladly trade my life to ensure their safety and security. It's how most parents are built. We're genetically hardwired to protect our children. Most responsible parents and decent human beings don't want to inflict unnecessary, lasting damage on their children. And yet it's parents who often destroy us, passing down disease and trauma, curses and a lifetime of pain, a hereditary suffering if the chain isn't broken. It can overwhelm generations.

In the past twenty years, my parents have never been able to properly say, "I am sorry for putting you through two decades of hell." There have been moments here and there where they have been apologetic and remorseful. It's clear they have understood that the "experience" set me back and harmed me. But they seemed incapable of truly reflecting on the immense, oppressive weight of it all, the heavy burden of carrying the Ali baggage.

When there were low moments for me—and there were many over the years—my parents often said, "Look at us, we didn't feel sorry for ourselves or get depressed, and we went through much worse! We were the ones in prison!" Or, they asked, "We've been going through this for twenty years, and we've been able to stay optimistic. We didn't get depressed. Why are you depressed?"

I've always tried to understand why two otherwise very smart and empathetic people were so disconnected from this realization. I've assumed that in prison they were so traumatized by their own pain they were unable to see this particular experience outside of their partnership. They never seemed to understand that they at least had a choice. They were able to write their own story, for better and worse. My story was written for me. My narrative was hijacked. My wife, a doctor who has spent years caring for victims of trauma, believes that if my parents were to truly acknowledge how much pain their actions caused me and the family, they would have broken down. They would have been unable to mentally and physically bear the truth because they loved me so much. Instead, they shielded themselves with this partial detachment and a "tough love" mindset. When I told my parents all this, they were deeply offended and hurt, adamant that they have always apologized for causing me so much pain. My mom said she still tells everyone, "Wajahat is our Rock of Gibraltar." I told them that I believed them, but that they never said it to me before. Often, the most important words we need to hear remain unspoken.

In moments of despair, I blamed myself. Why did I help? I could have left. Maybe I should have left and washed my hands of all of it and started my own life. But I knew I'd never leave. My grandmothers wouldn't have survived without me. I knew it was the right thing to do. I was, after all, a "good son."

About a year after their arrest, my parents were able to reestablish some normalcy and take over the business and the daily routines. We were now all crammed together at Yasmeen Phuppo's house, dependent on each other for money and paying the bills.

I was twenty-two years old and was suddenly adrift. I had no job. I had no credit. I was in debt. I wasn't in school. My parents came in and took control of the business and relationships and finances, so I had nothing left to do, except exhale and finally rest.

That's when my body started breaking down. I was unable to hold liquids and my bladder felt like it was being pierced by a thousand daggers, forcing me to run to the bathroom and relieve myself at least eight times a day. If I were chugging gallons of water and Mountain Dew, this would have made sense, but it happened regardless of water intake. I went to a urologist, who coincidentally was a Bellarmine high school alum. He examined me and said he'd only seen this in men above the age of fifty or in individuals who have undergone a very traumatic, stressful event. I didn't offer any details, thanked him for the explanation and the medicine, and went along my way.

I was unable to sleep at night. I'd stay up until 6 a.m. despite my best efforts, and I'd wake up early in the afternoon. I'd roll into the office by

3 p.m., and my parents would often ask, "Beta, why are you here when it's time to close?"

The answer was I had nowhere else to go.

After my parents were released, they spent the next decade appealing their case. Throughout my twenties, the sword of Damocles hung over our heads. At any moment my parents could lose their appeal and immediately be whisked to jail for several years, and I, an aspiring law student and wannabe writer, would be stuck, again, taking care of their mess.

The government seemed to stop caring about the case after they got the headlines. Seven government attorneys cycled through the ordeal. There was literally no movement on the case until my parents filed a motion to dismiss. Rather than granting the motion, and demonstrating there is no such thing as a neutral magistrate, the judge proactively urged the government to amend the indictment to cure the problems my parents and Cannon pointed out.

Ideally, I should have applied for a job, any job, but when you're stuck in limbo, you're in a state of mental and emotional paralysis. I kept thinking, "How can I pursue any long-term work or education when I have no idea what's going to happen tomorrow? If I go to grad school, I'll have to leave as soon as they lose their case. Or, if I move to NYC, I'll have to give up everything and move back."

I lost my spark and humor. I became a deeply serious and reserved person. People assumed I was a decade older than I was. My father was the first one to say and acknowledge the "trauma" word. He said I needed to see a psychiatrist to help me get back on track. But I took self-destructive pride in my ability to persist through the pain. I wasn't fragile. I wasn't weak. I was emotionally and mentally resilient. Unlike my peers, I never break. I am the brown Wolverine. I didn't cry once during the ordeal, and I wouldn't begin now.

In hindsight, obviously, this was ridiculous. There is no weakness in confronting your trauma and pain. In fact, healing your mental and emotional scars, acknowledging and defeating your inner demons, will be one of the most challenging, exhausting, terrifying, and brave fights of your life.

In early 2003, I finally relented and went to the psychiatrist I had visited five years earlier for my OCD. In our hour-long session, in addition to the traditional chat, he asked me to fall backward and let him catch me. He also asked me to lie on the floor and push up against his palms. I apparently revealed enough of myself in these exercises that he concluded: "You don't trust people. You trust no one. That's the main problem. You're going to have work on this. This will take a lot of work if you're willing to commit to it," he said.

Instead, I decided to white-knuckle it the rest of the way. My parents kept trying to encourage me to start my life. I'd laugh and respond, "What life?" Ami said, "At the very least, finish the play."

In hindsight, that advice helped save my life.

Chapter 7

Become a Domestic Crusader

"You're a playwright, you just don't know it. Dialogue and characters are your strengths," Ishmael Reed, famed novelist and poet, told me in his office after our short story writing class one afternoon in October 2001.

I chose Ishmael Reed's class because I dug his name, "Ishmael." I had no idea he was a MacArthur "Genius" Grant winner and two-time Pulitzer-nominated writer. I asked my science fiction English professor, Ojars Kratins, to describe the style of each of three professors offering the class so I could make my pick. He leaned back in his chair, and said, "Ishmael, well, he kind of lets you do your own thing."

That did it. Cool first name and he will give me more freedom than the other two teachers? I was sold. I submitted my application for one of the limited spots in the class five minutes before the 4 p.m. deadline and slipped it into the box outside the English Department in Wheeler Hall.

The application asked us to submit a ten-page short story writing sample. I did not have a ten-page short story writing sample, and because I procrastinated the night before, I didn't find the time to write one, and even if I did have the time I would have used it to play NBA 2K. The only original piece I had was *All This for an Ass?*, which I had written and directed for our comedy troupe, a ridiculous, twisted fantasy about two English noblemen who are impatiently awaiting the return of Gerf, the simple peasant boy with the simple task of collecting the annual taxes from the plebians. Along the way, Gerf encounters a witch who trades him the bag of money for a talking ass. Hijinks ensue.

This is what I submitted to Ishmael Reed, the MacArthur Genius, to gain entry to his prestigious workshop.

The actual class was intimidating as hell. My first story was about a female mosquito from the suburbs who was obsessed with hip-hop culture even though she had no Black friends. She was having an existential crisis because all her other friends had their first suck (literally, biting into flesh and drawing blood) and she was still a virgin. My peers laughed at all the right parts. Professor Reed seemed a bit concerned. He applauded the creativity but wrote "easy on the stereotypes" and underlined it twice. He assumed I was appropriating Black culture, but my piece was meant to describe many of my suburban peers who loved Black culture but didn't know Black people. Either way, I was mortified and realized that often your intention doesn't matter, but what matters most is how people hear and respond to your words. I was embarrassed and vowed to do a better job for my second story, which was due in a few weeks.

Then there was 9/11 and everything changed. I didn't go to classes for three weeks because of my newfound unpaid vocations as an accidental activist, community representative, and media spokesman. Around 3 a.m., the morning my story was due, I came up with an idea about a married couple who loathe each other and secretly plot to kill the other on their fiftieth wedding anniversary. The couple were in fact giant ogres with Scottish accents. The students *loved* the short story and Professor Reed told me to follow him to his office after class. I thought he would chew me out for missing three weeks. Instead, he told me to drop everything and write a play.

"You ever read those American classics like *Death of a Salesman* or *A Raisin in the Sun*?" he asked.

"Yes," I replied.

"Great. Write me something like that but with, you know, where is your family from again?"

"Pakistan."

"Yeah, Pakistan. OK. So, a Muslim family, you know, in America, but from Pakistan. You have two months to give me twenty pages, OK?"

I spent the next ten minutes begging him to reconsider, and to please let me just continue on with the class.

He shot me down: I would be wasting my time and talents in the short story class. He was paying attention to how Muslims and Islam were being covered in the media in the aftermath of the terror attacks—Muslims would get "hazed" for at least the next ten years and I'd have to be prepared. "Black people have endured and survived this for over four hundred years. We know what's coming," he said. His people had "fought back" through art and culture, through storytelling. All that Americans have ever seen and would see of Muslims would be stories about terrorism and violence and the Middle East, but if I could give them a story about an ordinary Muslim American family, it could help change minds. So, now I not only had to learn how to write a play but single-handedly counter America's disastrous foreign and domestic policy? Awesome.

"OK, well, good luck. See you in December. Bye," he said bluntly as he turned his chair around and faced his computer.

I started writing the play on my twenty-first birthday. A month later, I submitted twenty pages of a play without a title about three generations of a single family forced to spend a weekend together at the old family home. I passed the class and thought this interesting endeavor was done.

Professor Reed did not. He would keep bothering me, even after I graduated, to give him "just five more pages." Two years later, on my twenty-third birthday, I finished the play as a present to myself. My mother forced me to sit down and finish the last few scenes, commanding me not to leave my chair until it was done. (Bathroom breaks were permitted.)

The only task left was the title. I couldn't release a play as "Untitled by Wajahat Ali." I spitballed the first ten potential titles that came to mind and wrote them on the paper. I immediately knew the title I'd eventually pick as soon as I wrote it. A good title, like a crush, like your favorite flavor, instantly delights, it just hits you, and you know, "Yeah, that's it. That's the one."

The Domestic Crusaders.

I thought I could booby-trap and reframe the historically and politically loaded word "Crusades" especially in light of President George W. Bush's use of it to describe the War on Terror. My brown-skinned Muslim characters—these alleged vicious savages, this Axis of Evil in our homeland, this potential suburban sleeper cell, these "Moslems"—happened to be . . . quite boring, actually, just living their ordinary lives, discussing marriage opportunities and squabbling over petty family grievances and lamb biryani.

The creative process of finishing *The Domestic Crusaders* saved my life. That sounds like melodramatic hyperbole, something an actor says during an awards acceptance speech. But the small play was in fact a testament to life. As everything around me fell apart, as everything I touched "turned to dust," I created this story with characters who would live and breathe on the page and on the stage. The universe was unable to take this one thing from me. So I invested everything in it.

I turned in my senior thesis to Professor Schweik and graduated with an English major from UC Berkeley in the summer of 2003. My entire family attended. I wore the cap and gown, did the walk, and even took pictures. It was a rare good memory and experience from that time, and we were grateful to have it.

Maqbool Nana and a couple of other elders whom I respected gave me the same advice: start socializing again. In fact, they gave me an unofficial command that I had to accept every invite. I was told it was necessary for my spiritual growth.

It was time to reenter the world. Professor Reed read the play and invited me and my parents to Sprenger's Grotto, a Berkeley staple that used to be a favorite of author Jack London. When I saw him, he had the play rolled up and I thought he would beat me with it. Instead, he said, "This—this is great. You did it." "I did?" I asked. "Yes! You should do a staged reading now." "What is a staged reading?" I asked. "Oh, Carla will help you, she's a pro," he said, pointing to his wife, Carla Blank. "I will?" she asked, surprised.

Carla, like Ishmael, is an artist of many talents and professions, a dancer, director, teacher, and author, who is the yin to Ishmael's yang, a calm, sober anchor who enjoys his playfulness and wit but also can keep him in check, sometimes.

"Be careful, she's of Russian Jewish descent," Ishmael warned me. "You'll never get a compliment from her. I've been waiting forty years," he said, cackling to himself. She rolled her eyes. "Also, they've got like five hundred words for suffering in Russian, but she'll be great. You guys will have fun," he assured us.

Poor Carla thought she was just helping her husband's former student put on a simple staged reading, an exercise where the playwright introduces the play to a small audience and has a few actors sitting on chairs just reading the script. She had no idea she'd end up being the director and dramaturge, and have her life overrun by Pakistanis for the next eight years.

How to Make "The People" Like an "Ethnic" Story

Throughout my journey in getting *The Domestic Crusaders* to the stage, producers and agents kept assuring me, "Ethnic stories have a hard time translating to the mainstream," or "Mainstream audiences will not identify with ethnic audiences." I always replied, "Well, we're all ethnic." Rumi is still one of the best-selling and most influential poets in America. He was a Muslim scholar and saint who lived over 700 years ago in Turkey and wrote in Farsi. Somehow, he translates to the mainstream.

My favorite movie is *The Godfather*, a movie about an Italian-American family originally from Sicily. There's not a single Muslim or Pakistani in the entire trilogy. Trust me, I checked. There's a scene where Michael Corleone, played by Al Pacino, speaks in Sicilian for a few minutes with Sollozzo, right before he retrieves the hidden gun from the bathroom and assassinates him and Captain McCluskey. I've seen this movie countless times, and to this day I have no idea what they're saying. I don't care. It doesn't matter. I don't need to understand everything to empathize and be hooked. The movie still mesmerizes me.

Growing up on the margins, you learn to do your homework and catch up. The dominant culture is white and Judeo-Christian, and everyone who isn't part of that tribe is just assumed to know everything about it, because privilege is often blind to its own power and to those around them who lack it. I had to learn the following on my own: bat mitzvah, streaky underwear, meatloaf, unconditional love, ham sandwiches, anything to do with alcohol, and, oh yeah, the English language.

My peoples were more than just cannon fodder or terrorists or the end of punch lines. Our stories, cultures, languages, religions, and lives were rich, infused with vibrancy that could benefit the world. We just needed some miners to dig them up and share them. I wanted to create stories by us, for everyone: culturally specific and authentic tales for a diverse, global audience. I refused to believe that, somehow, I was genetically gifted and an outlier able to consume and appreciate literature, art, and culture made by artists of different ethnicities. Did my mother feed me imported breast milk from Nordic countries? Did she watch European foreign-language movies while I was in the womb? Yet I, a brown, Muslim kid, was able to empathize and identify with white characters who lived in white communities and interacted with mostly other white people. If I could do this, I had faith that white people, often referred to as "the mainstream," could cross the road without difficulty and with maybe just a little bit of hand-holding and appreciate a story populated by brown folks.

Carla and Ishmael agreed with me that I should first get the buy-in and support of my South Asian and Muslim community. We did everything grassroots. Carla and I initially held auditions at the Oakland Public Library. Only six people showed up. A few weeks later, two dozen showed up. If you build it, they will come . . . hungry.

I later moved the auditions to Chandni Restaurant and Mehran Restaurant, two popular South Asian joints located in the same shopping center in Newark, California. Chandni was the same place where two years earlier my Yasmeen Phuppo had convened a community meeting for people to help my parents who were in jail. Now the owners of both joints let me use the back space for auditions if I could somehow convince ten people to buy buffets. (I did.) Eventually, the staff and the restaurant managers, who were intrigued by the script, auditioned for the roles of the father and grandfather. (Sadly, none were cast but they gave a spirited effort.)

We ended up casting Kashif and Atif, who both tried out and were perfect for the role of Sal, the eldest son, and Ghafur, the young brother whose twenty-first birthday reunites the family at the home. The six-person cast was rounded out by nonprofessional actors, all South Asian, who worked for food and $50.

I went to Mehran and asked the owner, Fiaz, to let me convert his restaurant into a "dinner dining experience." I promised to pack the house with 250 people. I asked him to imagine how other artists would see Mehran as more than just a place where Desis got married, but instead as a potential venue for art and culture. I asked him to give me a five-course buffet meal and the hall for a "good price." He offered it to me at $10 a head, which is a perfectly reasonable price.

I went home and told my dad who felt personally insulted. "Come with me," he said. We drove back to Mehran. My father rolled up his sleeves, asked for Fiaz, and once he arrived, he launched into him, "Fiaz, how many times have I given you business? My son is here, willing to give you a dinner dining experience, and you charge him ten dollars a head? Ten dollars? Why do you insult me like this? Why? No. You will give us the hall, a five-course meal, dessert, and chai for six dollars a head."

It worked. I was a Padawan in awe of my father's Jedi uncle negotiator status.

I knew my brown peoples. They needed food. I had to give them a buffet to entice them to come. They wouldn't fork over money just for a play. If I gave them a two-act play, but kept an intermission with an amazing buffet, they'd at least stay for the first half. If they stayed for the second half, I knew they actually dug the play.

I called my own uncle, Mujjahid Chacha, my flesh and blood, to test my theory. I asked if he would come see my play if I also promised to give the audience a five-course Pakistani buffet meal for $15.

"Well, if you make it ten dollars, I'll think about it," he replied.

I did the staged reading at Mehran for $10 with a five-course buffet meal, chai and dessert included. The capacity was 250, but we ended up selling 350 tickets. The audience, mostly Pakistani and Muslim, stayed for the buffet, devoured it, stayed for the second half, and then gave us a huge standing ovation.

We realized we had something special.

Nonetheless, an uncle still came up to me afterward and said, "Beta, what is this playwriting? Do something useful—like protest."

The next year we performed the play at the Berkeley Repertory Theater and San Jose State University as special engagements. This time, I wanted to prove that this "ethnic" play would win over a diverse, "mainstream" audience.

We had no money, so we did everything ourselves. I made the program with Kashif and Atif at their house. We created the musical cues and soundtrack. My friend from college, cartoonist Connie Sun, created the poster that I plastered at every single South Asian restaurant and mosque in the area. My mother fed the entire cast and theater crew during rehearsals. We dressed the set with our own furniture, stripping our house bare for a few weekends. My grandmother entered the family room one day and asked if we were moving and, if so, how come nobody told her. My dad drove the U-Haul, and I learned how to become a producer and assistant director.

Carla and I went to check out the space. It was the Thrust Stage of the Berkeley Repertory Theater, and we caught a matinee of one of the shows. After I sat in the darkened theater, I played "the counting game."

There were only 11 of us in a crowd of nearly 300.

Actually, 10.5 but I rounded up.

That's it—10.5 people of color.

What did you expect? The play we were seeing in Berkeley, a stone's throw from Oakland, had an all-white cast, a mostly white crew, and was marketed to affluent, suburban whites—the foundation of the theater industry.

That's when I first encountered the reality of WAT: White American Theater. In fact, the theater industry is so white that more than 300 theater artists of color signed a letter in 2020 saying American theater is a "house of cards built on fragility and supremacy. And this is a house that will not stand." The signatories include Pulitzer Prize–winning playwrights Lynn Nottage, Suzan-Lori Parks, and everyone's favorite Hamilton, Lin-Manuel Miranda.

I made a vow to sell out the shows with diverse crowds of color. I also learned from my experience with our comedy troupe at UC Berkeley that if you reach out to people, invite them, and make them part of your journey, then many will invest in you and appreciate the gesture. I found every single South Asian and Muslim nonprofit, religious group, and collective in the Bay Area I could and asked them to sponsor my play. No financial investment, I just wanted them to put our play's website on their marketing material and help me promote the showings to their listservs and emails. In return, I offered some comp tickets.

It worked. The shows sold out. The audiences were diverse. They laughed at all the right spots. They gave it a standing ovation.

And despite all this, after every show, at least one Desi uncle and aunty would come up and ask, "But, what do the people think?"

"Aunty, you saw. The people liked it," I replied to one elder.

"No no, the people, beta. What do the *people* think?" she stressed.

She wasn't referring to South Asians in the audience, or Asians, or Blacks, or Latinos. She was referring to white people. It wasn't enough that we had a diverse crowd of so many different ethnicities all enjoying the play; the validation and support of the "people" reigned supreme. It was a realization that the needle wouldn't move unless the Whiteness blessed this small play with a touch of approval.

A few months later, on the fourth anniversary of 9/11, we did the play at the San Jose State University Theater. Same result. Sold out, diverse crowds. Standing ovations. More uncles and aunties approached me and asked about the "people." Well, the "people" had responded. We got a fantastic write-up in the *San Jose Mercury News* and the *San Francisco Chronicle*, which ran a photo of me looking like stern terrorist #3 from a bad Video on Demand action movie. A BBC reporter caught the Berkeley performance, and she did a ten-minute feature on us released around the same time.

A small play put on entirely with a shoestring budget returned its money and made a minor splash. Despite the mini success, an agent, who was introduced to me by Ishmael Reed, told me I needed "white characters" in my play to make it more mainstream, so that white audiences would care. She then urged me to add at least one white character in my next play or script. She, and a few others along the way, recommended I either strip the script of all the Urdu and Arabic or print a glossary at the end. But if I could work through words like *paesan*, *infamia*, and *pezzonovante* in *The Godfather*, I was confident people could work through a few words in Urdu and Arabic.

A Hollywood producer wanted to bring the play to LA. I took a phone call with him, and he was enthusiastic. However, he had one note, as all Hollywood producers do. I said, sure, hit me with it. "Well, what do you think about casting Ted Danson . . . as the Pakistani immigrant father?" he asked. I laughed for several seconds. "That was good. Good one," I said as my laughter died down. I might have even wiped away a tear.

He was not laughing. He was dead serious.

"Well, audiences like Ted Danson. I mean he's a big name, but they'd be comfortable with him as the dad," he explained.

"Yeah, but Salman is a middle-aged Pakistani immigrant," I replied, somewhat confused as to why we were entertaining this suggestion.

"Well, it's acting, right? We can just put on makeup and it'll be fine," he countered.

I have nothing against Ted Danson. I like Ted Danson. But until I see Pakistani actors playing Sam Malone in a *Cheers* remake, let's just say we have work to do.

Still, I assumed all this positive energy would lead to new creative projects and subsidize my dreams of becoming a writer, but nothing happened. It all fizzled.

At the age of twenty-three, I had decided to reapply to law school. I was accepted to UC Davis King Hall law school and, thanks to loans and grants, I was (barely) able to afford the tuition. Also, Davis was about seventy minutes away from Fremont. My parents had been out of jail for several months, but in case everything unraveled again, I could quickly return home and resume my duties of cleaning up the Ali family crap.

I assumed that a law degree would be a powerful tool in my "Batman utility belt," which is how I described my unorthodox and expanding skill set. I could practice law, help clients, make some money, and then at night write my way to creative and financial freedom like John Grisham and other attorneys-turned-writers who just needed some time before they could fulfill their artistic ambitions.

Throughout the application process, and for most of the first year of law school, I kept anticipating inevitable chaos. I was initially distant, reserved, and deadly serious compared to my colleagues. I stood apart and made very few friends. Just a few years earlier, I was hosting friends at my UC Berkeley apartment every night, and now I had forgotten how to socialize. I entered law school completely hardened and numbed, and it took me nearly two years to open up.

Instead of being judicious and prudent and pursuing lucrative corporate internships during the summer of my first year, I used all my time and scant resources to premiere the play at the Berkeley Repertory Theater and San Jose State University Theater for limited, weekend engagements.

The play was very well received, but it didn't open up any financial opportunities.

I graduated in 2007, passed the California bar exam, and assumed I'd be able to score a job and begin my life again at the age of twenty-seven. By that time, I had decided to forfeit these "ethnic stories" along with my dream of becoming a writer. I had honorably tried and failed to "make it." Unlike some of my peers who left for New York or Hollywood to pursue their dreams, I couldn't afford to dream. I couldn't indulge or entertain selfish desires like becoming my own man, starting a family, and pursuing my passions. My parents' litigation was still ongoing, and my family again might need to rely on me to survive if the shit hit the fan.

Instead, I was a licensed attorney, living back at home, completely broke, and driving my busted Toyota Camry without a driver's-side door handle to get my mother vegetables from the grocery store and take my grandmother to her doctor's appointments. I used to wake up every day and find a five-dollar bill in my wallet. My father told me, "Beta, no man should be without at least five dollars."

I spent hours every day writing cover letters and submitting my résumé to literally any legal job in the Bay Area and was greeted with rejections from attorneys who were impressed with my play and urged me to instead pursue a writing career. One young bankruptcy attorney interviewed me for a new practice he had started. He spent the entire conversation convincing himself *not* to hire me. Instead, he pleaded with me to leave law. "But, I really need the money, and I just can't afford it," I told him. "Yeah, I know, but just hack it as a writer if you can," he responded. "Trust me, I'm doing you a favor by not giving you this job."

I couldn't see the charity.

In hindsight, this time of poverty, rejection, and failure was a blessing for creativity. One day, on a whim, I decided to convert a paper I had written in law school on private military firms operating in Iraq into an op-ed. I submitted it to an online publication, CounterPunch, which immediately accepted it, published it the next day, and wrote back asking for more pieces. Over the next six months, I furiously cranked out interviews, commentary pieces, political essays, and movie reviews. I started my own blog, used social media outlets, built up a mailing list, and began receiving invitations to panels as a "social media journalist."

I had no business card, but I did have one fancy sports jacket and a busted Fujitsu laptop with a giant yellow ethernet cable attached to the modem.

Eventually, I became a contributor to the *Huffington Post* and the *Guardian*. I was still broke and living at home, but by this time I had a few clients thanks to word of mouth who retained me for services ranging from writing contracts to helping them avoid foreclosure. At night, I concentrated on this new, strange, social media journalism career that gave me access to free books, advance movie screenings, and interview opportunities with brilliant writers and academics.

In 2008, everyone expected Hillary Clinton to emerge as the Democratic candidate for president, but a young senator from Chicago started winning primaries. It was almost impossible to believe at the time, but it seemed white America would actually allow a Black man named Obama to become president.

Maybe now was the time for the play? If they were about to elect an alleged Muslim, maybe the "people" would embrace a play about a Muslim American family?

I knew that if I waited for the "people" to come to me, I'd be waiting forever, stuck in my room, an old man, or a corpse hunched over my laptop, before I was ever given a meaningful chance. "Fuck it. We'll do it ourselves," I said to myself with a *Braveheart* battle cry. I made a vow to premiere the play in New York on September 11, 2009.

Now I just had to get the money, a theater, a cast, and a crew.

Ishmael used his contacts and got me a meeting with the famous Nuyorican Poets Cafe on the Lower East Side in NYC. The artistic director Rome Neal dug the play but didn't think there was an audience for a play about Pakistanis. Still, he trusted Ishmael and said if I could raise the funds, which included insurance money, then they'd give me a five-week run in the fall of 2009.

During the day, I continued working as an independent attorney, and at night I kept cranking out political essays and interviews for more online outlets, this time expanding my portfolio to *Salon*, *Slate*, and the *Washington Post*. Late at night and early into the morning, I plotted how to bring *The Domestic Crusaders* to NYC. I made a vow to myself that I would *will* the play into existence. I made a commitment every day that I would work myself to death if necessary to make it happen. I would either succeed or I would die. That was it. Nothing in between. I believed this would be my last shot to finally emerge as my own man, able to create my own destiny, the way I had always imagined when I was that shy kid from Fremont who made homemade movies and dreamed of becoming a storyteller.

I created a list of "people," famous and well-known writers I respected, whom I assumed, in my delusion, would positively review this play no one had ever heard of. I wrote their names in one Excel sheet column, and in the column next to it added their contact info, which I found by scouring the internet and following up on leads. I then spent a year basically cold-emailing them my pitch on why they should read the play, why it didn't suck, and how a positive review from them would mean everything.

I eventually found the email of one such "people": actor and writer Emma Thompson. I sent her the most charming, funny, disarming, honest email I could, asking if she could please read the play. Her agent asked me to print and mail a copy to an address in England. I paid the hefty price and assumed I'd never hear from her again. A few months later, I received a two-page handwritten letter from Emma saying she was a "luddite" with computers, apologizing for the delay, and that she loved the play. Not only did she give me a review blurb, she also gave me a check to help my goal toward the $25,000.

I leaned on my friends from elementary school, high school, college, and law school to vouch for me and spread the word. Most of these fools would come over to my apartment in college and eat my mom's food and sleep on my couch, so I was shamelessly calling in favors from all over California. My first fundraiser was held by my high school friends, Tuan and An Pham, at their home, where I netted about $1500.

Word spread of this "dude who is putting on this Muslim play" in NYC thanks to social media and one degree of brown separation. Zeba Iqbal, who was a connector in NYC, read one of my passionate, desperate, enthusiastic posts to support my endeavor and was moved to help me. She believes in the arts and storytelling and wishes more of our community members would invest in young talent. She invited me to NYC to attend dinner for single Muslim American professionals held in a bougie South Asian restaurant for a "networking" event that was really just an excuse for a bunch of single Muslim folks to mingle and eyeball each other in hopes of some love connections. After dinner, Zeba introduced me to the crowd of 150 people who had never heard of me or my play. I gave an impromptu, passionate speech, tracing the journey of *The Domestic Crusaders* and why I thought we had to invest in our stories, especially at a time when our people were being marginalized.

The crowd was hooked. I just had to ask for money. Children of South Asian immigrants are not raised to gloat, boast, brag, flex, or compliment ourselves. We are like the anti–hip hop stars. We'd rap about how "We're kinda OK, I guess. I mean not bad, you know?" I said something like, "Well, if you don't mind, and if, you know, you can afford it, you can please donate. If you'd like."

Zeyba Rahman was sitting in the audience. She's a big-time baller who works at the Doris Duke Charitable Foundation, and her aim is to invest in cultural workers and storytellers to enrich and expand America. I didn't know any of this at the time. But this woman whom I'd never met was really angry at me. She stormed right up to me with her eyebrows furrowed. She took my hand and placed a wad of cash in it, and looking me in the eye said, "Listen, your ask for money? That was pathetic. Really pathetic. What are you doing? Do you want my money or not? Well, do you?"

"Y-y-yes," I stammered.

"Good, then ask for it. Be bold. You are asking for us to invest in you and your product. There's no reason to be shy. Next time, just say it. OK? I'm rooting for you," she said, then left.

I ended up with another $1500 that night. Zeba set up mini fundraisers around the East Coast. A few of my old friends did a couple in the Bay Area and LA. I went around with my one black Samsonite bag and one black sports jacket like a Pakistani P. T. Barnum making the pitch to anyone who would listen. I took Zeyba's advice and confidently asked for money, being as transparent as possible. I crashed on couches, ate PB&J sandwiches, slept never, and a few weeks before the play's premiere had enough money to take care of all the costs.

In the summer of 2009, Carla and Ishmael relocated to NYC for the summer to prep the cast, all South Asian actors who were paid in samosas and chai from the Punjab deli on Houston Street and on Rome Neal's famous banana pudding. I bought an insane deal on JetBlue, a summer special where for $500 you could fly round-trip from the Bay to NYC for eight weeks.

I would be in the Bay Area from Monday to Thursday working as a solo attorney and taking care of my clients. Then, on Friday mornings, around 5 a.m., I drove my '97 Toyota Camry to Park SFO, took the shuttle to the airport, got on the plane, slept the entirety of the flight, landed at JFK airport in NYC, woke up, took the subway to Manhattan, arrived at the Nuyorican Theater, worked with the cast and crew, walked from the Lower East Side to Midtown where I was staying at a friend's apartment, and along the way picked up dinner at Haandi's at 27th and Lex. I took the Sunday flight back home to SFO, where I took the shuttle to Park SFO, drove my car home, slept a few hours, woke up, did my legal work for a few days, and repeated the process.

We served as our own publicists. We hoped to score some media right before the play's premiere on 9/11 to generate buzz and ticket sales. Two weeks out, we had nothing. Finally, the week of the play we got a big feature in the *New York Times*, a mention in the *Wall Street Journal*, and several TV spots.

The night before the premiere, we did a special show for the late Miguel Algarín's birthday. He was the cofounder of the Nuyorican Poets Cafe, and it was an "intimate" gathering of one hundred friends, artists, and poets that included people like Ishmael Reed and Amiri Baraka. The audience was mostly Black, Puerto Rican, Italian, and Jewish American. My mother, who had flown in for the premiere, was the only Pakistani in the crowd. It was a potluck, so I asked my mom to make us all biryani. The day before, she went with Pope, our stage manager, to his tiny apartment in Queens where she somehow cooked amazing goat biryani for fifty people. Her dish was the hit of the night.

The lights went down. The audience of luminaries swallowed the marinated goat meat and sat down to watch *The Domestic Crusaders*.

Intermission.

Lights up.

I'm standing in the booth in the back.

"Excuse me? Are you the playwright? Well, I just wanted to shake your hand. That's good writing there. It reminds me of Jewish theater," said a pleased attendee.

Audience went back to their seats for Act 2.

Lights fade.

End of the play.

Silence.

Applause.

More applause.

A standing ovation.

"That reminded me of how we yell in our Puerto Rican house," Miguel's sister said to him after the play.

I exhaled.

The "people," my people, the Amreekan people, dug the play.

That's when I knew we'd be fine. After five weeks, Rome Neal, the artistic director, told me our little play had broken the Nuyorican's box-office records. His only regret was that he didn't extend the play's run.

The day of the last show, a Sunday matinee, Ishmael told me we were going to hang out with his friend. That friend was writer Toni Morrison. Before the show's premiere, we sat in the French café next door and had dessert and coffee. My entire goal during that ninety-minute sit-down was to not say anything embarrassing or stupid in front of two living legends. Meanwhile, Toni Morrison just wanted to discuss Wanda Sykes's latest comedy special. She tried to repeat all the sex jokes but kept interrupting herself with laughter. I was a fly on the wall between these two titans of literature who discussed racism, the treatment of Barack Obama by the US media, and their different literary styles. Mrs.

Morrison said Ishmael Reed was like a brute-force boxer and she was more subtle in her attacks, but both of them were peers, friends, and used their talents to tell stories of their communities and to confront white supremacy.

Then she looked at me and said, "You know how it is with us fellow writers. The creative process is most exciting in the imagination. It begins as something, but then it grows and grows."

"Fellow writer"? The shy, awkward kid from Fremont, California?

I ate my muffin, nodded, and stuck to my mission to not say anything embarrassing or stupid. We walked over to the theater and I sat behind Toni Morrison, who was in the second row. As soon as the play ended, I jumped on stage and in front of everyone, with chutzpah and courage, asked Toni what she thought of the play.

Pin-drop silence. All eyes on the Nobel Prize winner.

Very slowly, with deliberation, Mrs. Morrison articulated, "This play is brilliant. Moving. Shapely. Clever. Funny." And with that, she gave me a nod and quickly left to avoid the adoring fans.

But the greatest validation and compliment came from the kids who brought their parents to the show. High school and college students, budding writers, Muslims who didn't want to become doctors, urging their parents to imagine another path. "If this dumbass Wajahat could do it, why not me?" A few of their parents met me afterward and one said, "You know, I was skeptical. My son brought me to this. But, you know, he is talented. And, if you can do this, why not him?"

Why not?

I used to tell people I just fell into playwriting and had no training, but my director Carla corrected me. "You and Kashif made all those movies when you were kids. You did that improv troupe and those sketches. That was all training. You just didn't realize it, but you've been doing this forever," she reminded me.

After the play's NYC run, the same Bay Area uncle, who six years earlier had mocked me and told me to protest, apologized. He had lived in this country for over forty years, he said, had done everything right, and yet each time he turned on the TV he was portrayed only as a terrorist or a cab driver. He said he wished he would have told one of his sons to become a writer. He wished me well and prayed for my success.

I still encounter many Muslims who lament the depiction of our faith and communities in mainstream media. They also often live in the past, wistfully remembering the glories of an Islamic civilization that produced Cordoba, the Ottoman Empire, and Rumi, who is still cranking out book sales despite living over 700 years ago.

There is a mourning in their reminiscence, a hope and prayer for a renaissance that passed us by. I reject this nostalgia. Instead, I ask all those who are still striving to be recognized as "Amreekan" to invest in the present and future Rumis of today. There is someone right now, reading this book, who has always dreamed of being a poet, or a play- wright, or a comedian, or a director, but has never had the encourage- ment. Sometimes, a nod of approval, or a compliment, from family or a friend is all it takes, the small gust of wind that lifts the sails.

Chapter 8

Die Hard 2: Die Harder in Amreeka

I was a writer. I practiced law. I was finally making my own name and gaining some fame and respect for my words. Yes, I was still broke, stuck at home, single, in debt, in bankruptcy, and my parents' case was now on appeal, but at least I was on my way out of the ditch. After eight years of living under the fear of the dangling sword, I felt our necks would be spared.

And then my parents lost their appeal and my father was arrested again.

The morning of August 25, 2010, I was sleeping in bed when the phone call came from my father's attorney informing me the appellate court had ruled against my parents. I remember that my left hand started trembling and I lost air for several seconds. For the past eight years, I had just hoped and imagined that somehow they'd be able to beat it.

My parents had come out of prison. They had rebuilt their lives. My grandmothers were still alive. We were all together. We had just come back from annihilation. And just like that, without a warning or a whisper, the sword fell.

It all turned to dust again.

The court ordered a five-year prison sentence for my parents and a $20 million restitution to Microsoft. The original headlines had claimed a $100 million loss, and we always wondered where the other $80 million went. Seems like a big chunk of change, no? The court affirmed twenty of the counts specifically relating to mail and wire fraud, and overturned ten counts dealing with money laundering.

Our house was subject to criminal forfeiture and now belonged to the government. During my parents' release, they were at least able to move back into our family home and pay the monthly mortgage. I enjoyed having a bedroom with walls instead of makeshift cardboard boxes that were taped together.

The judge gave us a month to move out and told my mother she could choose to wait six months to self-report to FCI Dublin, a low-security federal prison without fences for female inmates. She decided to take it and help settle all the family affairs for their five-year journey. I was living at home with my parents, and we were pooling all our money. I was almost finished with my Chapter 13 bankruptcy, but my credit was still in tatters.

I had done this entire dance eight years ago, so I had experience and muscle memory.

There weren't any splashy headlines this time. No printed copies of the news to be found in the mosque. No community gossip. Mostly, when people found out they just felt bad. Having seen my parents over the past few years, most assumed they had settled the case or served their time and moved on with their lives. They were shocked it had gone on for so long.

We held another garage sale. Another storage unit, another pile of boxes, this time much smaller. A week before we had to move, I called the Tri-City Homeless Shelter and inquired about temporary rooms. My aunt, who was suffering from health and financial problems by that time, decided to take in my grandmother and keep her with two renters in her home. We were officially homeless.

My Patata Dadi by that time had left for Pakistan. A year before, she was showing signs of dementia. She kept repeating actions, forgetting where she placed her glasses and clothes, and a blank look washed over her face. She was my grandmother's sister-in-law, married to her elder brother who had tragically passed away early in the marriage. She had one son, Hamid, whom she loved more than the world, but he also died in his early thirties when they were both doing Hajj in Mecca. All alone, she became my grandmother's companion and helper, a role she patiently fulfilled with both love and quiet resentment. I never understood why a loving God would be so unkind to a pious woman of immense spiritual strength. Her every happiness was taken from her.

We were very close and she said I was her "hamdard," an empathizer, to whom she could unburden her sorrows from time to time. Her greatest fear, she said, was that she would die alone, because she had no close blood relatives left to take care of her. We kept assuring her that she was our family, and my parents always treated her with the highest level of love and respect. She was always appreciative, but her worry persisted.

I promised her that once I established myself financially I'd help take care of her and she'd never have to worry about being forgotten or left alone.

My parents were concerned about her safety and health if they were to end up in jail. They made arrangements in Pakistan, based on assurances that she would be taken care of properly, in a private home, with extended family members. The last time I saw her was when we dropped her off at San Francisco International Airport. I just had a feeling I'd never see her again. But I said all the predictable things: "Oh, everything will be fine soon, and inshallah you'll come back when Abu and Ami are more stable."

Her condition deteriorated in Karachi. Those entrusted to take care of her eventually washed their hands of her, placing her in a senior center home, which was severely "lacking" in resources. My mother's sister, Fareesa, went to visit her and was horrified by her wasted state. Patata Dadi is buried in the same cemetery as my Nana, my mother's father, down the street from their family home in Karachi.

Every time I visit Karachi, I pay my respects. Every time, I apologize for failing to keep my promise.

Back in 2002, during my parents' first arrest, it was me, my grandmothers, and my aunt. Now? It was me and my mom. At the last second, my father's first cousin, Mujjahid, said we could stay in a bedroom in the

Union City home he shared with his three young kids. He was the same uncle who said he'd come to my play in Mehran if I offered it for $10. He was going through a nasty divorce, and he thought my mother could be a positive role model and a Mary Poppins for the house. He didn't ask for any money, but we gave what little we could.

I was about to turn thirty. People thought I was "killing it." My peers from college and law school said I was the one who "made it." I felt like I was in a comedy and a horror movie. I was living in a bedroom I shared with my mom in my uncle's house because every other possession was lost. However, I was also being invited to different cities across America and the world to give talks, speak at panels and festivals, or present at workshops. My passport, which was completely barren at the age of twenty-one, had collected numerous stamps by the end of the decade.

No matter who I told about my struggles, no one would believe me. They'd just laugh it off and say, "Oh, Waj, you're just so self-deprecating." I'd counter, "No, really, I'm homeless, and I'm struggling to pay my bills," and, unable to process the information or purely out of discomfort, they'd change the conversation. Eventually, I stopped telling anyone and just kept it all hidden. What was the point? I had one foot in success and the other foot in poverty. Everyone thought I was achieving the American dream while I was living an American nightmare.

For two months, every single job opportunity I pursued was a dead end. Muhajjid uncle, an immigrant from Pakistan who became a successful salesman from scratch, could never understand how I could be an attorney and not make any money. Since I was twenty, I had outworked everyone. I had tried to make the most of my talent and my opportunities. I had a good education. I was careful and frugal. And I had a growing reputation as a writer. But I never had money. I was always financially crippled despite my best efforts. With every success, I found myself warning my family and friends: "The Ali curse will strike. Just watch. It's still chasing me. Too many good things have randomly happened in a row. Something terrible is about to happen." My parents thought I was too cynical.

And it did strike, time and again. But, each time I was about to fall, like Maqbool Nana predicted, some hidden hand from the ghayb, the unseen, lifted me up. Al-Husein, a friend, called me and said the Center for American Progress, a think tank in DC, was looking for a lead writer and researcher to do a report on Islamophobia, which eventually became "Fear, Inc.: The Roots of the Islamophobia Network in America." They had me on the short list and were following my career but didn't know if I'd be interested. Considering I was broke and living in a bedroom with my mom, I said, "Sure, I'll do it." They hired me for almost nothing, but it was money, an opportunity, and an activity that at least kept me busy. In addition, around this time, writer Dave Eggers called me and said HBO was after him to pitch a series. We had previously worked together on a piece for *McSweeney's*, the publication he founded based in San Francisco. Dave had read a *New York Times* article about Muslim immigrant cops joining the force and wondered if we could create a genre cop show as a Trojan horse to introduce a complex Muslim protagonist. He asked me to come up with an idea and pitch it with him. Two days later, we're on the phone with HBO trying to sell them on a dramatic show about a young, brilliant Yemeni Muslim detective in the Bay Area who is navigating the "old-boy" racism of his San Francisco Police Department while fielding suspicion and mistrust from his own community. An executive at HBO told me, "We have over a hundred fifty years of experience here and, literally, no one has ever heard of you. But, we like the idea and we like Dave, so we'll give you guys a contract to submit three drafts of a pilot."

Every few months, Dave and I would work on a draft, turn it in, split the payment, and I'd get enough money to survive for a while.

My mother and I had to bide time until March 10, 2011. That's when my mother had to self-report to prison.

It's strange driving your own mother to prison. It was a calm, Bay Area morning. Nothing memorable or extraordinary. We got up, had a simple breakfast. She drank her chai. She had said goodbye to Mujjahid Chacha and his kids the night before. We went in my '97 Camry on

680 North toward Dublin. There were no melodramatic speeches, no confessions or regrets uttered, no promises or grandiose statements. We tried to find and enjoy the humor in it, all of it, but very little was to be found. I kept telling her inshallah one day this will end and just to have faith. This, too, shall pass. She put on a brave face, wiped away some tears, and nodded.

I walked with her through the office door. She checked in. The officers asked her to step through the gate and walk through the metal detector. We gave each other a hug. She walked forward, looked back to wave, and for the next three and a half years I only saw her during my weekend visits to jail.

Soon afterward, my father was transferred from the Santa Rita penitentiary in Dublin, California, to a low-security camp in Oregon. Even though I wouldn't be able to see him, we knew this was a blessing and he'd be able to survive three to four years there in less severe and punishing conditions.

My aunt by this time had lost her home due to her declining health and financial resources, but we still had to take care of Dadi. A family friend, Afshan aunty, respected my grandmother and always felt terrible about what happened to our family. She needed renters as her teenage kids were going to college and she thought it would be a win-win. My grandmother, my aunt, and I stayed there for several months until we were able to find a nearby apartment in Fremont. We pooled money and somehow we were able to pay rent and take care of the bills.

By the fall of 2011, I was being invited to give more keynote addresses. I picked up projects here and there. I could at least take care of our basic necessities. From nothing, to having money for two weeks, to having money for the month, I now had enough savings to survive for one and a half months!

I was moving on up!

Until I almost died—again.

I Strongly Recommend Having a Near-Death Experience

Throughout my twenties, I always felt I was being chased. Like I was in the horror movie *It Follows*, unable to see a malevolent force or act of nature that I knew, deep in my bones, nonetheless was coming after me. I had to outrun it. I had limited time, and I just knew it would get me despite my best efforts.

I have no physical proof or documentary footage of jinns and poltergeists doing morning stretches before embarking on their daily run to chase me. I just had a hunch. I also had the advantage of experience. Pakistan tried to get me three times: a hit-and-run accident, pneumonia, and malaria. I was a sick kid with terrible allergies. I had OCD.

An early end felt inevitable. The only question was "How?"

I woke up with my back on the floor of the local 24 Hour Fitness looking up at the young, blonde trainer who was staring at my crotch. My legs were spread apart and I was wearing baggy gym shorts and boxers. I closed my legs and tried to figure out what had happened. "You're awake! Thank God. How are you?" asked a nice man, kneeling beside me. It was the same man who had just told me, "Hey, man. You don't look too hot," as I was sitting on the stationary bike, collecting my breath, before everything went woozy.

Now I was on the floor. My heart was still racing and pounding.

I had just turned thirty-one years old and was relatively healthy. I didn't smoke, drink, or party. I went to the gym pretty frequently and did cardio. I had even lost weight. Earlier that day, I had some free time so I decided to come in to do some light elliptical for about thirty minutes. As soon as I started my mild workout, my heart rate spiked, my head became heavy, and my eyes dimmed. The world around me moved in slow motion. This was a common experience whenever I was about to pass out, but it usually happened gradually and I'd be able to return to a normal state with some breathing exercises. This time, I didn't have the luxury. I knew that if I didn't sit or lie down I'd be knocked out within seconds. The closest thing to a chair I could find was a station-ary bike. I lumbered over there, had that brief chat with the nice man, and next thing I know I'm surrounded by concerned, terrified faces.

A final hereditary gift, or curse, from my father's side was heart arrhythmia. It seems my grandmother, my father, my aunt, and a few of my cousins have all inherited milder forms of this condition where your heart sounds like an experimental tabla playing in a remixed version of *Bitches Brew.*

I had the most severe case of all my family members—something called supraventricular tachycardia, which produces rapid heartbeats even at a resting state. If OCD is caused by an electrical misfiring of the brain, this was an electrical misfiring in the heart. I could be completely relaxed, and randomly my heart rate could spike to 150 beats per min-ute and stay there for an hour. (The normal heart rate for most men is around 60 to 100 beats per minute.) Sometimes my heart rate would just skip around with an irregular rhythm.

The first time this happened was when I was fourteen and fasting during Ramadan. About fifteen minutes before iftar, the sunset meal when Muslims open their daylong fast, I was overcome with exhaustion. My heart rate spiked, and I remember just lying on the couch only to wake up with my family and my cousins standing over me and shouting. I had completely passed out for about 90 seconds. The same thing hap-pened a couple more times in high school. During college, I had a few episodes but I was able to keep myself from passing out. I could now rec-ognize the signs, and I'd sit down, breathe, or lie down to "reset" myself.

The episodes became much more frequent after I turned twenty-four. I remember playing soccer with a bunch of colleagues and students during law school. I sat down on the bleachers to catch my breath, and the next thing you know thirty of my peers were hovering over me, with a few convinced I was going into cardiac arrest or dying. "Hey, guys. It's all good! I know that was scary, but I just have this condition, where, like my heart rate just randomly spikes, and sometimes it causes me to pass out, but the good news is when I do, it resets it! So now I'm all good!" I said, with a big smile.

My cardiologist recommended I go for an ablation, a heart surgery where they take electrodes through your groin and up to your heart to eliminate the faulty electrical pathways. I was down for it, but my father with his OCD and trauma kept researching alternative treatments and exercises. My episodes were only a nuisance at that stage, and I wasn't above the age of fifty, so no one was worried about strokes resulting from blood clots. So I indulged him and decided to postpone it.

"Yeah, I should've gotten that ablation," I thought to myself as the EMT came and two paramedics took me inside the ambulance. They checked my heart rate. "Whoa!" the young paramedic said after seeing 220 bpm on the screen. She checked it again and it was around 220 to 235 bpm. They pumped me full of drugs, assuming that would do the trick, as it had in the past. Nope. Heart rate was still at 220 bpm.

They rushed me to Washington Hospital, which thankfully was across the street. My small corner of the emergency room soon became the most popping place on the floor. It was packed with nurses and the emergency room doctor, a man who looked like Danny DeVito with bushier eyebrows and a thick Eastern European accent. The medicine wasn't working so they went for a cardioversion. This is where they send electrical shocks to your heart with the hopes of resetting it. You know that scene in TV shows where they place the paddles on a person's chest and yell "3–2–1. Clear!" (ZAP!)? Yeah, it's just like that. One "ZAP!" usually does the trick.

They had to cardiovert me three times.

You're supposed to be knocked out during the process thanks to the drugs. Of course, I happened to wake up right before each time they zapped me. Being cardioverted is like swallowing an angry, tiny mule that rests in your lungs, digs deep, and then with a violent force kicks its hind legs back, expanding your chest outward. I would not recommend this experience.

None of those electrical shocks worked.

I scanned the room, and the faces of the nurses, techs, and doctor were ghost-white. Usually, when the medical staff looks terrified, it's not a good sign. I started coughing up yellow phlegm and mucus. I couldn't lie down because it felt like I was drowning, so they had me hunched over and I kept vomiting. I had pulmonary edema. My lungs were filled with fluids.

I was having congestive heart failure at the age of thirty-one.

The myth says you see a "tunnel of light" when you're about to make your exit, and your whole life flashes before your eyes. What happens instead is that you just know your time is up. You don't need to ask the doctors or look at the charts. Your body just knows. I've talked to many people who have survived near-death experiences, and there are five common stages.

First, you end up asking for more time. It's clichéd, I know, but that's the first instinct. Doesn't even matter if you're religious, you feel compelled to reach out to the universe and ask for a one-up. "Allah, this can't be it. I need more time!"

Second, you begin bartering. "OK, God, check it, check it. Look, if you give me more time, I *promise* you I'll spend my time being more pious and righteous. I'll help out people more, I'll volunteer, I'll be a better man. I promise."

Third, you realize your pathetic negotiations are getting you nowhere, and your body is telling you time is running out. This is where you do an audit of your life. Everything becomes crystallized, focused, the excess filtered out, and you somehow pinpoint key moments and experiences in life that you haven't thought of in years. I saw a privileged brown Muslim kid who grew up in Fremont, loved by his family, able to see amazing sights around the world, obtain a valuable education, and write and publish his play. I felt I had no standing to whine or complain. These images and thoughts all rushed through my mind like a montage.

Fourth, you think of your relationships and loved ones. I felt bad for my parents and my grandmother. I realized this would pain them greatly. I didn't know if they'd ever be able to recover. I prayed that Allah would give them sabr, some peace, and make it easy for them.

Finally, you think of your relationship with God or the universe. I asked Allah to forgive me for my numerous mistakes and how I wasted so much of my privilege and potential. I felt I could have done so much more, but I just got lost and stuck along the way. Still, I was grateful for everything and thankful for a good life. That's the one thing about faith that the cynics can't knock, even if it is a crutch: it gives hope. It's in those final moments of this long, often difficult journey called life that faith gives you immense comfort. You feel that you are not alone as you exit this Earth—a loving God will embrace you on the other side.

At the end, I did have one regret, though. I kept telling myself I should have invested in a family. I let my fear and pain keep me from opening up and taking a risk in relationships. I assumed that a woman could not, would not, possibly take a chance on me with all my baggage and chaos. Instead, I had just worked, nonstop, day and night, trying my best to write, publish, and work on projects that I hoped would push the needle forward. I should have at least tried to find love. That's what gnawed at me as my heart kept racing at 220+ bpm and liquid was pouring out of me, as my chest felt like raw fire.

As soon as I had this realization, my heart rate stabilized. Another doctor came in and recommended a dosage of a medication and, for whatever fortuitous reason, this time it worked. Just like that. Back to normal. The entire room exhaled. The doctor admitted me to the hospital overnight. The next day, he visited me and said, "Holy shit, man! You really fucking scared us!"

I left the hospital knowing I just got extra time. How can you not be humbled and affected after an experience that nearly left you dead in your oversized gym shorts and white sneakers? Everything looked new again for a few days. I paused and found beauty in the ordinary experiences I took for granted: a child riding a bike for the first time in a park; an elderly Sikh uncle jogging during the afternoon; the taste of a hot cup of freshly made chai; the beautiful tan hills of Fremont; the ability to walk, to laugh, to breathe deeply and fully. After many years, I felt rejuvenated.

If it wasn't for my near-death experience, I wouldn't have finally gotten the ablation, which settled my "electrical misfiring" once and for all. I also wouldn't be married with a family today. Less than a year after that freakish episode, I ended up eloping with Sarah in Washington, DC.

At the age of thirty, before my mother went to prison, she dropped the "immaculate fatwa." While putting the groceries in the trunk of the Camry in the Safeway parking lot, my mother randomly turned to me and said, "You know what? It's OK if you don't marry a Desi girl. Desis have too much drama. You're a simple guy. We won't care if you marry a white girl or whomever. But, it'd be nice if she was Muslim . . . *just saying*." The " . . . you can marry a white girl or whomever" fatwa drops when Desi parents have completely given up hope their thirty-year-old child will ever settle down. Obviously, grown men have the agency and ability to marry, or not marry, whomever they want, but this magical fatwa is a gift from the heavens, and it removes all potential guilt, shame, and passive-aggressive drama from a potential interracial coupling. "Oh, if only I had this fatwa when I was eighteen," I thought to myself. Still, I didn't entertain the idea of dating at the time because I was broke, my father was in jail, my mother was about to go to jail, I was homeless and working like crazy. What woman would ever invest in me?

Sarah was finishing up her residency training in family medicine at UCSF and finalizing her divorce. Despite the fact that she had had two divorces in her twenties—its own kind of social leprosy and stigma for women—every Desi and Muslim man from Fremont to London still desired her. She was a beautiful, brilliant doctor with a CV nearly twelve pages long who was known to be kind, approachable, and humble.

We shared social acquaintances and kept bumping into each other at events. We started talking on GChat, platonic but flirtatious conversations, and one day she hit me with, "Listen, I don't talk to men for this long on GChat unless I'm interested in them, so—." I immediately panicked, apologized for misleading her, and decided to engage in a massive suicide cockblock and remove myself from the equation as a potential love interest. There was just no way I could be in a relationship. There was too much chaos.

Nonetheless, we remained friends over the next year. She moved to DC to do a fellowship in community health. I kept going to DC to do research for a report I was working on about the Islamophobia industry, and each time our mutual group of friends used to hang out. Her friends Uzma and Lena kept playing the role of Muslim Cupids, whispering flattering insinuations about me to Sarah for months while telling me that Sarah was the one girl who wouldn't mind that I was broke and that she would actually marry me for love.

After my near-death experience, I knew I had to allow myself to open up to the possibility of happiness and love and expose myself to pain if necessary. I decided to take a bold step. I told Uzma to ask Sarah if it was OK for me to approach her with the intention of "talking to her." Uzma laughed for three minutes and then said, "You're such an idiot. Why are you such a fool? Both of you! My God, man, of course she'll be OK with it! Oh, my God! I can't believe I have to tolerate both of you!"

Uzma informed me that Sarah agreed to "talk," so I gave her a call that same night. For the first few minutes, it was as hilariously awkward as you can imagine where two platonic friends are now formally talking to each other with the potential of maybe creating a romantic relationship, but after some laughs, a conversation started flowing, about our hopes, our futures, and what we imagined a successful marriage and partnership would be like. We talked for three hours. After three days and three very long phone calls, I knew. (When you know, you know.) By the start of the fourth phone call, I said in a very romantic and poetic way, "Listen, I love you. I want to marry you. So, let's just do this, OK?"

Like I said, very romantic. So smooth. A month later, we were married with our parents' blessing. My parents remembered meeting her one time at my cousin's birthday party a few years before in Fremont. She had played Ping-Pong with my mother. They were impressed by her, and my mom even remarked, "You know, beta, you should marry a girl like that one day."

Now, both my parents were in jail but were highly supportive of the marriage. Fortuitously, I met her parents when they were visiting Fremont. Sarah's brother had just married a woman who lived there, and they all came up from Florida to visit her family. Sarah flew in from DC and told me to come have lunch with them at Shalimar Restaurant in Fremont. Later, I took them to Fenton's Ice Creamery in Oakland, where her father asked about my parents' arrest, which he had read about, just to satisfy his curiosity and concerns. Neither of them mocked or judged me, or made condescending or cruel remarks, and at the end of my tale they felt bad for what we had endured. Instead, her mother's only request was that I would promise to love and respect her daughter. Her parents had their own trauma of seeing Sarah divorced twice within ten years. Thank God for low bars.

My mom lent me her wedding ring, because I was too poor to afford one, and told me to retrieve it from the safety deposit box at the Chase bank in Fremont. It fit Sarah perfectly. When we married in 2012, all I had was a '97 Toyota Camry without a driver's-side door handle, the black Samsonite bag I used for my *Domestic Crusaders* travels, a PS3, some clothes, some books, and about $600 left in the bank account.

For our wedding night, I took Sarah to Ravi Kabob in Arlington and we had the "Ravi Kabob Special" with boneless chicken boti and seekh kabab. The total was under $20, and she was very happy with the meal. We went to her apartment, made love, and watched *Conan the Barbarian* on TV.

I promised Sarah that one day I would "make it rain" and to just be patient and that I had a lot of potential despite having very little at the moment. She looked at me and said, "Wajahat, I'm not marrying you for your potential. I'm marrying you for the man you are right now." I immediately recognized I was a very lucky man.

After years of sadness and despair, I felt joy again. I didn't have to imagine the possibility of starting again, I was living it. I was no longer alone. I was writing the next chapter with my wife. This was my rebirth.

And then Dadi passed away.

My Heart

Dadi by this time was in her eighties, and over the past several years, I had frequently driven her to the hospital for her multiple appointments since her son and daughter-in-law were both behind bars. The doctors and nurses all knew us by name. She was a regular customer. She told us she kept living to see her son one last time and to see me marry a good woman who would love me.

I was able to fulfill one of her wishes.

Before I eloped with Sarah, I asked for Dadi's blessings, and she promised to keep my wedding a secret. I flew to DC, married Sarah, and went on a five-week work trip for the State Department, where I was an independent consultant hired to teach storytelling, social media, and leadership skills to young change agents in three countries. I enjoyed our honeymoon in the Maldives, Nepal, and Sri Lanka using Skype to connect with my new bride in the morning and night. Instead of moving to DC, I returned home to Fremont. I told Sarah I couldn't leave Dadi while my parents were in jail. She agreed and said we'd make it work long-distance.

Dadi wanted a proper wedding celebration for her beloved grandson and new bahoo. She said she would borrow money if she had to, but she couldn't just sit and welcome my wife without any festivities. I adamantly refused. There was no way I would indulge in the ridiculous and hypocritical pomp and circumstance of a traditional wedding, inviting people who for the most part had abandoned us to celebrate as my parents sat in jail. Dadi marshaled all her South Asian powers to induce guilt—which were considerable and fearsome—to turn my hardened heart, but I was a stubborn goat, proud and unyielding.

We finally agreed on two big buckets of halal KFC, a tray of haleem, and some shami kabobs. Sarah visited in November, about three months after our wedding, to finally meet Dadi and Phuppo. Dadi was ecstatic. She embraced and kissed Sarah, gave her a piece of her own jewelry and some nice South Asian clothes. She made me buy mithai (sweets) and flowers. Dadi invited Khalil uncle and Wasia aunty, our relatives who lived close by, to partake in the festivities. Sarah is the daughter of a doctor, but she was raised in Okeechobee, Florida, to humble, immigrant parents who weren't ostentatious or elite. She went to the local public high school and grew up with mostly non-Muslim friends from middle-class neighborhoods who enjoyed the local rodeo, running track, shooting guns, drinking sweet tea, and making homemade videos in her spacious front yard. She thought this was better than any fancy party. Who could go wrong with halal KFC, haleem, and shami kabobs?

We all felt joy—and for my grandmother and me, it was the first time in a long time. My grandmother smiled the way I remembered before the great unraveling. When Dada was alive. When we were all in the big, brown, triangle house in Fremont. That smile.

"You know, Wajahat, he's my heart," she told Sarah. "My heart," she repeated in her accented English, tapping her chest.

A month later, we buried her.

I traveled to Cincinnati, Ohio, for a speech, and on the way back I stopped in DC to spend time with Sarah. My aunt had assured me that Dadi was recuperating from her heart valve surgery. She had encouraged me to go to the speech, make money, and see Sarah on the way back. I told them if anything, God forbid, went wrong to immediately let me know and I'd come home. I called Dadi, and she picked up the phone from the hospital and said she felt fine and was looking forward to seeing me in two days.

Within half an hour of that phone call she suffered a massive stroke. The right side of her face and body went numb. She couldn't speak. Her brain was hemorrhaging. My aunt informed our family members, and my cousins, who grew up with me in Fremont and were living in LA, flew in to be with their dying grandmother.

Dadi's face lit up when she saw me enter the room. The 49ers and Patriots game was on TV. Kaepernick carved up Brady and New England that Sunday. I told everyone they could take a break, and I'd spend time with Dadi. She kept looking up at me, and I assured her everything would be fine. I caressed her arms and that lovely mound of underarm fat that I played with as a kid. She smiled and fell asleep.

She never woke up again.

During those final few days before she took her last breath, I desperately tried to have my father released on a furlough to attend the funeral. I got referrals, letters, help from attorney friends, and frantically called his correctional facility to go through all the procedures. At the last second, the warden denied the request. My father was shattered.

Hundreds came to pray for her at her funeral. I was shocked to see so many old, familiar faces. People who had come to our homes during our religious events and song parties in the '80s were there. People who abandoned us a decade ago were there. People who were cruel, people who were kind, people who were acquaintances. Our entire past came out to show respect. The only ones not there were my parents. Sarah flew in to be with me, and she took my mother's place to help wash and clean the body.

Muslim men lend their shoulder and carry the casket to the grave. Then, close family members, usually two or three people, step inside the grave and help place the body in the dirt. I was the first one in the grave and I was the last one out. I remember how light her body felt. We live an entire life only to depart wearing a simple, white shroud. I gave her a kiss on the forehead and left the grave, rejoining the living, those of us left behind.

My father called the day of the funeral. It was one of only two times I've ever heard him cry. Both times he apologized, and I assured him there was nothing to apologize about. A son is allowed to cry for his dead mother. A son should bury his mother, not miss the funeral because he is behind bars. The cost of the curse, the nazr, the jadu, the bad choices, it became too much.

One day, the white towel would have to be thrown from the heavens. It was time.

My mother was released in July 2014 after serving three and a half years in prison. She wore an ankle bracelet for three months. I had already moved to Virginia by this time to be with Sarah and build a new life, my own life. Ami initially stayed at Shaheen aunty's house where Kashif and I made all those homemade movies. A year later, my father was released. My parents then stayed in a room at the house of Riffat and Arshad uncle, who had stayed in touch over the years and always assisted when asked.

After a few months, they moved into a small home, where they rent a room and the generous landlord lets them pretty much use the entire first floor.

My parents went into prison optimistic and hopeful and left the same way. There are no prison tats and six-pack abs. If they are bitter and resentful at the universe, they don't show it. They didn't make a *Kill Bill* list and vow revenge. They don't curse all the people who stabbed them in the back and did gheebat. They didn't weep over all their lost possessions or lose their faith in God.

In fact, my parents consider themselves lucky. Both of them say that things are much worse for most people. They say, "Look at people who are tortured, or look at innocent people who spent years in Guantanamo. At least we are alive and able to get out." My father remains defensive about the litigation against the government and Microsoft, but it's more disgust than rage. My mom doesn't spend any energy on it.

They are humbled and more aware. In prison, my mother shared a room with four other incarcerated people. Everyone at the camp referred to her as "Mrs. Ali" out of respect. She became an ESL teacher for women who were trying to learn English. She also taught knitting classes. She said she found those experiences and relationships with other women to be very rewarding. These were resourceful, intelligent women. Many were in there for drug offenses. A majority happened to be African American, Latina, or Native American. My mother was never a fan of the US criminal justice system, but after enduring the prison experience, she is convinced it is cruel and ineffective. It crushes poor women, especially women of color, who sometimes just need some counseling, help, and kindness.

I asked my mom if she thinks being Muslim and Pakistani immigrants worked against them. "Being brown? For sure. They nailed us. In prison, we were all minorities mostly, and it was post 9/11," she said. My father's language is more blunt and coarse when talking about the criminal justice system. You will hear words like "corrupt," "racist," "broken," and "flawed."

My father became the imam of the Muslims in the Oregon camp. They asked him to lead the weekly Jummah Friday prayers where he gave the khutbah, or sermon. Fifteen incarcerated people asked my father to help them become Muslim by reciting the shahada. He also taught business classes and English as a second language.

The "dream" finally made sense to me. Why did my grandfather take me to the barber shop? Cutting the hair in some Native American tribes signifies remembering and acknowledging the loss of a loved one, and the growth of new hair represents the continuation of life after their passing. As Maqbool Nana had told me years ago, in Islam, there is a tradition of cutting your hair after completing the Hajj, the pilgrimage to Mecca, symbolizing a spiritual rebirth. My hair was cut.

For me, it meant I survived. I was exorcised. I was cleansed, standing anew after a forceful and painful shedding of my youth and innocence. I emerged from that awful decade. Wiser, older, scarred, but still alive. I still feel anxiety whenever I return to the Bay Area and remember the past. I can never feel completely at ease. The bad memories remain and sometimes cloud all the years of good. But, I'm trying. I'm still trying to let go.

Maybe it will help me re-create that perfect sleep.

★ Chapter 9

Elect a Muslim President, but Beware of Economic Anxiety

Like many immigrant parents who came here after 1965, my parents unconsciously chased Whiteness for most of their lives. They didn't admit it because they weren't even aware of it. Prison made them realize they were actually always closer to Blackness. They were now stamped as alumni of the prison industrial complex like so many Black and brown people in this country. If anything, they have emerged much more progressive in their politics, advocating for criminal justice reform, immigration reform, racial justice, and higher taxes on the rich. They've survived the horrors of prison. They've seen firsthand the tragedy that inequity produces.

All of that didn't keep them from being shocked by the emergence into the limelight of an American politician with the Blackest and most Muslim-y name ever: Barack Hussein Obama.

The only way it could be even Blacker and more Muslim-y would be if he added a Muhammad at the beginning and an X at the end. It was our inshallah Hail Mary pass and Mashallah Immaculate Reception at the same time. Muslims joked that we went from invading and toppling a statue of one Hussein in the Middle East to elevating another to the highest office in the land all within the same decade.

Go ahead, roll your eyes all you want, but many Americans after all this time still believe Obama is a Muslim, or they aren't sure about his religion.

If President Barack Hussein Obama is a Muslim, let me assure you the dude is the worst Muslim of all time. He eats bacon openly, drinks alcohol, never recites the Quran while facing Mecca, believes Jesus Christ is his savior, goes to church, and says he is a Christian. It's safe to say we won't be naming him our caliph after we take over America one Subway and halal food cart at a time.

Remember the lady in the red shirt? At a town hall meeting in Lakeville, Minnesota, in October 2008, she said, "I can't trust Obama. I have read about him, and he's not, um, he's an Arab."

Senator McCain cut her off, grabbed her microphone, and replied, "No, ma'am. He's a decent family man [and] citizen that I just happen to have disagreements with on fundamental issues, and that's what the campaign's all about. He's not [an Arab]."

When Senator McCain passed away in September 2018, this clip was used to hearken back to a political climate of civility and mutual respect. McCain was praised for interrupting the lady in the red shirt and defending Obama from racist slurs. He stood in direct contrast to the 45th president, who said, "I think Islam hates us."

While watching that clip, I realized two things. One, the birther conspiracy conflated Obama with being Arab and Muslim and Black, all interchangeable, and made him appear to be an insidious villain with a secret anti-American plot. Second, although most of America thought McCain's interjection was praiseworthy, it was actually *kinda offensive* to the rest of us.

I mean, why can't an Arab, and by extension a Muslim, be "a decent family man [and] citizen?" I would have loved for McCain to have instead said, "He is not Arab. Even if he were, that doesn't give us an excuse to be racist or doubt his loyalty and love for this country."

It took a Republican and one of the architects of the War on Terror, General Colin Powell, to come out and finally say the right words on national television. Two weeks before the 2008 election, the former secretary of state appeared on *Meet the Press* and asked:

Is there something wrong with being a Muslim in this country? The answer's no, that's not America. Is there something wrong with some seven-year-old Muslim American kid believing that he or she could be president? Yet, I have heard some senior members of my own party drop the suggestion, "[Obama] is a Muslim and he might be associated with terrorists." This is not the way we should be doing it in America.

I really appreciated General Powell's comments, even though for me it wasn't enough to absolve his complicity in the disaster he helped create in Iraq and Afghanistan. Regardless, most Muslim Americans welcomed and celebrated his words. Many who voted for President Bush and Republicans eight years prior—assuming that Bush would be the most pro-Muslim president ever—had been shellshocked by the seven-year hazing unleashed by his administration after 9/11. In 2008, the overwhelming majority had learned from their mistake and voted Democrat.

Still, we had to confront the problem of electing a Black Christian man with an "ethnic" name who might lose critical votes in battleground states because white voters were afraid he belonged to our religious tribe. "Rust Belt voters," by the way, should include Blacks, Latinos, Asians, and Muslims, but the term usually refers only to white Christian voters. To court this coveted demographic during the intense 2008 Democratic primary, Hillary Clinton wore flannel shirts and drank beer in Midwestern pubs, while Obama rolled up his sleeves and threw a bowling ball. For many of those voters, nothing these candidates could ever say or do would matter because one had ovaries and the other was Black.

On the other hand, we Muslims didn't get Clinton drinking chai with us while wearing a colorful, pashmina hijab, or Obama playing basketball with a bunch of brothers after Jummah prayer while wearing a kufi and dhikr beads around his wrist.

Nope. We were treated like a contagious venereal disease. During the 2008 campaign, Muslims and Islam were worse than herpes. If you hung around it too often you might catch it. We would linger forever and ruin your political life. That's how it felt to those of us desperately trying to get out the vote for Obama and throw the atrocious Bush administration into the dustbin of history, or at least catapult him into a successful painting career. President Obama's campaign volunteers removed two Muslim women wearing hijab who were standing behind the podium at his Detroit, Michigan, rally in the summer of 2008 so they wouldn't appear in photographs.

Two months before the election, I was given a free ticket by my friend to a ridiculously expensive Silicon Valley fundraiser for Obama that I otherwise would never have been able to afford. It was attended by Howard Dean, the chairman of the Democratic National Committee at the time. I asked him why the Democrats weren't openly embracing Muslim voters and doing more to push back against anti-Muslim fear-mongering. "Why? The election is just two months away," he replied sternly.

The fundraiser was hosted and attended by Muslim Americans.

You want our votes and our money, but you don't want to date us publicly? Got it. That was the message. But for the sake of the country we decided to take the humiliation.

In America, communities of color have always put our "economic anxieties" second to placate the economic anxieties of "real Americans" from the "Rust Belt." We just pray and hope they will do the right thing and vote for a qualified candidate who *doesn't* want to put babies in camps. Sometimes it works, and other times we get Trump. If we are to be honest with ourselves, the group that has historically always played identity politics is white voters, and the rest of us have been hijacked by their rage, fear, and anxiety. Theirs are the grievances of "regular Americans from the heartland." When we voice our concerns, we are "playing the race card," engaging in victimhood, not pulling ourselves up by our bootstraps, abusing political correctness, and enforcing cancel culture and affirmative action.

Even though President Obama and Democrats didn't openly embrace us, we embraced them. An overwhelming majority of Muslim Americans again voted for our alleged brother in Islam in 2012 when he ran for reelection. Obama's farewell tour was bittersweet. Unlike other Obama voters, I never held him to be the Chosen One or the progressive savior. He behaved exactly like I thought he would. He was a center-left Democrat who was intelligent, cautious, and spent far too many years playing nice with an obstructionist Republican Party that was committed to making him a one-term president.

I compared Obama to an Etch A Sketch. You could impose upon him whatever you wanted. He was *your* American dream. That was the beauty of the "hope and change" message emblazoned on his face. He was the promise of what America could be and become for everyone if the nation overcame its racism and cruelty. A scrawny kid born to a Muslim Kenyan father and a white mother, who grew up in Indonesia, ate biryani with his Pakistani roommate in college, and graduated from Harvard Law School, ended up being one of the most beloved politicians in the modern era and the most powerful man in the world.

Maybe a Pakistani kid could become president? If America voted for Obama twice, then why not our kids? *That* was the power of Obama. He allowed the nation to imagine "What If?" Commentators, mostly white, said Obama's election proved that America was now a "post-racial society."

But a Black man had ascended to the White House and "replaced" forty-three previous white men. A Black man and his Black family had "replaced" a white family and were now sleeping in the White House once occupied by the Founding Fathers. Historically, whenever Black people and people of color made progress in America, the demons of white rage would rise with a fury to choke and wrestle this country back to 1953, before *Brown v. Board of Education of Topeka*. It was inevitable that Obama's election would unleash and invigorate the same malevolent forces that had always existed and corrupted America's promise for the rest of us. I knew it. Many people of color knew it and lived it. Even Obama knew it.

During the first year of his presidency, Obama addressed Muslims overseas at Cairo University and gave his first foreign interview to Al Arabiyya, but visiting a mosque at home was too toxic until the man was literally about to leave office. Unlike President Bush, Obama didn't step inside a Muslim American mosque until the final year of his presidency in 2016, just as Donald Trump was campaigning on a Muslim Ban.

President Obama addressed the crowd of Muslims gathered at the Islamic Center of Baltimore and urged the country not to give in to fear and hate. He left us with a warning: "We will rise and fall together."

Muslims were finally invited to the party. We had finally made it. Some of us actually believed we were wanted. Our invitation was about to be rudely revoked right as we were about to walk through the front door.

Economic Anxiety for Them, Perpetual Anxiety for Us

I was in New York City at the Democratic headquarters waiting for the results and covering the 2016 election for the *Huffington Post*. I was looking forward to the balloons dropping from the Javits Center ceiling. Hillary Clinton would be announced as the first female president of the United States of America. The balloons would gently fall down, there would be mirth and alcohol, and the world could exhale without ever wasting another precious moment worrying that an incompetent buffoon and reality-TV star could come so close to occupying the Oval Office.

Sixty-three million Americans voted for the former host of *The Apprentice*. The man who promoted the "birther" conspiracy. The guy who bragged on the *Access Hollywood* tape about grabbing women by the pussy.

I was disappointed and shocked by the election, but I was also reporting and maintained my professional composure. I had training as the "Muslim ambassador" and "Muslim fireman" after 9/11. All of us had endured the trauma and failure of the Bush administration, and despite all the chaos, it eventually led to eight years of Obama. Maybe communities could unite and resist four years of Trump? Maybe we could emerge stronger, if somehow we survived it? If anything, I attempted to give the viewers some hope and perspective. I said something like the Earth will continue to spin on its axis and tomorrow we will wake up and still be alive and all is not lost.

Most journalists of color knew it was predominantly racism that was the primary driver for Trump's base. We also knew we were in for a rough four years. Trump was going to go forward with his useless wall across the southern border, his war on immigrants, his Muslim Ban, and his tax cuts for the rich.

I covered the Democratic National Convention held in Philadelphia in 2016 for the *Huffington Post* and asked both Clinton and Trump supporters if they would come visit me in the Muslim camps if Trump were elected. I was mostly serious. Most of the white interviewees laughed, said that was silly, and furthermore believed that his proposed Muslim Ban was just a political ploy to win the election. It would never happen, they said. Black people I interviewed knew it could go down. Thankfully, everybody, including Republicans, promised they'd help smuggle in halal cheese steaks.

I've even had this conversation with a few Muslim voters for Trump. (Yes, they exist.) Many I talked to were for him because he was going to be great for the economy, offered lower taxes for the wealthy, and was going to be tough against the "bad immigrants," referring to the undocumented and Mexican laborers who, according to them, take welfare and don't contribute to America. They also believed that the Republican Party, led by a man who said his personal Vietnam was not getting sexually transmitted diseases, would promote "family values" such as ending abortion and gay marriage.

However, America's gatekeepers weren't ready to acknowledge the primary driving factors behind Trump's win. Instead, we were deluged with endless commentaries and stories on the alleged "economic anxiety" of the white working class that felt betrayed by elites and fell into the arms of Trump. This disproven theory is like the Freddy Krueger and Michael Myers of American politics, incapable of dying, always coming back to haunt us in reboots and sequels.

It's funny how enduring poverty and economic ruin didn't transform me and so many other people of color into racists and xenophobes who committed a violent insurrection against the country and overtook the U.S. Capitol on January 6, 2021, or maybe we're just unique and come from a better "culture" and "civilization"?

For the past five years, the research has consistently shown that racial resentment was the most important factor in driving Republican voters for Trump. Specifically, a 2019 study concluded that "the nativist narrative about 'taking back America' and anti-immigrant sentiment became stronger forces than economic issues" for Trump voters.

I didn't see much "economic anxiety" when I interviewed Trump supporters at a Maine rally a month before the election. For nine hours, I was immersed in an ocean of diversity. There was every type of white under the sun. Any and every white you could imagine had assembled for Trump. I talked to bikers for Trump, veterans for Trump, suburban moms for Trump, college kids for Trump, gun owners for Trump, business owners for Trump, seniors for Trump. It was a buffet of Whiteness. I talked to as many of them as I could. None expressed "economic anxiety" as their primary motivation for voting Trump. They loved how he was "politically incorrect," and "hit back" and "took on the libs" and "kept it real" and "wasn't afraid" and "took on the elite." They didn't apologize for his racism, but excused it as him being an equal opportunity bigot. The xenophobia and sexism were like a *Pulp Fiction* adrenaline needle right to the heart. "Oh, he takes on everyone. That's why I love him," a white biker told me. Trump didn't take on White supremacists or Putin, who interfered in the US election, but that was somehow fine.

In front of me was a middle-aged father in glasses, dressed in a yellow polo shirt and khakis. From appearances, he appeared to be upper middle class. He was accompanied by his son, who was around ten years old. He looked up to his father for cues, following his lead, clapping and

hooting in sync as Trump addressed the fawning crowd. He kept looking for affirmation, and his father every so often would look down and
nod and the boy would smile. I'll never forget it. "Economic anxiety" is
performed, taught, mimicked, and passed on from father to son, generation to generation. It's an American birthright.

Even the rich suffered from it.

In 2017, I was invited by the Aspen Forum to discuss "Racism in
America" after Trump's election. Aspen is wild. It's the winter getaway
for the rich and powerful, who take their private planes to their vacation homes to ski on the gorgeous slopes. It's called "Billionaire Mountain." It's where the 1 percent, the insanely wealthy and white, hang
out and relax. I was invited to this small gathering by a millennial staff
member who specifically wanted me to talk honestly and bluntly about
the challenges of being Muslim and a person of color during the Trump
administration. I knew I had to ease the crowd into the triggering topics
of "white supremacy" and "white privilege."

I used kid gloves. I used humor. I took my time, carefully parsing out
the nuances. About ten minutes in, I hit them with "white privilege."
As soon as I said it, I saw the face of one of the attendees contort, like
I had stabbed her with a fire poker of rage right in her cold heart. Let's
just call her Aspen Karen. I lost her right there and then.

Sometime after my talk, I had the chance to speak with her one-on-
one. Our conversation was a beautiful microcosm of every awkward,
painful conversation I've had with white women when it comes to
racism. Aspen Karen never raised her voice but kept shooting arrows
through every loaded, subtle comment. She talked about "meritocracy"
and how everyone she knows became wealthy through hard work. She
said "the most qualified" are the ones who get the leadership positions,
which explains, of course, how white men and women are always at the
top. She recommended I read Hillbilly Elegy and offered to set up a public discussion between me and its author, J. D. Vance.

I gave her my email address and told her to contact me anytime. I'm
still waiting for the email.

I'm sure she doesn't consider herself racist. In fact, I've yet to encounter anyone in America who has openly admitted to being a racist. Nothing is more offensive to an American than being called a racist. We'll forgive you sooner for punching our mother in the throat or kicking our beloved puppy in the face. Even white supremacists don't consider themselves to be racist. They're just "racial realists" or "American Identitarians" who believe in preserving the purity of the white identity.

Trying to call out racism in America is like being trapped in that classic *Twilight Zone* episode where William Shatner was the only flight passenger able to see the horrifying goblin trying to destroy the plane. He tried his best to warn the other passengers, but everyone thought he was crazy. At the end of the episode, he is taken away in a straitjacket as the camera pans to reveal a damaged airplane wing. This is how I felt. My terror wasn't at 20,000 feet. It was at ground level in the United States of America.

Many journalists, writers, and academics of color, including myself, called out the goblin from the start. My eyes were always wide open, but I never took any joy in being a brown Cassandra. During the 2018 midterm elections, instead of touting the country's economic success to rally support for Republicans, Trump zeroed in on a single message: he will protect Americans from the impending "invasion" of a migrant caravan filled with undocumented Latino immigrants, Middle Easterners, and terrorists. We now had the president of the United States openly promoting a fringe conspiracy theory that originated among white supremacists.

The same month that Trump and right-wing media incessantly warned Americans about an "invasion" that never occurred, Robert Gregory Bowers walked into the Tree of Life Synagogue in Pittsburgh during Sunday services and killed eleven people. On Gab, a social network used by right-wing extremists, he posted rants accusing "the filthy evil Jews" for "bringing the filthy evil Muslims into the country." Hours before the shooting, Bowers posted, "[Hebrew Immigrant Aid Society] likes to bring invaders in that kill our people. I can't sit by and watch my people get slaughtered. Screw your optics, I'm going in." A domestic terrorist echoed the same exact language and manufactured fear of "invaders" as the president and used it as justification to murder eleven innocent people. A terrorist had walked into a synagogue and committed a massacre. What would stop another from shooting up a church, like white supremacist Dylann Roof had done in Charleston in 2015?

Or a mosque?

For the first time, my neighborhood mosque hired armed security during Friday prayers. Local synagogues started doing the same for their services. There was something absolutely unnerving about seeing a buffed Afghan-American man with a Glock 19 around his waist, vigilantly scanning the mosque parking lot. I had lived in this country for three decades, and this was the second time people felt afraid to go to their houses of worship; the first was right after the 9/11 terror attacks. These extremists were united in their hatred of all of us: Muslims, Jews, Blacks, Latinos, and immigrants of color. Again, if you haven't noticed, bigots aren't really into nuance.

After Trump's election, I was invited more frequently to give commentary on CNN and MSNBC, quickly gaining favor with the producers and hosts for being "good TV," which meant I came in prepared, could speak in short, punchy sound bites, and had chemistry with the hosts. They kept introducing me as "Muslim journalist—Wajahat Ali," even though I was not part of an interfaith panel or theological debate about monotheism. I was invited to discuss politics, current affairs, and the Trump administration. When was the last time you ever heard anyone announce a reporter as "Here's the Christian journalist . . ." and now let's bring out the "Jewish journalist"? Even viewers called it out on social media. I just smiled.

I was also told that I was funny. In my experience, many gatekeepers are shocked that practicing Muslims have a sense of humor. In New York City several years ago, a successful literary agent, who is well traveled, intelligent, and a graduate from an Ivy League university, was courting me as a potential client. He took me to a fancy seafood restaurant after reading a few articles I had written in *Salon* and the *Guardian*. He admitted, "You know, I just didn't know Muslims could be funny. I mean, it's a stupid thing to say, of course you can be funny, but I just assumed you are, you know, like—"

"Constipated?" I asked, going off the pained and stern expression on his face.

"No, no, just very, very . . . serious," he replied.

Then he went on a five-minute monologue interrogating himself as to why he would actually make that assumption and how it was unfortunate and that he actually knows Muslims, and they are funny. During this entire time I just kept nodding, and most of my attention was captured by the delicious branzino fish and delectable grilled octopus I was having for the first time.

A few years ago at an interfaith event in New York, I told the crowd of white liberals that being Muslim in front of them often felt like being stared at by curious and terrified zoologists who are amazed I learned how to lift my knuckles off the ground and walk erect for the first time. The audience responded with awkward silence.

After years of my being seen predominantly as some combination of an exotic zoo animal and commentator on all things Muslim, Chris Hayes of MSNBC invited me on his evening show to talk about the future of the Democratic Party. That's it. The conversation had nothing to do with Trump bashing Muslims or Islamophobia. It was so . . . refreshing. I was called to do my job as a writer and commentator, a student and witness to American politics, invited based on my skill and expertise. I wasn't "the Muslim guy," or "the funny Muslim guy," or "the liberal Muslim guy." I was just a guy. An American guy. It was liberating. This is what Whiteness feels like. It's like having Red Bull coursing in your veins. It gives you wings. You can just be.

I was no longer just talking about Muslims, Islam, Ramadan, Hajj, or terrorism. I was talking about the news of the day and American politics. I was holding court with superstars and I was doing just fine. My numerous appearances finally gave me respect with my Pakistani community. There's something about appearing on CNN that finally vaults you to "respectable" status in the eyes of immigrant uncles. My play didn't do it. The speeches didn't do it. Even writing in the *New York Times* failed to accomplish it. But being on CNN, interviewed by

Anderson Cooper, holding my own, that's what squeezed that pure tear of pride from their stingy eye.

"That Wajahat. I knew him since he was a little boy. He was very fat, but a good boy," they said, finally acknowledging my existence.

Still, I had concerned community leaders give me unsolicited advice. "Don't be too passionate! They'll think you're angry!" they said. "Wait, I never get angry," I replied. "No, but you become excited and energetic, and then the people will think you have rage," they countered.

Again with "the people." Colonialism, and Whiteness, does wonders. It infects your bones, your very soul, making you a self-conscious performer your entire life, always wary and aware of Sauron's gaze. We have to always police our emotions to placate the assumed anxieties and fears of "the people." We were not even allowed righteous rage as Trump spread hateful conspiracy theories and promoted a Muslim Ban. We were not allowed to be "mad as hell" and "politically incorrect." Respectability politics trumps all. Meanwhile, my mother's only comments after every TV appearance were that I slouched and that they messed up my makeup.

Covering the Trump administration as a Muslim made me feel like I could join Cirque du Soleil if they accepted overweight individuals skilled at mental gymnastics.

Many in the media played the "both-sides" sporting game, creating a false equivalence between two competing teams, normalizing the president's racism and outright cruelty. I always thought it was maddening and downright comical that throughout the four years of Trump's presidency his racism was sugar-coated by white colleagues as "racial flare-ups," "inflammatory rhetoric," and "racially charged" language.

What over-the-counter medicine is recommended to deal with the inconvenient, occasional "racial flare-up"? Whitewash?

After a while, it becomes journalistic malpractice to play Taboo and not to call something for what it actually is.

When people asked me why the media engaged in absurd double standards with Trump, often giving him a free pass for his obnoxious conduct and racism, they expected me to reply with "because of the ratings," or "access," or "future book deals," or "proximity to power." Certainly, all were true. I recall being in the CNN green room in DC, waiting to go on-air, and chatting it up with a reporter of color. I was lamenting how toxic Trump's presidency had been both for journalists and for people of color, as he riled up his base in a frenzy against us. "Yeah, but it's all good for our careers. I mean, I get on TV a lot more now," she replied, finishing the last touch of makeup before heading into the studio.

I was on set in New York for a CNN roundtable in which we finished a discussion about Trump's latest "racially charged" outburst. He had just told four progressive Congresswomen of color to "go back and help fix the totally broken and crime infested places from which they came." All four are U.S. citizens, and three of them were born in America. The host of that particular show turned to me and said, "You know, I really don't think Trump is a racist. He's just doing this for his base." I'm not God or a heart surgeon. I don't know what's inside someone's heart or their soul or their thoughts. I can only judge them by their actions, rhetoric, and behavior.

To be sure, many excellent reporters held Trump and his administration to account, did fantastic investigative reporting, asked tough questions, uncovered scandals and shady money trails, and suffered death threats and abuse simply for doing their job well. Also, most journalists of color didn't play this "both-sides" game. They called out the hate and racism and fascism exactly for what it was, and history will remember them accordingly.

But for those who did play the game, the main reason they gave him a pass is because they simply didn't care. They just didn't give a shit.

Now, this might seem harsh, especially to those reporters and journalists and media professionals who imagine I am pointing at them. Of course they were disgusted! Of course they didn't agree with his racism! Of course he was a terrible president and in hindsight it's so clear how he was a failure on so many levels! They aren't racist or hateful and they never, ever agreed with his comments!

But they also really didn't care.

You know how I know it's true? Because if Trump had launched his presidential campaign by promoting anti-white bigotry, hatred, and conspiracy theories, he'd never have been elected president. It wouldn't be a different playbook, it'd be a whole different ball game. He wouldn't get free airtime to rant and rave. He wouldn't get deferential treatment. He wouldn't get whitewashed language to cover up his hate. He wouldn't be welcomed for his sensationalism and entertaining presence by producers and TV execs. He wouldn't be praised for finally having the right "tone" for a speech he read off the script or having a "very different tone" a day after inciting a violent insurrection that left five people dead.

His hate never affected them, so they didn't care.

It didn't affect their parents, their spouses, or their children. There was no ban proposed against their community. Hate crimes didn't spike that made them think twice about going to their houses of worship. No one was chanting "go back" to their ancestors' original European countries. They weren't being called invaders and rapists.

They were removed from it all, spectators, able to observe the shit show from a distance. They were able to delude themselves into thinking they were neutral with their inaction.

The chaos never went down in their neighborhoods. They didn't hear it or feel it, but they could report on the casualties with detached objectivity. It didn't hurt that it made for some great TV.

Build the Multicultural Avengers (Capes Optional)

So, how do we fight back? I suggest we build our own multicultural Avengers. It's a "coalition of the willing," to quote President George W. Bush, but this time it is dedicated to life and restoration instead of death and annihilation.

We must unite to take on our most dangerous foe: Thanos, a mad titan who wants to decimate half of living creation to bring forth his maniacal vision of "balance" and peace to the universe.

America's Thanos is the Whiteness. It seeks control of government, finance, media, law enforcement, violent extremist groups, and social media messaging to restore "balance" that will make America great again. It has allies all across the globe.

US national security experts have warned that white power movements are growing, organizing, and plotting. They feed off the same information ecosystem that also sustains Republican politicians and right-wing cable-news hosts. They are fueled by conspiracy theories and fear. Unlike most of their fellow travelers, they believe in the use of violence to further their absolutist ideology.

The fringe has become mainstream and is assembling its own super-villain coalition.

We are dealing with our own Black Order, Thanos's ruthless army of stormtroopers and Blackshirts who loyally serve him in furtherance of his genocidal agenda.

One of my main fears during the Trump administration was that Trumpism would outlast Trump. Frankenstein's monster had escaped the lab and turned on its masters. Hate and fear still sell. They work. They feed a 24/7 news cycle. They prey on rage and pain and ignorance and loss. They have a fertile global playground. All hate needs is a new host, a new avatar, someone who is more polished, more competent, less prone to gaffes, and not compromised by debt or self-destructive tendencies.

We all have to rise up together and stop this because it will affect our present and future generations.

Suppose you end up having kids one day. Suppose they end up marrying someone outside of your race, religion, national origin, gender identity, sexual orientation, or political leanings. Nature, love, porn, alcohol, lust, and/or boredom do their job and eventually nine months later a beautiful baby is born. No matter how much you loathe your child's partner, you will immediately fall in love with this precious grandkid whom you have decided, without any field data or evidence, is the most ridiculously cute baby in the world and whom you adore to infinity and beyond.

Suppose your Gerber model grandkid is of mixed race, with gorgeous brown skin and a multisyllabic name, born and raised in the United States of America.

How would you feel if this beloved king or queen of yours was mocked and ridiculed for their skin color? Bullied into believing that they could never be president of the United States because of their name and gender? If every day they were reminded they will never truly be an American?

What happens if America told them, "Go back to where you came from!"?

Why would you want to be responsible for helping create such an intolerant, miserly environment that would punish your own blood, the light of your life, for simply existing?

What if you could help, in some meaningful way, change that future based on your actions today?

Wouldn't it be worth the effort?

The truth is that America is already a multicultural coalition of the willing. We are the ethnic Avengers, but some of the side characters just haven't gotten their solo movies yet.

However, I sincerely believe every person alive has their own unique talents and gifts. Let me go all in with the comic-book analogy and call it a superpower. You don't have to be a super soldier like Captain America or infused with photon energy like Captain Marvel to make an impact. In fact, deferring to a solitary hero or leader to save us from all our problems brings us authoritarians and strongmen. We tap out, wait on the sidelines, and outsource all the work.

When people come together around shared values, investing their time and talents to create solutions to a problem, that's when movement and change happen. I'm also not a naive, wide-eyed optimist. We won't win over everyone. We've permanently lost a good chunk of this country for at least my lifetime. But we can still get the majority.

I remember "the Hill." That's the name we gave to the mound of grass we sat on every day during lunch at Bellarmine. "The Hill" was a sanctuary. After a while, our core group of five or six friends expanded to include nearly a dozen and a half students who occupied the lofty perch. We never discriminated against anyone. All were welcomed. If you took a snapshot of our crew, it'd be representative of America. A Muslim, a Hindu, a Buddhist, a bunch of lapsed Catholics. Filipinos, South Asians, Vietnamese, Black, white. We were missing women, but it is an all-boys school so cut me some slack. It is a Catholic high school whose purpose of being is to help create "men for and with others": people dedicated "to bringing all their God-given talents to fullness and to living according to the pattern of service inaugurated by Jesus Christ."

I didn't even have to be Catholic to be down with that.

Basically, it's the same concept: create a community of service that looks out for each other and helps those in need. You know, like superheroes.

If you are asking how you can be an ally, that means you have the desire and perhaps also some privilege—some power—to help.

To quote Peter Parker, who quoted Uncle Ben, who quoted Voltaire: "With great power . . . comes great responsibility."

Now, let's use it to build a multicultural Avengers and defeat Thanos. Don't make the same mistake Thor did in *Infinity War* when he axed Thanos in the chest and let him live.

Remember: go for the head.*

* (Figuratively, not literally.)

Chapter 10

Invest in Hope, but Tie Your Camel First

My parents left everything behind in Pakistan and ventured on a journey across the Atlantic Ocean. What ultimately inspired them to get on that plane, like so many others, was hope.

Hope.

In America, they would make their dreams into a reality.

In America, they would have an opportunity and the freedom to be something more, something better, something bigger than where they came from.

In America, they would defy the odds and thrive in a country that segregated and brutalizes Black people, denied women the right to vote until the twentieth century, passed legislation to ban people who looked like them from arriving on its shores, and sent bombs to kill and young men to die in Vietnam.

In America, they would be accepted in spite of their brown skin, their religion, and their accents.

In America, they would plant new roots with meaning and purpose, roots that would endure and flourish.

America is an insane country. Everyone has to be a little bit mad to live here. We love comeback stories and fictitious larger-than-life characters. Heck, we sometimes ask them to be our leaders. We elected a reality-TV show star and failed businessman over an experienced, competent woman because Hollywood convinced us he had mastered the Art of the Deal. In the 1980s, we elected another actor to help us end the Cold War abroad as he unleashed the War on Drugs at home against Black and brown communities.

In America, we're terrified of socialism but we love giving tax cuts to the rich who don't need them. We hate affirmative action but we're fine with legacy admissions at Ivy League schools for wealthy families. We hate spending money on education, infrastructure, and health care but we will balloon the deficit and explode our debt for failed wars in the Middle East. We are a pro-life nation but we're fine with hundreds of thousands of Americans dying during a pandemic because, hey, the markets and economy have to get going.

Like I said, it's an insane country.

But it's still so lovable.

It's hard not to be smitten with a country that has a giant statue of Lady Liberty holding a torch welcoming immigrants with the words of a Jewish poet, Emma Lazarus, tattooed at her feet: "Give me your tired, your poor, Your huddled masses yearning to breathe free, The wretched refuse of your teeming shore."

How can you not be romantic about America when you find out Lady Liberty was sculpted by Frenchman Frédéric-Auguste Bartholdi, originally modeled after a Muslim woman dressed in traditional Egyptian dress, and given as a gift for the centennial of the Declaration of Independence?

The story is as American as apple pie, which was originally made by the Romans.

Lady Liberty represents the idea of America as the new colossus, a country that represents something more noble, far grander, and more magical than its actual, often horrific reality and lived history.

My father believed in *that* America.

He is now seventy-four years old. For the first time in his life, he made plans to leave the country in case Trump won reelection in 2020. It would be a clear sign to him that we were no longer welcomed. He mainly feared for his grandchildren and their safety.

He spent time researching different "safe" locations for Muslims. He says Vancouver looks beautiful from all the pictures and, according to his research, is "immigrant friendly" but unfortunately also pretty expensive. Right now, New Zealand is high on his list. The island is spacious and beautiful, it has hobbits, and the prime minister is educated and believes in science. Also, there's halal meat.

I've had many conversations with friends who told me their immigrant parents have shared similar fears and concerns about America becoming unwelcoming to them and their community.

"But where can we go that's safe? Where?" I've been asked this question by friends trying to find an ideal location that provides security but also excellent Wi-Fi and halal options just in case this country turns on them overnight.

I don't think such a place exists. We can't escape the horrors.

There's an unspoken realization that our generation is facing an onslaught of absurd challenges. It's like God decided to push "Play" on his "Fuck Shit Up" mixtape.

A once-in-a-lifetime pandemic has killed over four million people around the world. Just sit with that stunning number for a moment. If there was anything positive to come out of this pandemic, it allowed us to see ourselves clearly, whether we choose to accept the vision or not. It has been a beautiful X-ray of our country, revealing us raw, naked, and exposed. We can see our sins, virtues, flaws, successes, angels, and demons.

We're also trying to recover from a global depression. We now hold the distinction of having the highest income inequality of all the G7 nations and the lowest minimum wage in terms of purchasing power (USA! USA! USA!). The wealth gap between America's richest and poorest families has doubled in the past thirty years. If the systems don't reform, they will eventually collapse under the weight of their corruption or be torn down by masses who will rightfully view them only as architects of their oppression.

Disinformation and propaganda have distorted the truth, which is automatically rejected by many if it doesn't fit our narratives, confirms our biases, or is validated by a news outlet we trust. A nation that can't unite over basic facts is broken, susceptible to exploitation, lies, flattery, dangerous propaganda, foreign interference, and an authoritarian iron rule.

And of course that good ol' fashioned racism and xenophobia will always be around. This loss of wealth, power, and security is a perfect atmosphere for extremism to thrive. In particular, white anxiety has increased with the empowerment of women and people of color. The death rattle of white supremacy has transformed into a death march, and its loyal adherents will become more radicalized, weaponized, and violent as they continue to lose power and numbers.

Even if the pandemic and racism are tamed, the world might be uninhabitable in a few decades due to climate change.

But I still want us to invest in hope.

Islam, like most world religions, spends a lot of time preparing us for death, the hereafter, and other awesome, extraordinary events. One would assume that amid all the doom there is utter nihilism or at the very least a command to abandon worldly concerns. After all, if it's all going to hell—literally—then what's the point, right? Let it burn, pray, and leave the rest to God.

Instead, the Prophet Muhammad said to plant a seed.

"If the Hour [the day of Resurrection] is about to be established and one of you was holding a palm shoot, let him take advantage of even one second before the Hour is established to plant it," he advised his companions.

Even now, we should invest in hope.

It sounds utterly foolish, I know. It's also masochistic.

Investing in hope means allowing yourself to be open to the possibility that life will improve and that change is just beyond the horizon. But it also means exposing yourself to disappointment and crushed dreams. It means voluntarily making yourself vulnerable to pain. It's wiser to curl up in a shell and protect yourself from life's numerous blows. Another natural defense mechanism is to laugh at hope and dismiss it as a delusional crutch of wide-eyed, naive fools. If you choose never to believe, then you can never be betrayed.

Trust me, I know. I've been there. You just spent over two hundred pages reading about it.

However, I refuse to embrace the alternative, which is cynicism and apathy. They are cheap and lazy, but so inviting and temporarily comforting. They require zero investment. You get to just sit in the cheap seats as a spectator and yell "Boo!" at the fools who decide to step in the ring and get their noses bloodied.

But it was hope that helped us endure our daughter's stage 4 cancer.

In April 2019, my wife called me, sobbing, as I was in my Vancouver hotel room preparing for my TED Talk. The previous month we had just found out Sarah was pregnant with our third baby. In three days, I was about to step onto the stage and deliver a twelve-minute talk making the case for having children, inspired by my son, Ibrahim, and my daughter Nusayba.

Sarah called me and said she felt a "bump" on Nusayba's stomach and took her to the emergency room, hoping she had some benign condition. Instead, the doctors told us they discovered bumps all over her liver. It was hepatoblastoma, a rare cancer that primarily affects children during the first three years of life.

My immediate reaction upon hearing the news was balling my fist in anger, punching the sofa, and yelling "No!"

The Ali curse had finally struck again. I had assumed it skipped my children. Perhaps my marriage had finally blocked it from passing on to my family. If it still existed, it would eventually catch up and claim only me. But I never expected this news.

I recited the "barter prayer," which is said by all parents, both religious and atheist. It's a trade to the universe: "Dear God, please protect Nusayba. I offer a trade: my life for hers." You wait for an answer you know will never arrive. I felt powerless in the face of a disease whose only design was to utterly ravage life without discrimination. I was just a dad. My job is to solve problems, "fix things," and knock out the mortgage. How do I fight cancer?

As I sat in my hotel room absorbing the news, I remembered a famous saying in Islam: "Tie your camel first, and put your faith in God." It means first exhaust yourself and do everything you can within your human powers, and after that, leave it to God.

Sarah and I made the decision that we'd do everything within our capacity to give our little girl a fighting chance. Thanks to Sarah's job at Georgetown Hospital, we had health insurance, or else Nusayba wouldn't have survived a month. In fact, the doctors were initially worried she wouldn't make it past May because she suffered from multiple complications that delayed her chemotherapy. Within two weeks, my daughter shriveled to her bones.

The percentages were not in her favor. The cancer had spread all over her liver and a spot had developed in her lung. Our two-year-old girl needed heavy chemotherapy, strong enough to knock out adults, and a full liver transplant. If we could find a liver, she'd still need two additional chemotherapy sessions to obliterate the cancer and would also need a lifetime of checkups and daily, life-saving medications.

For the entire summer of 2019, we were "hospital parents" and abandoned any semblance of normal life. Cancer doesn't care about your abs routine, your Netflix queue, your weekend plans, your fantasy football league, or your job prospects. Cancer plays for everything. A "good day" used to be getting solid sleep, eating a tasty meal, having enough money in the bank account, playing with the kids, and having nobody yell at me. Now a "good day" meant that Nusayba's numbers stayed normal, she didn't vomit, and there were no fevers that would require us to rush to the hospital.

Every night, as my family slept, I stayed up until the early morning. I couldn't rest. I spent hours preparing myself for every scenario, every timeline, every future that could emerge. I sat on my couch like Dr. Strange using his Time Stone and imagined seeing every outcome, including Nusayba's death. How would I respond, what would I tell her brother, her grandparents? How would I bury her? How would I live a full life with a void in my heart? How would I pretend to be normal for the sake of my wife and my son's happiness?

This was an act of self-preservation. I had to confront the harsh truths and facts in front of me. I kept looking at the percentages. I couldn't afford to be blindsided by tragedy. I had to acknowledge that despair and pain were in the bag waiting to greet me at the end of the rainbow.

But I also spent nights imagining Nusayba receiving a full liver transplant, recovering from her sickness, eating whipped cream, Reese's Pieces, and Smarties, making her trademark weird noises and goofy faces and finding a way to live life fully again with a giant scar across her belly.

I preferred that story.

We needed a liver donor and time was running out. I used my network to share Nusayba's story. We were hoping a few people with O blood type would step up and volunteer to endure the battery of tests to see if there was a compatible match with our daughter.

We received a call that an anonymous donor had volunteered and this time it was a grade A Wagyu liver match. The surgery would be happening within a few days. Super-pregnant Sarah told me to take Nusayba into the operating theater after she was heavily sedated. I wore the hospital scrubs, the closest I'd ever come to resembling a real doctor, picked up my daughter, and laid her on the table. She briefly opened her eyes. I recall saying, "Be brave. Your Baba loves you very much. I'll see you soon." I kissed her on the cheek and I let her go.

After that, there's nothing else a parent can do except hope and pray.

A few hours later, Dr. Fishbein joined us in the waiting room and said it was one of the cleanest and easiest surgeries he'd ever performed. Everything went "perfectly." This was echoed by all the nurses and attendants. We bumped into the donor's surgeon who told us, "I've done this many times. Usually, when a donor wakes up, the first thing they ask is, 'When can I go back to work?' or 'Am I OK?' Nusayba's donor is a good man," he said with tears in his eyes. "You know the first thing he said when he woke up? 'When can I donate blood again?' Your daughter has a good man's liver in her," he told us again, before walking away.

We later met the anonymous donor whose name is Shawn Zahir, a Pakistani Muslim American who was living with his wife Rida nearby in Washington, DC, at the time. It turned out that Rida followed me on Twitter. Although we had never met, she kept updated with all my posts about Nusayba. Shawn is the anti-millennial who didn't have any social media profile. One day, Rida was sitting on the couch, scrolling through Twitter, when she read aloud my tweet looking for a donor. Shawn grabbed the phone, read the thread, and said, "I'm O blood type. I could apply."

A stranger risked his life to step up and help a girl he had never met—to give a piece of his liver so she could live.

He was one of five hundred people, mostly strangers, who were willing to donate a piece of their liver. Dr. Fishbein, the head of the MedStar Georgetown Transplant Institute, said it was the first time supply had outmatched the demand. He was floored.

By sharing Nusayba's story, we not only helped save her life, but some of those donors were later matched with other kids in need of livers. Georgetown is now creating a center in Nusayba's honor to expand the scale and scope of their transplants. There were people who volunteered their liver, their money, and their kindness who actively loathed my politics. I know because they told me.

It was important for me to experience this because I was becoming bitter and losing my faith in so many of my fellow Americans. How could millions support a man who wanted to ban my people and keep kids in cages? But I realized that people, even those who have atrocious politics, still have the capacity for decency and kindness. I firmly believe most people still have the desire to do good in this world.

I often remind myself of this because I look on so much of the cruelty and ugliness and say, "Nope. I can never forgive or forget. There's no hope. People won't change."

But I remember that, sometimes, some people do change.

If you had told me as a high school senior in the Bay Area that a daytime talk-show host would be a lesbian married to a woman, I would tell you to pass the weed, which I wouldn't inhale. Growing up, I thought this country would never elect a Black man president in my lifetime. If they did, they certainly wouldn't have a Black female vice president. Impossible. Absolutely impossible. We're just too racist in America. It's in our DNA.

In 1949, Paul Blanshard's *American Freedom and Catholic Power* spent eleven months on the *New York Times* bestseller list. In the book, he sounded "the alarm over the flood of Roman Catholic immigrants to the United States." He said they were a "profound threat to democracy, equality, and secular values." He warned they wouldn't integrate, and they would impose their beliefs on Americans. In 1960, America elected its first Catholic president, John F. Kennedy, who had to assure the nation he wasn't loyal to the pope. In 2020, America elected its second Catholic president, Joe Biden, who wasn't required to make such assurances. In 2021, six of the nine Supreme Court justices are Catholic and two are Jews.

This story isn't new. Communities persist and thrive, even as they suffer, face persecution, and are humiliated.

They endure.

Sometimes, all you have is hope that when the page turns it'll bring with it a better story that doesn't end in tragedy.

I'm a romantic at heart. I can't help it. Despite my attempts at cynicism, I still believe that some people can change, and the future can bring bright days ahead.

How can I not?

I was supposed to be dead. I should have flatlined in my oversized gym shorts and worn-out sneakers.

But here I am, finishing the first draft of this book as a present to myself before my fortieth birthday. I'm sitting on the family room couch with my laptop burning my thighs. My wife, Ibrahim, and Nusayba are all sleeping in our bedroom, having successfully kicked me out to the guest bedroom. Our baby daughter, Khadija, who was born a month and a half after Nusayba's liver transplant, is knocked out in her crib after receiving the most delicious, organic, fresh round of breast milk.

I take none of this life for granted.

People are also reconnecting with their families, their friends, and their frenemies due to the coronavirus pandemic. The virus flattened us, unequally, and reminded us of the fragility and necessity of human relationships and communities, something most of us ignored as we were notching up a high score on a game on our phones or multitasking deep into the night as we binge-watched our favorite shows.

We survived. Many did not.

As a parent, I can't afford to be cynical and lazy. I have three kids and I have to prepare them for this harsh world. As such, I ask myself: what's my role? Sometimes, I think I'm Hodor from *Game of Thrones*, the character whose sole purpose is to sacrifice his life and block the door so his friends have enough time to escape the rampaging horde of demons.

Other times I think I'm a janitor, a man who must spend the rest of his life cleaning up my generation's mess so my kids' generation at least has some untainted living space.

When I'm truly idealistic, I hope to be a gardener. Maybe through whatever small talents I might have, I can plant a seed. Hopefully, my children's generation can find comfort in its shade. If I have a green thumb, maybe my work bears some delicious fruits. If I'm really lucky, I'll be able to sit with them and taste it. (Mangoes and pomegranates in this dream, please.)

The challenge for America is whether or not it will live up to its narrative of being a sanctuary, a haven for all, a place where anyone can come and achieve success and freedoms. Laborers keep coming to this country as undocumented immigrants even after they are criminalized, because they believe there is a chance for them and their family. Their children who came here as minors were eventually given a path toward a legal status based on satisfying certain qualifications. They are called the DREAMers. They bravely expose themselves, risking detention and deportation, in the hopes their stories can appeal to this country's basic humanity and decency to implement immigration reform that finally recognizes them as fellow Americans.

The way America deals with Islam and its Muslim residents will also be a critical test. Unlike the Irish Catholics or the Eastern European Jews, we are mostly non-white. We won't blend in or be accepted by the

Whiteness. We are also not included in the Judeo-Christian narrative of Western civilization even though we've been here since its founding. Islam is still a civilizational threat that allegedly "hates us," according to many Americans. Its adherents must be profiled. Its Sharia and mosques must be banned. Hinduism and Buddhism are fine, as long as they stick with yoga, mindfulness, the Beatles in 1968, henna, and Richard Gere.

But will America stretch and expand for us?

I must keep hoping that it can and will.

As you know by now, my family is big on dreams. I'll share one last one before my time is up.

My father told me about this dream twice, years apart, and while the fine details were altered in the retelling, the plot remains the same.

He saw himself, Dada, and me in a beautiful, spacious mosque filled with people. The muezzin had just made the adhan, the call to prayer, and people were standing up, filling the rows and preparing for the imam to lead them in prayer. We kept walking toward the front.

After a while, my grandfather stopped. He told us to continue onward. My father asked him to keep walking with us, but he said this was as far as he goes. My father and I continued, nearing the front, close to the imam and the minbar, the pulpit.

In the first retelling, my father said he stopped, and he urged me to go on. Then he woke up. In the second retelling, we both kept advancing forward. Then he woke up.

Every generation's pain, trauma, dreams, hopes, and successes affect and shape the next generation. We are all connected, even when we feel so distant and untethered to each other's truths and realities.

When I have this dream, and I suspect I will, I hope I'm walking alongside Ibrahim, Nusayba, and Khadija, and that the inheritance I've left them is filled with wisdom, love, truth, and joy. I hope it sustains them. I hope it makes them proud. I hope they can forgive me for my numerous mistakes and look at me with understanding and kindness instead of scorn and pity.

At the end, we want our children to reflect the best of us, but the truth is they inherit all of it: the good, the bad, the ugly, the male-pattern baldness, the entire baggage.

I just want to increase the percentages in their favor, and I thought I'd start with their names.

Sarah let me "advise" her on naming all three kids. If we were going to have a boy, I always knew he'd be an Ibrahim. I remembered the small gift Maqbool Nana gave me when I was in so much pain, immersed in so much difficulty during my parents' initial trial. It was a verse from the Quran: "We said, O Fire! Be thou cool, and a means of safety for Abraham." The name Ibrahim was a prayer. I hoped the fires of this world would be cooled by and for his generation. Ibrahim has since lived up to his name. He's grown to be a thoughtful, sensitive, and curious child with an elephant memory, who is attentive to his two sisters and their needs and who finds a way to make easy friends with just about anybody. Just don't mess with his impressive LEGO creations, or criticize him too harshly, and you'll get along fine with him.

For our second child, Sarah wanted to name her Asiya, who was the pharaoh's wife and the adoptive mother of Moses. She found him in the crate as a baby and loved him as her own son. It's a beautiful name. You can't go wrong. Rock-solid. But it was between that and Nusayba, my first preference. As Nusayba was literally making her entrance into the world, my wife, in labor, looked up at me and said, "She's a Nusayba." She was a famous warrior feminist of early Islamic history who rushed into battle to save fallen soldiers and protect the Prophet's life. She suffered twelve major wounds. She asked the Prophet why the Quran was addressed only to men and not to women. Afterward, a powerful verse was revealed that refers to both men and women as spiritual equals in the sight of God. I have no time or patience to raise a damsel in distress. If the goblins ever come after me, I'm expecting my daughters to throw down and kick ass to save my life. It seems our baby girl has already lived up to her namesake. The world needs more Nusaybas for the challenges ahead.

To complete the trilogy, we went with a Muslim All-Star and named our youngest girl Khadija, after the beloved wife of the Prophet, known as one of the four perfected women and the first convert to Islam. She was a successful businesswoman and widow who hired the Prophet to manage her caravan. Impressed with his character and reputation, she's the one who proposed marriage to him. He accepted even though she was wealthier and fifteen years his senior. When asked about Khadija, the Prophet said, "She believed in me when no one else did; she accepted Islam when people rejected me; and she helped and comforted me when there was no one else to lend me a helping hand."

Our Khadija's arrival reminds me that life goes on. She was our little gift who brought joy at the end of a painful and terrifying journey. It's always the Khadijas of the families and communities who end up saving the day. They rarely get the spotlight or the A plotline, but without them it will all fall apart. With their strength, love, and resilience, America will always have a chance.

✳   ✳   ✳   ✳

I don't know if I've convinced you, but I have tried to make an appealing, rational case for you to consider investing in hope, and tying your camel in the face of absolute horrors and chaos.

To quote a proverb of the original Americans, "You can't see the future with tears in your eyes."

If you were willing to take this final leap of faith with me, then allow me to congratulate you on successfully becoming an American.

My father has been inspired by the results of the 2020 election and the enthusiasm and passion of young people who came out to vote and are out on the streets, leading and organizing for change.

The demonstrations and protests against the murder of George Floyd in the summer of 2020 had a profound impact on my parents, in particular my father.

It moved him.

He said he came to the United States in 1966 as a young student and personally witnessed the country's "chaos" as it struggled for equality.

He believes the fire is different this time. He says that, back then, the white majority didn't stand with the call for justice and change, but instead they fled to Nixon, soothed by his comforting racist dog whistles. But now, he believes, "they are with us."

My father, a Muslim, an immigrant from Pakistan, included himself with American communities still struggling for freedom and dignity and respect.

"This time, they are with us," he repeated.

"Us."

I was encouraged and told him, regardless of what happens, I plan on staying in Amreeka and fighting until the end.

When they tell me, "Go back to where you came from," I'll say, "Thank you. I'm already here."

In the meantime, I look forward to throwing the best American BBQ potluck on the block, inviting all my diverse neighbors to bring their ethnic food, where everyone dances to a dope, international playlist, while I make fresh, hot chai in a white apron. I recommend you all attend. My only condition is you must bring an open mind, a generous heart, and be willing to reach out to those who have never received an invite to finally come take a seat and enjoy a delicious meal at our everexpanding table.

Acknowledgments

How can a lifetime be acknowledged in a few brief pages?

A book, like a person, cannot live or survive long and well without the care and attention of others. Like people, it requires some selfless, unconditional love and random acts of kindness to endure the journey until the end. Even though this book bears my name on its cover and its spine, it could only come to be after a lifetime of collaborations.

I won't be able to finish my speech in thirty seconds. In about two paragraphs the orchestra will start playing that gentle but passive-aggressive music that tells you to wrap it up. You can get up and use the restroom or skip to the end, and I won't be offended. But allow me for the last time to try to hold your attention.

God is great. Allahu Akbar. Thanking an omniscient deity for success is often trite and induces well-earned eye rolls, because after all, it seems performative and also cynics are right to ask, "Well, how come you didn't thank God during all the bad shit?" Agreed. But I believe it's important to take time and tell the universe that I am aware. I acknowledge all of it. The entire journey. The good, bad, ugly, sublime, ridiculous, hilarious, maddening, frustrating beauty of the entire ride—all the bumps, all the failures, all the glory.

Without the mileage I wouldn't be able to write these words you have just read. Every scar tells a story. I am grateful for all of them.

I'm at the age now where death and birth hit you in waves. The elders who shaped you, the titans whom you thought would live forever, are being buried, and your childhood friends, who'd agree with you that they have no business procreating, are having babies.

I often think of my grandmother and grandfather, Mirza Mustafa Ali and Muneer Unissa Begum, and the generation of elders who now remain only as memories and blessings. They would have been proud of this book. My Dadi and Patata Dadi would have enjoyed sitting with me, listening to me read a chapter, as we ate papri chaat from that Indian aunty on Fremont Boulevard who made it extra crispy. I miss them.

I'd like to thank that generation for their sacrifices. They endured the Partition, war, trauma, and pain, but they still did their best to hold on to traditions and faith and managed to live, love, and laugh through it all. I hope this book in part is another chapter in the ongoing story, one that could not have been told without their parts, the original protagonists.

I'd like to thank the elders who are still living—from my father's and my mother's side—both here in Amreeka and in Pakistan. Maybe now they can finally say, "Well, even though he didn't become a doctor, he turned out OK."

My parents' generation has now replaced my grandparents as the elders. They often say, "We won't be here for that long, so be sure to call," which generally adds another two years of life to their timeline. Mainly, they want to know they've led a good life and that they tried their best. I hope my parents know that I appreciate their love and devotion. We don't come from an "I love you" family. But I love them very much, and I am proud to be their son. I look forward to reading their story, but if they don't want to share it, then that's fine as well. They've earned a good rest.

I'd like to thank my Yasmeen Phuppo for scooping me up and taking me to the hospital in Pakistan, probably saving my life. She's always seen me as the kid she never had. My Nani, Masood Mamoo and Ami's family in Pakistan always helped during the darkest of times. In fact, Masood Mamoo helped wire money at the last second so I could take the Barbri LSAT courses and pass the bar exam. And . . . I ended up becoming a writer, alas. Regardless, it's one of his many acts of generosity. My family from my father's side throughout the years helped step up during times of multiple crises. Again, thank you to Mujjahid Chacha for letting us stay in his house when we were homeless.

No one wakes up and becomes a writer by themselves. All Jedis have masters who taught and mentored them along the way. I've been incredibly lucky to have brilliant teachers who always believed in me and challenged me to unearth whatever talent they saw in a chubby, insecure, awkward kid who was just trying to find his voice and not sweat profusely in front of girls. Much love and respect to the teachers at Child's Hideaway Preschool, James Leitch Elementary School, Harker (It's finally "Game day," Mr. Walsh!), Bellarmine, UC Berkeley (thanks, Professor Susan Schweik, for giving me time to finish my thesis!), and the UC Davis School of Law.

I want to give a shout-out to some English teachers who are no longer with us. Mrs. Mittelstet was my writing teacher in sixth grade who encouraged me. Years later, while waiting in line for a movie at Century 22 Theaters, I recognized her. She remembered an essay I had written for her years ago and said, "That was very good. You were a really good writer." Mrs. Harp put the fear of God in us in eighth grade, and all we wanted was to earn her approval. But behind her stern demeanor was a razor-sharp, kind, and encouraging teacher who helped me refine my skills. I maintain that some of the smartest and fastest minds I've ever met were in my Honors English class in Bellarmine High School. Every day was like an All-Star game. Nearly the same group of about thirty kids had Mr. Alessandri and Mr. Harville from sophomore to senior year. Those two treated us with respect, expanded our creative and intellectual horizons, challenged us to be better, and helped shape us into becoming better writers and people. They remained my fans until they passed, and I am indebted to both of them.

I'm so glad I took Professor Kratin's advice and applied to Ishmael Reed's short story class. What a sliding door moment. I often wonder if I'd ever have become a writer if it wasn't for that fateful decision. For the past twenty years, Ishmael and Carla have mentored, encouraged, helped, and counseled me in this strange, eventful path toward becoming a paid writer. They owed me nothing, but they either really believed in me or were really bored and ended up devoting years of their time to help. I can't pay them back, so I can only hope to pay it forward.

Along the way, I've been really lucky to meet friends and collaborators. We've gotten up to some good mischief. Thanks to Dave Eggers and the McSweeney's crew for inviting me to participate in their projects and entertaining my crazy ideas. My people at the Before Columbus Foundation are always holding down the fort to expand and stretch what it means to be American, page by page, word for word, and we'll never stop. Miguel Algarian created something beautiful with the Nuyorican Poets Cafe, a home for the rest of us, where we could stand up and be heard. Much love to Rome Neal and the Nuyorican crew for giving our play *The Domestic Crusaders* shelter when everyone else turned us away.

The Naqvis have been our "phone a friend" family and helped us throughout the years. My mom even stayed at their place after she was released for the second time. I hope they know I acknowledge and appreciate their kindness. Riffat aunty and Arshad uncle have always lent a hand, their home, their food, and their warmth. The late Hisham uncle and Afshan aunty rented rooms in their house to us when we didn't have a place to go, but their entire family treated us like their own. Thank you.

We're a religious family and we've had our fair share of interactions with interesting characters, from shady numerologists to people with fake smiles who wear kufis and hijabs, but there are so many men and women who truly help, with either prayers and guidance, kindness and wisdom, simply because they've decided to give their lives to love and service. That's another face of faith that's often unseen, clouded by the cruelty and the ugliness. It's that beauty that makes us cynics hold on and stay seeking.

As you can tell, I have a tendency to talk a lot when I'm excited. You should be grateful this book wasn't four hundred pages. I was able to whip it into shape with the precise, careful, and brilliant guidance of my awesome editor, Alane Mason of W. W. Norton. She dragged her teenage son to see a conversation between me and Hasan Minhaj years ago in New York. Afterward, she approached me and said I should write a book. We stayed in touch. I sent her the proposal, and from her thoughtful comments I immediately knew she was the right one to shepherd this book to completion. She even taught me some Italian words along the way.

P. J. Mark of Janklow & Nesbit told me to write a book more than a decade ago. He signed me up hoping I'd deliver him a manuscript in 2012. It took about nine years, but we eventually got it done, PJ. There's a reason he's one of the most respected agents in the business. He's smart, deeply invested in his clients, and actually cares about making the world a better place.

Charles Yao signed me as a talent for the Lavin Speaking Agency back in the day mostly because he enjoyed talking with me over the phone and he appreciated my arcane '80s pop cultural references. A recommendation from Reza Aslan convinced him to take the call. But that entire crew really went out of their way to help me over the years, and I'm deeply appreciative.

A lot of editors over the years have gone to bat for me and given me opportunities to write in my voice for large, international audiences. Thanks to Rachel and Jenee at the *New York Times*, Harry and Noah at the *Daily Beast*, Matt when he was at the *Guardian*, Sarah and Kerry when they were at *Salon*, Shahid and Zahed at *Altmuslim*, Scott and Jeff at *The Atlantic*, Michelle and Sarah at the *Washington Post*, and Jeffrey and the late Alex over at *Counterpunch*.

Thanks to the brilliant Rim-Sarah Alouane, an expert on French law and religious freedoms, who took time out of her PhD to help me with research and fact-checking, and who once sent me a very important email at 3 a.m.: "Serious question: should I cite Voltaire or Spider-Man, or both?"

Special shout-out to Uzma Sabir and Lena Albibi, who have been like sisters to me and to my wife, Sarah, and not only assisted in us getting married but have loved our kids like their own and have always been around to give a helping hand.

Shawn Zahir literally gave us a piece of his liver. He was the anonymous donor who stepped up to help save a little girl he had never met. I am forever indebted to him and his wife, Rida. How can I pay him back? I always ask this question and hope the universe one day gives me the right answer. I'd also like to recognize and celebrate Megan Black, who volunteered to donate her liver and was ready to go until the doctors decided at the last second that the surgery was too much of a health risk.

Thank you to all the health care professionals and workers at MedStar Georgetown Transplant Institute and Children's National Medical Center who helped save Nusayba's life. They're not miracle workers, they're just people, and they deserve to be paid and treated with respect. I'd also like to thank my wife for having health insurance. Without it, my girl probably wouldn't be alive today. It's a sin that millions of our fellow Americans won't even have a chance to survive because they don't have access to affordable health care in the world's most powerful and wealthy country. Hopefully, our generation can remedy this madness.

I want to apologize to all my friends over the years. I know I haven't been the best, but I was always trying. I'm still trying. I got stuck along the way. I aim to do better. At the very least, you can never say I wasn't entertaining. Thanks especially to my former roommates Ahsan Shaikh and Jason Moy for tolerating me.

I've been incredibly lucky to have strong, supportive women in my life. My love and respect always to Jessica Zweng, Saman Chaudry, Reema Dodin, Connie Sun, Julia Mendoza, and Lisa Gohil.

My in-laws, Afshan and Zafar Kureshi, have always treated me with respect, never guilted or shamed me for being poor or having parents who went to prison, and have rejoiced in every success and helped during every trial. My brother-in-law Faraz and his wife Najla, along with their two rug rats, and my sister-in-law Farah always supported me in my unorthodox writing career, even when it didn't seem likely that there'd be a happy ending. Thank you.

If I've forgotten anyone, forgive me, I'll make it up in the paperback edition.

My hope and prayer are that one of you is reading this right now and asking yourself, "Wajahat isn't all that. I mean the book is OK. It ain't bad. But if he can write a book, why not me? I also have a story to tell." You're absolutely right. "Why not you?" I never thought I could write or speak in front of an audience, but here I am, with a published book that you have decided to read. There's no reason why you can't pick up a pen and write your own. There are many stories in America that have yet to be written, which need to fill in the missing pages and complete our expanding narrative. Don't let anyone tell you that your story doesn't matter or doesn't belong.

I will (finally) leave you with my four wins in life.

If all else fails, if this book sinks like a crater, annihilated and torn to shreds with scathing reviews or, worse, ignored and forgotten, if there's no worldly success or admirable accomplishment to my name, no awards, no credits, no plaudits, nothing remotely notable to distinguish my mundane life from any other living soul, then I can still make my exit with a smile on my face knowing I've done the following: married Sarah Kureshi and helped her co-produce Ibrahim, Nusayba, and Khadija.

Being a father is the greatest achievement of my lifetime. Every day is a blessing, and maybe I'm slightly biased, but I have immense confidence in my kids, who are obviously totally badass and brilliant. I look forward to seeing their generation lift us all up and push us forward.

For my children, I hope your Baba makes you proud.

For Sarah, my beloved, thank you for believing and investing in me when I had nothing except a '97 Toyota Camry without a driver's-side door handle and some hope for a better future. My love eternal.

Notes for the Fellow Nerds

Introduction

1   **Gandhi was also racist:** Desai, Ashwin, and Goolam H. Vahed, *The South African Gandhi: Stretcher-Bearer of Empire* (Stanford, CA: Stanford University Press, 2015); Frayer, Lauren, "Gandhi Is Deeply Revered, But His Attitudes on Race and Sex Are Under Scrutiny," NPR, October 2, 2019, www.npr.org/2019/10/02/766083651/gandhi-is-deeply-revered-but-his-attitudes-on-race-and-sex-are-under-scrutiny.

4   **we left-handed people are a highly productive:** Sala, Giovanni, and Fernand Gobet, "Are Left-Handed People More Gifted than Others? Our Study Suggests It May Hold True for Maths," *The Conversation*, June 14, 2017, theconversation.com/are-left-handed-people-more-gifted-than-others-our-study-suggests-it-may-hold-true-for-maths-79059.

6   **always asked to be welcoming but are still never welcomed:** This line was inspired by a poem recited by Afaq Mahmoud at "The M Word: Muslim-American Stories of Hope and Resistance" event held at Columbia University on February 24, 2017, https://www.facebook.com/penmword/posts/903206049819182.

9   **now branded as "chain migration":** Qiu, Linda, "What Is 'Chain Migration'? Here's the Controversy Behind It," *New York Times*, January 26, 2018, www.nytimes.com/2018/01/26/us/politics/the-facts-behind-the-weaponized-phrase-chain-migration.html.

9   **Uh Oh Pasghettio!:** "Uh-Oh! 5 Things You Didn't Know about SpaghettiOs," Campbell Soup Company, March 19, 2021, www.campbellsoupcompany.com/newsroom/campbell-history/uh-oh-5-things-you-didnt-know-about-spaghettios/.

13 **the Supreme Court in *Brown v. Board of Education of Topeka*:**

Brown v. Board of Education of Topeka, 347 U.S. 483 (1954). See also Kluger, Richard, *Simple Justice: The History of Brown v. Board of Education and Black America's Struggle for Equality* (New York: Vintage Books, 1977).

1.   Create Your Own Superhero Story

15   **Out of the top ten most populous countries:** "U.S. Census Bureau Current Population," *U.S. Census Bureau*, March 25, 2021, www.census.gov/popclock/print.php?component=counter.

18   **"Race Mixing is Financed and Led by Jews!":** Miller, Michael E., "The Shadow of an Assassinated American Nazi Commander Hangs over Charlottesville," *Washington Post*, June 12, 2020, www.washingtonpost .com/news/retropolis/wp/2017/08/21/the-shadow-of-an-assassinated -american-nazi-commander-hangs-over-charlottesville/.

21   **the "Einstein visa":** "Employment-Based Immigration: First Preference EB-1." *USCIS*, November 23, 2020, www.uscis.gov/working-in-the -united-states/permanent-workers/employment-based-immigration-first -preference-eb-1.

21   **Melania Trump was a Slovenian model:** "Melania Trump—the First Lady in Our Nude Photo Shoot," *British GQ*, November 8, 2016, www.gq -magazine.co.uk/article/donald-trump-melania-trump-knauss-first-lady -erections.

29   **According to one sahih hadith:** "Sunan Ibn Majah | Chapter: 32 | The Chapters on Food," *Ahadith*, ahadith.co.uk/chapter.php?page=2&cid= 188&rows=10.

29   **"One ought not to eat with one's left hand":** Ansari, Bilal Ali, "Commentary on the Hadith of Shaytan and Eating with the Left Hand," *Bilal Ali Ansari*, February 14, 2014, bilalaliansari.com/2014/02/14/ commentary-on-the-hadith-of-shaytan-and-eating-with-the-left-hand/.

31   **In 1846, John Frémont was sent:** "John C. Frémont: A Continent Divided: The U.S.-Mexico War," *Biographies: John C. Frémont: A Continent Divided: The U.S.-Mexico War*, University of Texas at Arlington, library.uta.edu/usmexicowar/item?bio_id=81&nation=US.

31   **Frémont and his men presided over:** Field, Margaret A., "Genocide and the Indians of California, 1769–1873," master's thesis, University of Massachusetts Boston, May 1993, https://scholarworks.umb.edu/ cgi/viewcontent.cgi?article=1142&context=masters_theses;   Nazaryan,

Alexander, "California's State-Sanctioned Genocide of Native Americans," *Newsweek*, August 17, 2016, www.newsweek.com/2016/08/26/california-native-americans-genocide-490824.html.

44 **40 percent of American adults weren't obese:** Galvin, Gaby, "America Has Gotten Much Fatter in the Past Two Decades," *U.S. News & World Report*, February 27, 2020, www.usnews.com/news/healthiest-communities/articles/2020–02–27/us-obesity-rate-passes-40-percent.

47 **"yank yo tooth out" dentist:** Rock, Chris, *Kill the Messenger*, HBO, September 27, 2008.

2. Say Hello to America's Oldest Friend

54 **Its core adherents believe that "white people":** McMaster, Geoff, "Scandinavian Studies Professor Debunks Idea of 'Racial Purity,'" *Norwegian American*, July 30, 2020, www.norwegianamerican.com/viking-racial-purity-van-deusen/.

54 **Just talk to Irish Catholics and Italian Americans:** Guglielmo, Jennifer, and Salvatore Salerno, *Are Italians White? How Race Is Made in America* (New York: Routledge, 2003); Harriot, Michael, "When the Irish Weren't White," *The Root*, March 17, 2018, www.theroot.com/when-the-irish-weren-t-white-1793358754; Massey, Douglas, and Karen Pren, "Unintended Consequences of US Immigration Policy: Explaining the Post-1965 Surge from Latin America," *Population and Development Review* 38, no. 1 (2012): 1–29, https://www.ncbi.nlm.nih.gov/pmc/articles/PMC3407978/.

54 **Skin color itself is a product:** Jablonski, Nina G., "The Evolution of Human Skin and Skin Color," *Annual Review of Anthropology* 33 (2004): 585–623.

54 **there were no "white" people in Virginia:** Allen, Theodore W., *The Invention of the White Race* (London and New York: Verso, 1994–97).

56 **Study the Rust Belt:** McQuarrie, Michael, "The Revolt of the Rust Belt: Place and Politics in the Age of Anger," *British Journal of Sociology* 68, no. S1 (2017): S120–52, https://onlinelibrary.wiley.com/doi/full/10.1111/1468–4446.12328.

56 **Be an "essential" worker during a pandemic:** "The Plight of Essential Workers During the COVID-19 Pandemic," *Lancet (London, England)* 395, no. 10237 (2020): 1587, doi:10.1016/S0140–6736(20)31200–9.

56 **Assume that wealthy and white immigrants are "expats":** Koutonin, Mawuna Remarque, "Why Are White People Expats When the Rest of

244 * Notes for the Fellow Nerds

Us Are Immigrants?" *Guardian*, March 13, 2015, www.theguardian.com/
global-development-professionals-network/2015/mar/13/white-people
-expats-immigrants-migration.

57   **Support free speech by trying to ban critical race theory:** Kearse, Stephen, "GOP Lawmakers Intensify Effort to Ban Critical Race Theory
in Schools," Pew, June 14, 2021, https://www.pewtrusts.org/en/research
-and-analysis/blogs/stateline/2021/06/14/gop-lawmakers-intensify-effort
-to-ban-critical-race-theory-in-schools.

57   **children of Latino immigrants as "anchor babies":** Villarreal, Alexan-
dra, "'Anchor Babies': The 'Ludicrous' Immigration Myth That Treats
People as Pawns," *Guardian*, March 16, 2020, www.theguardian.com/us
-news/2020/mar/16/anchor-babies-the-ludicrous-immigration-myth-that
-treats-people-as-pawns.

57   **"welfare queens" for being lazy:** Foster, Carly Hayden, "Anchor Babies
and Welfare Queens: An Essay on Political Rhetoric, Gendered Racism,
and Marginalization," *Women, Gender, and Families of Color* 5, no. 1
(2017): 50–72.

58   **Refuse to accept Santa Claus:** John, Arit, "There Really Is a Global
War on Santa," *The Atlantic*, December 12, 2013, www.theatlantic.com/
international/archive/2013/12/there-really-global-war-santa/356077/.

58   **but end up quietly voting for him:** Fadel, Leila, "Majority of Muslims
Voted for Biden, But Trump Got More Support Than He Did in 2016,"
NPR, December 4, 2020, www.npr.org/2020/12/04/942262760/majority
-of-muslims-voted-for-biden-but-trump-got-more-not-less-support.

3.   Do Something Useful

61   **the primary murder weapon of choice for immigrant mothers:** Eddie
Murphy described how his mother was similarly skilled with throwing
shoes and using them as a boomerang in his 1983 stand-up comedy special,
Delirious. It seems Pakistani mothers and Black mothers share strategies.

67   **According to the 2020 Hollywood Diversity Report:** Hunt, Darnell, and Ana-Christina Ramón, *The Hollywood Diversity Report 2020:
A Tale of Two Hollywoods*, UCLA, 2020, https://newsroom.ucla.edu/
releases/2020-hollywood-diversity-report.

67   **93 percent are held by white people:** Darnell and Ramón, *Hollywood
Diversity Report 2020*.

67   **In 2019, we bought the majority of tickets:** Darnell and Ramón, *Hollywood Diversity Report 2020*.

68 **A Brief Hall of Fame and Tour of Recent Whitewashing:** Tierney, Dolores, "From *Breakfast at Tiffany's* to *Hellboy*: The Ongoing Problem of Hollywood 'Whitewashing,'" *The Conversation*, September 5, 2017, theconversation.com/from-breakfast-at-tiffanys-to-hellboy-the-ongoing-problem-of-hollywood-whitewashing-83331.

69 **In media, framing theory:** Davie, G., "Framing Theory," *Mass Communication Theory*, retrieved from masscommtheory.com/theory-overviews/framing-theory/.

69 **I became Islamic Rage Boy:** Butt, Riazat, "All the Rage—Victim of US Bloggers' Cartoon Hits Back," *Guardian*, July 23, 2007, www.theguardian.com/world/2007/jul/23/india.digitalmedia.

70 **"I am not happy with people joking":** Butt, "All the Rage."

70 **In 2015, a *Public Policy* poll:** Somin, Ilya, "Political Ignorance and Bombing Agrabah," *Washington Post*, December 18, 2015, www.washingtonpost.com/news/volokh-conspiracy/wp/2015/12/18/political-ignorance-and-bombing-agrabah/.

70 **Muslims and the Prophet Muhammad have been demonized:** Tolan, John V., *Faces of Muhammad: Western Perceptions of the Prophet of Islam from the Middle Ages to Today* (Princeton: Princeton University Press, 2019).

71 **This poem, revered as a "masterpiece of epic drama":** Feffer, John, *Crusade 2.0: The West's Resurgent War Against Islam* (San Francisco: City Lights, 2012), 27–28.

71 **a "purple skinned, big lipped, hook-nosed monster":** Arjana, Sophia Rose, *Muslims in the Western Imagination* (New York: Oxford University Press, 2015), 29.

71 **In his masterwork, *The Divine Comedy*:** McCambridge, Jeffrey B., "Dante and Islam: A Study of the Eastern Influences in the Divine Comedy," master's thesis, Indiana University, 2016. See chapter 5: "The Prophet Muhammad in the *Divine Comedy*."

71 **Voltaire portrayed the Prophet Muhammad:** Brockopp, Jonathan E., *The Cambridge Companion to Muhammad* (New York: Cambridge University Press, 2010), 241; Voltaire, *Le Fanatisme Ou Mahomet Le Prophète: Tragédie* (Paris: Mille Et Une Nuits, 2015).

71 **"divinely inspired messenger":** Brockopp, *The Cambridge Companion to Muhammad*, 241–42; de Boulainvilliers, Henri, *The Life of Mahomet* (Piscataway, NJ: Gorgias Press, 2002), 222; Munir, Hassan, "Voltaire, Rousseau, and Napoleon on Prophet Muhammad," iHistory, 2015, http://www.ihistory.co/enlightened-french-disbelievers-on-prophet-muhammad/.

72 **Rousseau, praises the Prophet Muhammad:** Brockopp, *The Cambridge Companion to Muhammad*, 242; Rousseau, Jean-Jacques, *The Social Contract*, CreateSpace Independent Publishing Platform, 2014, 55; Fatih, Zakaria, "Peering into the Mosque: Enlightenment Views of Islam," *French Review* 85, no. 6 (2012): 1070–82, doi:10.1353/tfr.2012.0147.

72 **Thomas Jefferson, who in 1765 ordered his first copy:** Spellberg, Denise A., *Thomas Jefferson's Qur'an: Islam and the Founders* (New York: Vintage Books, 2014); Manseau, Peter, "Why Thomas Jefferson Owned a Qur'an," *Smithsonian Magazine*, January 31, 2018, www.smithsonianmag .com/smithsonian-institution/why-thomas-jefferson-owned-qur-1– 180967997/.

72 **Nearly 30 percent of the enslaved were originally Muslim:** Khan, Saeed A., "Muslims Arrived in America 400 Years Ago as Part of the Slave Trade and Today Are Vastly Diverse," *The Conversation*, April 11, 2019, theconversation.com/muslims-arrived-in-america-400-years-ago-as-part-of-the-slave-trade-and-today-are-vastly-diverse-113168.

72 **we had Goethe rejecting Voltaire's depiction:** Tolan, *Faces of Muhammad*, 1; Einboden, Jeffrey, *Islam and Romanticism: Muslim Currents from Goethe to Emerson* (Oneworld Academic, 2014).

72 **The Prophet Muhammad also got love from Napoleon:** Tolan, *Faces of Muhammad*, 1.

72 **Edward Said described this phenomenon:** Said, Edward W., *Orientalism* (New York: Pantheon Books), 1978.

73 **In *Reel Bad Arabs:*** Shaheen, Jack G., *Reel Bad Arabs: How Hollywood Vilifies a People*, 3rd ed. (Northampton, MA: Interlink Publishing, 2015).

74 **we have what Gayatri Spivak referred to:** Spivak, Gayatri Chakravorty, "Can the Subaltern Speak?" *Die Philosophin* 14, no. 27 (2003): 42–58, doi:10.5840/philosophin200314275.

74 **First Lady Laura Bush rationalized the War on Terror:** Gerstenzang, James, and Lisa Getter, "Laura Bush Addresses State of Afghan Women," *Los Angeles Times*, November 18, 2001, www.latimes.com/archives/la -xpm-2001-nov-18-mn-5602-story.html.

74 **At least 37 million people have been displaced:** Vine, David, et al., *Creating Refugees: Displacement Caused by the United States' Post-9/11 Wars*, Brown University, 2020, watson.brown.edu/costsofwar/files/cow/imce/ papers/2020/Displacement_Vine%20et%20al_Costs%20of%20War%20 2020%2009%2008.pdf.

74 **"viagra for Western cultural imperialists":** Ali, Wajahat, "'Sex and the City 2's' Stunning Muslim Clichés," *Salon*, January 3, 2013, www .salon.com/2010/05/26/sex_and_the_city_cultural_tone_deafness/.

74 **According to a Gallup study of over one billion Muslims:** Esposito, John L., and Dalia Mogahed, *Who Speaks for Islam? What a Billion Muslims Really Think* (Gallup Press, 2007); Esposito, John L., and Dalia Mogahed, "Who Speaks for Islam," *Charlie Rose*, May 9, 2008, charlierose.com/videos/12664; interview with the coauthor Dalia Mogahed.

74 **The *New York Times* portrayed Islam and Muslims more negatively:** Arshad, Owais, et al., *Are Muslims Collectively Responsible? A Sentiment Analysis of the New York Times*, 416Labs, 2015, http://static1.squarespace .com/static/558067a3e4b0cb2f81614c38/t/564d7b91e4b082df3a4e2 91e/1447918481058/nytandislam_study.pdf.

75 **Muslims accused of plotting violence received:** Rao, Kumar, et al., *Equal Treatment? Measuring the Legal and Media Responses to Ideologically Motivated Violence in the United States*, ISPU, 2018, www.imv-report .org/.

75 **perpetuated stereotypes that associate people of color:** Eberhardt, Jennifer, *Biased* (Cornerstone Digital, 2019); Edwards, Blake, "Acting Black: An Analysis of Blackness and Criminality in Film," master's thesis, University of Southern Mississippi, 2019, aquila.usm.edu/cgi/viewcontent.cgi?article=1718&context=masters_theses; Pierson, Eric, "Black on Black Crime: Hollywood's Construction of the Hood," Ericarchive, 1997, files.eric.ed.gov/fulltext/ED410329.pdf.

75 **The repeated association of violence with brown and black skin:** Stanley, Jason, *How Propaganda Works* (Princeton: Princeton University Press, 2015), 121–24, 213–15.

79 **temporarily iced by Clear Channel radio stations:** Krovatin, Chris, "164 Songs That Were Banned from American Radio After 9/11," *Kerrang!*, September 11, 2019, www.kerrang.com/features/here-are-the-164 -songs-that-were-banned-from-american-radio-after-9–11/.

4. Be Moderate So America Will (Maybe) Love You (Conditionally) One Day (Inshallah)

81 **"Where are the moderate Muslims":** Mahdawi, Arwa, "The 712-Page Google Doc That Proves Muslims Do Condemn Terrorism," *Guardian*, March 26, 2017, www.theguardian.com/world/shortcuts/2017/mar/26/ muslims-condemn-terrorism-stats.

81 **among the nearly four million Muslim Americans:** "American Muslims' Views on Terrorism and Concerns about Extremism," Pew Research Center's Religion & Public Life Project, July 26, 2017, www

.pewforum.org/2017/07/26/terrorism-and-concerns-about-extremism/; Lipka, Michael, "Muslims and Islam: Key Findings in the U.S. and around the World," Pew Research Center, August 9, 2017, www .pewresearch.org/fact-tank/2017/08/09/muslims-and-islam-key-findings -in-the-u-s-and-around-the-world/; "Joint Statement Against Anti-Black Police Violence," *Muslim Advocates*, muslimadvocates.org/ joint-statement-against-anti-black-police-violence/; Diamant, Jeff, et al., "U.S. Muslims More Likely to Say Blacks Lack Equal Rights," Pew Research Center, September 18, 2017, www.pewresearch.org/ fact-tank/2017/09/18/muslims-more-likely-than-americans-overall -to-say-blacks-lack-equal-rights-in-u-s/; Younis, Mohamed, "Muslim Americans Exemplify Diversity, Potential," Gallup, March 2, 2009, news.gallup.com/poll/116260/muslim-americans-exemplify-diversity-potential.aspx.

82 **"If you're a Muslim and you love America":** Wang, Frances Kai-Hwa, "Muslim Americans React to Bill Clinton's Tuesday Night Speech," NBCNews.com, July 28, 2016, www.nbcnews.com/news/asian-america/ muslim-americans-react-bill-clinton-s-tuesday-night-speech-n618886.

83 **"You have sacrificed nothing—and no one":** Khan, Khizr, "'You Have Sacrificed Nothing—and No One!'" BBC News, July 29, 2016, www.bbc .com/news/av/election-us-2016–36911159.

86 **Bhagat Singh Thind:** *United States v. Bhagat Singh Thind*, 261 U.S. 204 (1923).

86 **In *Takao Ozawa v. United States*:** *Takao Ozawa v. United States*, 260 U.S. 178 (1922).

86 **historically, many South Asians, Arabs, and Latinos:** Parvini, Sarah, and Ellis Simani, "Are Arabs and Iranians White? Census Says Yes, but Many Disagree," *Los Angeles Times*, March 28, 2019, www.latimes.com/projects/ la-me-census-middle-east-north-africa-race/; Demby, Gene, "On the Census, Who Checks 'Hispanic,' Who Checks 'White,' and Why," NPR, June 16, 2014, www.npr.org/sections/codeswitch/2014/06/16/321819185/ on-the-census-who-checks-hispanic-who-checks-white-and-why; Varathan, Preeti, "For One Year, All the South Asians in the US Were Considered 'White,'" *Quartz*, September 2, 2017, qz.com/india/1066287/ for-one-year-all-the-south-asians-in-the-us-were-considered-white/.

86 **The census, after all, was used:** Aratani, Lori, "Secret Use of Census Info Helped Send Japanese Americans to Internment Camps in WWII," *Washington Post*, April 6, 2018, www.washingtonpost.com/news/ retropolis/wp/2018/04/03/secret-use-of-census-info-helped-send-japanese -americans-to-internment-camps-in-wwii/.

87   **A 2015 U.S. Census Bureau study:** Mathews, Kelly, et al., United States Census Bureau, 2017, *2015 National Content Test Race and Ethnicity Analysis Report*, www2.census.gov/programs-surveys/decennial/2020/program-management/final-analysis-reports/2015nct-race-ethnicity-analysis.pdf.

88   **"Beta, we see Blacks on TV shows":** Edwards, "Acting Black," https://aquila.usm.edu/masters_theses/661.

89   **The "model minority" myth is a dangerous drug:** Dixon, Travis L., *A Dangerous Distortion of Our Families: Representations of Families, by Race, in News and Opinion Media*, Color of Change, 2018, colorofchange.org/dangerousdistortion/.

89   **42 percent of Americans couldn't name a single prominent Asian American:** Jones, Dustin, "42% In The U.S. Can't Name A Single Prominent Asian American, A Survey Finds," NPR, May 16, 2021, https://www.npr.org/2021/05/16/997346466/80-of-asian-americans-say-they-are-discriminated-against.

89   **Asian Americans are the least likely group in the U.S. to be promoted to management:** Gee, Buck, and Denise Peck, "Asian Americans Are the Least Likely Group in the U.S. to Be Promoted to Management," *Harvard Business Review*, May 31, 2018, https://hbr.org/2018/05/asian-americans-are-the-least-likely-group-in-the-u-s-to-be-promoted-to-management.

89   **Vicha Ratanapakdee, an immigrant from Thailand:** Fuller, Thomas, "Daylight Attack on 2 Asian Women in San Francisco Increases Fears," NYTimes.com, *New York Times*, May 5, 2021, https://www.nytimes.com/2021/05/05/us/asian-attack-san-francisco.html.

90   **"Chinese and infecting people with coronavirus":** Kim, Yeon Ju, "Report: Sam's Club stabbing suspect thought family was 'Chinese infecting people with coronavirus," Kxan.com, April 8, 2020, https://www.kxan.com/news/crime/report-sams-club-stabbing-suspect-thought-family-was-chinese-infecting-people-with-coronavirus/000.

90   **"the Chinese virus" and "Kung Flu":** Stop AAPI Hate, National Report, May 6, 2021, https://stopaapihate.org/national-report-through-march-2021/.

90   **"despite its intent to treat all immigrant groups":** Lee, Erika, *America for Americans: A History of Xenophobia in the United States* (New York: Basic Books, 2019), 244.

91   **fear of a "population explosion" from:** Lee, *America for Americans*, 235–37.

91   **President Johnson's policies would bring "swarms":** Lee, *America for Americans*, 239.

91   **"driven by racist and xenophobic fears":** Lee, *America for Americans*, 249.

91   **drastically reduced the number of Mexican laborers:** Lee, *America for Americans*, 246–47.

91   **this would bring more European relatives here:** Lee, *America for Americans*, 243.

91   **Instead, the number of immigrants from Europe fell:** Pew Research Center, Modern Immigration Wave Brings 59 million to U.S., Driving Population Growth and Change Through 2065, September 28, 2015, https://www.pewresearch.org/hispanic/2015/09/28/modern-immigration -wave-brings-59-million-to-u-s-driving-population-growth-and-change -through-2065/; Lee, *America for Americans*, 252.

92   **"effectively eliminated most avenues for legal immigration":** Lee, *America for Americans*, 248.

92   **"Rarely is the question asked":** Weisberg, Jacob, "The Top 25 Bushisms of All Time," *Slate*, January 12, 2009, slate.com/news-and-politics/2009/01/ the-top-25-bushisms-of-all-time.html.

93   **many Arab and South Asian immigrant voters:** "Exit Poll: Muslims Voted as a Block for George W. Bush." *Beliefnet*, November 17, 2000, www.beliefnet.com/faiths/islam/2000/11/exit-poll-muslims-voted-as-a -block-for-george-w-bush.aspx.

93   **"I'm not in favor of abolishing the government":** Weisenthal, Joe, "Grover Norquist Continues to Make One Big Error on Economics," *Business Insider*, November 27, 2012, www.businessinsider.com/grover -norquists-big-error-thinking-taxes-enable-spending-2012–11?IR=T.

93   **Bush's promise to "restore honor and dignity":** Bruni, Frank, "Bush Calls on Gore to Denounce Clinton Affair," *New York Times*, August 12, 2000, www.nytimes.com/2000/08/12/us/2000-campaign-texas-governor -bush-calls-gore-denounce-clinton-affair.html.

93   **As a candidate, Bush actually met with Muslims:** "Muslim Leaders Meet with George W. Bush," Pluralism Project Archive, Harvard University, October 5, 2000, hwpi.harvard.edu/pluralismarchive/news/ muslim-leaders-meet-george-w-bush?page=2; Merelli, Annalisa, "Read George W. Bush's 'Islam Is Peace' Speech, Delivered Days after 9/11," *Quartz*, September 11, 2017, qz.com/1074258/911-video-and-text-of- george-w-bushs-islam-and-peace-speech/.

93   **He also spoke out against racial profiling:** Blumner, Robyn E., "The Outrages of Secret Evidence by Our Government Continue," *Tampa Bay Times*, September 3, 2005, www.tampabay.com/archive/2002/03/24/the -outrages-of-secret-evidence-by-our-government-continue/.

94   **up to 90 percent of Florida's 60,000 Muslim votes:** Abdelkarim, Riad

Z, and Basil Z. Abdelkarim, "American Muslim Voters Come of Age with Bloc Vote," *Washington Report on Middle East Affairs*, 2001, www .wrmea.org/001-january-february/american-muslim-voters-come-of-age -with-bloc-vote.html.

94 **"because of the Muslim vote":** Foer, Franklin, "Fevered Pitch," *New Republic*, November 12, 2001, newrepublic.com/article/83799/ norquist-radical-islam-cair.

97 **murder of Balbir Singh Sodhi:** Sikh American Legal Defense and Education Fund, 2011, *The First 9/11 'Backlash' Fatality: The Murder of Balbir Singh Sodhi*, saldef.org/wp-content/uploads/2011/08/Balbir_Singh_ Sodhi_First_Backlash_Murder.pdf.

97 **no Muslims in New Jersey celebrated the deaths:** Bradner, Eric, "Donald Trump on Muslim Claim: 'I'm Not Going to Take It Back,'" CNN, November 30, 2015, edition.cnn.com/2015/11/29/politics/donald -trump-new-jersey-muslims-celebrating-9–11.

98 **The *New York Post* published a piece:** Gorta, William J., "Missing—or Hiding?—Mystery of NYPD Cadet from Pakistan," *New York Post*, October 12, 2001, nypost.com/2001/10/12/missing-or -hiding-mystery-of-nypd-cadet-from-pakistan/.

98 **"I want to see it in my lifetime":** Candiotti, Susan, "Mom Wants Muslim Son's Name Moved to Be Among First Responders at 9/11 Memorial," CNN, September 11, 2012, https://religion.blogs.cnn.com/2012/09/11/ mom-wants-muslim-sons-name-moved-to-be-among-first-responders-at- 911-memorial/.

100 **"We do not want this war, this violence":** Sisario, Ben, "The Dixie Chicks Change Their Name, Dropping the 'Dixie,'" *New York Times*, June 25, 2020, www.nytimes.com/2020/06/25/arts/music/dixie-chicks-change-name.html.

100 **After 9/11, the school paper, the *Daily Californian*:** Cavna, Michael, "9/11 ART: From Honor to Anger, 10 Cartoonists Reveal Feelings Behind Sunday's Funnies to Mark Anniversary," *Washington Post*, September 9, 2011, www.washingtonpost.com/blogs/comic-riffs/post/911 -art-from-honor-to-anger-10-cartoonists-reveal-feelings-behind-sundays -funnies-to-mark-anniversary/2011/09/08/gIQA4ASwEK_blog.html.

101 **Since then, she's supported Holocaust deniers:** Edmunds, Donna Rachel, "Michelle Malkin Shunned by Conservatives Over Support for Antisemites,"*Jerusalem Post*,November 20, 2019,www.jpost.com/american -politics/michelle-malkin-shunned-by-conservatives-over-support-for -antisemites-608349; Lancaster, Jordan, "Conservative Group Cuts Ties with Michelle Malkin," *The Hill*, November 18, 2019, thehill.com/home news/media/470974-conservative-group-cuts-ties-with-michelle-malkin.

101 **She published a column titled "Berkeley":** Malkin, Michelle, "Berkeley: Some Kind of Foreign Country," *Kitsap Sun*, September 26, 2001, products.kitsapsun.com/archive/2001/09–26/0001_michelle _malkin__berkeley_some_ki.html.

104 **"The face of terrorism is not the true face of Islam":** Bush, George W., "'Islam Is Peace' Says President, Remarks by the President at Islamic Center of Washington, D.C.," The White House, National Archives and Records Administration, September 17, 2001, georgewbush-whitehouse.archives .gov/news/releases/2001/09/20010917–11.html.

104 **"Overall, Americans took 9/11 pretty calmly":** Haltiwanger, John, "Twitter Users Dunk on the New York Times' Paul Krugman After He Said 9/11 Didn't Lead to a 'Mass Outbreak' of Islamophobia or Violence," *Business Insider France*, September 11, 2020, www.businessinsider.fr/us/ twitter-paul-krugman-new-york-times-backlash-911-tweets-2020–9.

104 **Krugman must have forgotten the 481 hate crimes:** Keng Kuek Ser, Kuang, "Data: Hate Crimes against Muslims Increased after 9/11," *The World from PRX*, September 12, 2016, www.pri.org/stories/2016–09–12/ data-hate-crimes-against-muslims-increased-after-911.

104 **Those tools happened to be used predominantly:** ACLU, *Blocking Faith, Freezing Charity: Chilling Muslim Charitable Giving in the "War on Terrorism Financing,"* 2009, www.aclu.org/sites/default/files/field_document/ blockingfaith.pdf.

105 **The Patriot Act also expanded money-laundering:** *The USA Patriot Act: Preserving Life and Liberty: Uniting and Strengthening America by Providing Appropriate Tools Required to Intercept and Obstruct Terrorism* (Washington, DC: U.S. Department of Justice, 2001).

105 **This included the Holy Land Foundation:** Bridge Initiative Team, "Factsheet: Holy Land Foundation," *Bridge Initiative*, Georgetown University, January 27, 2020, bridge.georgetown.edu/research/ factsheet-holy-land-foundation/.

105 **In 2003, FBI director Robert Mueller:** Kar, Debi, "Ten Years After Patriot Act, Time to Restore America's Freedoms," *Muslim Advocates*, October 27, 2011, muslimadvocates.org/2011/10/ten_ years_after_patriot_act_time_to_restore_america_s_freedoms/.

106 **We didn't need a modern Muslim registry:** ACLU, "National Security Entry-Exit Registration System," www.aclu.org/issues/immigrants-rights/ immigrants-rights-and-detention/national-security-entry-exit-registration.

107 **In 2016, an Iraqi-American college student:** Kindervatter-Clark, Caitlin, "'Allahu Akbar' Isn't a Scary Phrase, But Terrorism Has Warped the Way We Hear Arabic," *Washington Post*, March 1, 2019, www.washingtonpost

.com/posteverything/wp/2016/04/20/arabic-can-sound-scary-when-your
-only-exposure-to-it-comes-from-stories-about-terrorism/.

107 **They accused the school of peddling "soft jihad":** Elliott, Andrea, "Critics Cost Muslim Educator Her Dream School," *New York Times*, April 28, 2008, www.nytimes.com/2008/04/28/nyregion/28school.html.

107 **"Arabic is not just another language":** Hing, Julianne, "The $43 Million Islamophobia Machine," *Colorlines*, September 1, 2011, www.colorlines .com/articles/43-million-islamophobia-machine.

108 **56 percent of Americans in a survey believe:** Baynes, Chris, "Most Americans Say 'Arabic Numerals' Should Not Be Taught in School," *Independent*, May 21, 2019, www.independent.co.uk/news/arabic-numerals -survey-prejudice-bias-survey-research-civic-science-a8918256.html.

109 **The NYPD spent eleven years spying:** ACLU, "Raza v. City of New York—Legal Challenge to NYPD Muslim Surveillance Program," August 3, 2017, www.aclu.org/cases/raza-v-city-new-york-legal-challenge-nypd-muslim -surveillance-program; Pilkington, Ed, "NYPD Settles Lawsuit after Illegally Spying on Muslims," *Guardian*, April 5, 2018, www.theguardian.com/ world/2018/apr/05/nypd-muslim-surveillance-settlement.

109 **"that mosques and religiosity are actually associated with high levels of civic engagement":** Harvard Kennedy School Belfer Center for Science and International Affairs, "Mosques are a Positive Force in America," March 9, 2011, https://www.belfercenter.org/publication/ mosques-are-positive-force-america.

110 **"If you want something done":** Étienne, Charles-Guillaume, *Bruis et Palaprat* (Paris: Madame Masson, 1807).

5.   Die Hard in Amreeka

115 **Men of color, especially Black men:** Fadulu, Lola, "Black Men in D.C. Are Expected to Die 17 Years Earlier than White Men. Here's Why," *Washington Post*, August 27, 2020, www.washingtonpost.com/local/black -men-in-dc-are-expected-to-die-17-years-earlier-than-white-men-heres -why/2020/08/27/8a679ca6-e805–11ea-a414–8422fa3e4116_story.html.

116 **It's called "fuku" in Junot Diaz's:** Diaz, Junot, *The Brief Wondrous Life of Oscar Wao* (New York: Riverhead Books, 2008).

121 **Karachi is one of the most densely populated cities:** Kolb, Elzy, "75,000 People per Square Mile? These Are the Most Densely Populated Cities in the World," *USA Today*, July 11, 2019, eu.usatoday.com/story/news/world/ 2019/07/11/the-50-most-densely-populated-cities-in-the-world/39664259/.

126 **"All of our brains have these naturally occurring":** Ali, Wajahat, "O.C.D., My Exhausting Best Friend," *New York Times*, October 13, 2018, www.nytimes.com/2018/10/13/opinion/sunday/ocd-my-exhausting -best-friend.html.

127 **the white majority in America, historically, is not as prepared:** Feagin, Joe R., *Racist America Roots, Current Realities, and Future Reparations* (New York: Routledge, 2000), 167; Assari, Shervin, "Black Americans May Be More Resilient to Stress than White Americans," *The Conversation*, September 16, 2016, ihpi.umich.edu/news/black-americans-may-be-more-resilient-stress-white-americans; Leavy, Patricia, *Privilege Through the Looking-Glass* (Sense Publishers, 2017), 40.

6. Avoid Jail

130 **swept up in Operation Cyberstorm:** Robert, Mullins, "FBI Arrests 27 on Computer-Fraud Charges," *Silicon Valley Business Journal*, April 19, 2002, www.bizjournals.com/sanjose/stories/2002/04/15/daily80.html.

138 **"It's a big club, and you ain't in it":** Carlin, George, "Life Is Worth Losing," Beacon Theater, New York, November 5, 2005.

148 **over two million incarcerated individuals in the United States:** Sawyer, Wendy, and Peter Wagner, "Mass Incarceration: The Whole Pie 2020," Prison Policy Initiative, March 24, 2020, www.prisonpolicy.org/reports/pie2020.html.

148 **Eighty-four percent of incarcerated people are poor:** Miller, Reuben Jonathan, *Halfway Home: Race, Punishment, and the Afterlife of Mass Incarceration* (New York: Little, Brown, 2021), 6.

148 **Nearly 20 million people live in America with a felony record:** Miller, *Halfway Home*, 8.

7. Become a Domestic Crusader

165 *The Domestic Crusaders:* Ali, Wajahat, *The Domestic Crusaders*, McSweeney's, 2011.

165 **I thought I could booby-trap and reframe:** Ford, Peter, "Europe Cringes at Bush 'Crusade' against Terrorists," *Christian Science Monitor*, September 19, 2001, www.csmonitor.com/2001/0919/p12s2-woeu.html.

166 **Rumi is still one of the best-selling:** Moaveni, Azadeh, "How Did Rumi

Become One of Our Best-Selling Poets?" *New York Times*, January 20, 2017, www.nytimes.com/2017/01/20/books/review/rumi-brad-gooch.html.

170 **American theater is a "house of cards":** Paulson, Michael, "Theater Artists Decry Racism in Their Industry," *New York Times*, June 9, 2020, www.houseytimes.com/2020/06/09/theater/theater-artists-decry-racism .html.

8. Die Hard 2: Die Harder in Amreeka

185 **was looking for a lead writer:** Ali, Wajahat, et al., *Fear, Inc. The Roots of the Islamophobia Network in America*, Center for American Progress, 2011, www.americanprogress.org/issues/religion/reports/2011/08/26/10165/fear -inc/.

185 **writer Dave Eggers called me and said HBO:** Eggers, Dave, and Wajahat Ali, "The First Half of MJ, a New Script by Wajahat Ali and Dave Eggers," *McSweeney's Internet Tendency*, February 6, 2015, www .mcsweeneys.net/articles/the-first-half-of-mj-a-new-script-by-wajahat-ali -and-dave-eggers.

198 **Many were in there for drug offenses:** Sawyer and Wagner, "Mass Incarceration: The Whole Pie 2020," www.prisonpolicy.org/reports/ pie2020.html.

9. Elect a Muslim President, but Beware of Economic Anxiety

200 **but many Americans after all this time:** Bailey, Sarah Pulliam, "A Star-tling Number of Americans Still Believe President Obama Is a Muslim," *Washington Post*, September 14, 2015, www.washingtonpost.com/news/ acts-of-faith/wp/2015/09/14/a-startling-number-of-americans-still-believe -president-obama-is-a-muslim/.

201 **"I can't trust Obama. I have read about him":** Stewart, Emily, "Watch John McCain Defend Barack Obama Against a Racist Voter in 2008," *Vox*, August 26, 2018, www.vox.com/policy-and-politics/2018/8/25/17782572/ john-mccain-barack-obama-statement-2008-video.

201 **"I think Islam hates us":** Hauslohner, Abigail, and Jenna Johnson, " 'I Think Islam Hates Us': A Timeline of Trump's Comments about Islam and Muslims," *Washington Post*, May 20, 2017, www.washingtonpost

.com/news/post-politics/wp/2017/05/20/i-think-islam-hates-us-a-timeline
-of-trumps-comments-about-islam-and-muslims/.

201   **General Colin Powell, to come out and finally say:** " 'Meet the Press'
Transcript for Oct. 19, 2008, Featuring Former Secretary of State Gen.
Colin Powell (Ret.)," NBC News, October 19, 2008, www.nbcnews.com/
id/wbna27266223.

203   **President Obama's campaign volunteers removed two Muslim women:**
Smith, Ben, "Muslims Barred from Picture at Obama Event," *Politico*,
June 18, 2008, www.politico.com/story/2008/06/muslims-barred-from
-picture-at-obama-event-011168.

205   **President Obama addressed the crowd of Muslims:** Fritze, John, and
Ian Duncan, "President Obama at Maryland Mosque: 'You Fit in Here,'"
Baltimore Sun, February 3, 2016, www.baltimoresun.com/politics/bs-md
-obama-mosque-visit-20160203-story.html.

206   **Instead, we were deluged with endless commentaries:** Chokshi,
Niraj, "Trump Voters Driven by Fear of Losing Status, Not Economic
Anxiety, Study Finds," *New York Times*, April 24, 2018, www.nytimes
.com/2018/04/24/us/politics/trump-economic-anxiety.html.

207   **Specifically, a 2019 study concluded:** Oberhauser, Ann M., et al.,
"Political Moderation and Polarization in the Heartland: Economics,
Rurality, and Social Identity in the 2016 U.S. Presidential Election,"
Sociological Quarterly 60, no. 2 (April 12, 2019): 224–44, doi:10.1080/003
80253.2019.1580543.

208   **It's called "Billionaire Mountain":** Hoffower, Hillary, "Step inside 'Billionaire Mountain,' the Wealthy Aspen Enclave Where the Bezos and
Dell Families Own Sprawling Mansions and Homes Go For as Much as
$49 Million," *Business Insider*, August 26, 2019, www.businessinsider.com/
aspen-colorado-billionaire-mountain-rich-famous-neighborhood-2019–8.

209   **They're just "racial realists" or "American Identitarians":** "Alt Right:
A Primer on the New White Supremacy," Anti-Defamation League,
www.adl.org/resources/backgrounders/alt-right-a-primer-on-the-new
-white-supremacy.

209   **the impending "invasion" of a migrant caravan:** Roberts, David, "The
Caravan 'Invasion' and America's Epistemic Crisis," *Vox*, November
1, 2018, www.vox.com/policy-and-politics/2018/11/1/18041710/migrant
-caravan-america-trump-epistemic-crisis-democracy.

209   **"the filthy evil Jews":** Turkewitz, Julie and Kevin Roose, "Who is Robert Bowers, the Suspect in the Pittsburgh Synagogue Shooting?," *New
York Times*, October 27, 2018, https://www.nytimes.com/2018/10/27/us/
robert-bowers-pittsburgh-synagogue-shooter.html.

209   **A domestic terrorist echoed the same exact language:** Stelter, Brian, "Pittsburgh Suspect Echoed Talking Point That Dominated Fox News Airwaves," CNN, October 29, 2018, www.cnn.com/2018/10/29/media/pittsburgh-suspect-invasion/index.html.

212   **his racism was sugar-coated by white colleagues:** Eligon, John, and Richard Fausset, "Obama Soothed. Trump Stirs. How 2 Presidents Have Tackled Racial Flare-Ups," *New York Times*, June 1, 2018, www.nytimes.com/2018/06/01/us/obama-trump-race.html.

212   **"inflammatory rhetoric" and "racially charged" language:** Mason, Jeff, "Trump Signs Order on Police Reform After Weeks of Protests about Racial Injustice," Reuters, June 16, 2020, www.reuters.com/article/us-minneapolis-police-usa-trump/trump-signs-order-on-police-reform-after-weeks-of-protests-about-racial-injustice-idUSKBN23N2NR.

213   **"go back and help fix the totally broken and crime infested places":** Smith, Allan, "Trump says Congresswomen of Color Should 'Go Back' and Fix the Places They 'Originally Came From,'" NBC News, July 14, 2019, https://www.nbcnews.com/politics/donald-trump/trump-says-progressive-congresswomen-should-go-back-where-they-came-n1029676.

214   **He wouldn't be praised for finally having the right "tone":** "CNN's Dana Bash Praises Trump's Message to Americans—CNN Video," CNN, March 17, 2020, www.cnn.com/videos/politics/2020/03/17/trump-coronavirus-tone-praise-bash-vpx.cnn; Baragona, Justin, "Dana Bash on Trump's Latest MAGA Riot Video: 'Obviously a Very Different Tone,'" *Daily Beast*, January 7, 2021, www.thedailybeast.com/cnns-dana-bash-on-trumps-latest-maga-riot-video-obviously-a-very-different-tone.

214   **It's a "coalition of the willing":** Beehner, Lionel, "The 'Coalition of the Willing,'" Council on Foreign Relations, February 22, 2007, www.cfr.org/backgrounder/coalition-willing.

215   **US national security experts have warned:** Kanno-youngs, Zolan, and David E. Sanger, "Extremists Emboldened by Capitol Attack Pose Rising Threat, Homeland Security Says," *New York Times*, January 27, 2021, www.nytimes.com/2021/01/27/us/politics/homeland-security-threat.html; Department of Homeland Security, *Homeland Threat Assessment*, 2020, www.dhs.gov/sites/default/files/publications/2020_10_06_homeland-threat-assessment.pdf.

217   **"With great power . . . comes great responsibility":** Before being popularized by Uncle Ben in *Spider-Man*, this quote was initially written by the Comité de Salut Public and addressed to the members of the French National Convention in 1793: "Ils doivent envisager qu'une grande responsabilité est la suite inséparable d'un grand pouvoir," which

translates to "They [the Representatives] must contemplate that a great responsibility is the inseparable result of a great power," *Journal Des Débats Et Des Décrets, Ou Récrit De Ce Qui S'est Passé Aux Séances De L'Assemblée Nationale Depuis Le 17 Juin 1789, Jusqu'au Premier Septembre De La Même Année*, vol. 41, Imprimerie Nationale Baudouin, 18; Cronin, Brian, "When We First Met—When Did Uncle Ben First Say 'With Great Power Comes Great Responsibility?'" CBR, July 15, 2015, www.cbr.com/when-we-first-met-when-did-uncle-ben-first-say-with-great -power-comes-great-responsibility/.

10. Invest in Hope, but Tie Your Camel First

219 **Lady Liberty was sculpted by Frenchman Frédéric-Auguste Bartholdi:** Blakemore, Erin, "The Statue of Liberty Was Originally a Muslim Woman," *Smithsonian*, November 24, 2015, www.smithsonianmag.com/ smart-news/statue-liberty-was-originally-muslim-woman-180957377/.

220 **We now hold the distinction of having the highest income inequality of all the G7 nations:** "Decile Ratios of Gross Earnings: Incidence of Low Pay," OECD.Stat, stats.oecd.org/Index.aspx?QueryId=64193.

220 **The wealth gap between America's richest and poorest families:** Schaeffer, Katherine, "6 Facts about Economic Inequality in the U.S.," Pew Research Center, February 7, 2020, www.pewresearch.org/fact -tank/2020/02/07/6-facts-about-economic-inequality-in-the-u-s/.

221 **"If the Hour [the day of Resurrection]":** Elias, Abu Amina, "Hadith on Trees: Finish Planting Trees, Even If the Hour Is Established," Daily Hadith Online, November 24, 2012, www.abuaminaelias.com/ dailyhadithonline/2012/11/24/plant-tree-ressurection/.

226 **"the alarm over the flood of Roman Catholic immigrants":** Saunders, Doug, *The Myth of the Muslim Tide: Do Immigrants Threaten the West?* (New York: Vintage, 2012), 115.

226 **a "profound threat to democracy, equality, and secular values":** Blanshard, Paul, *American Freedom and Catholic Power*, 2nd ed. (Boston: Beacon Press, 1958); Herberg, Will, "American Freedom and Catholic Power, by Paul Blanshard," *Commentary Magazine*, August 1949, www .commentarymagazine.com/articles/will-herberg/american-freedom-and -catholic-power-by-paul-blanshard/.

226 **In 1960, America elected its first Catholic president:** Roos, Dave, "How John F. Kennedy Overcame Anti-Catholic Bias to Win the Presidency," *History*, November 20, 2019, www.history.com/news/jfk-catholic-president.